An Incredibly

Foolish and Dangerous

Thing To Do

Also by Daniel Reiver:

Black Star, a novel

Coming Soon:

Jersey Devils, a novel

Source Material, a novel

Stories of Children, short stories

An Incredibly Foolish and Dangerous Thing To Do

Backpacking through China in 1995

A Memoir

Daniel Reiver

Copyright © 2025 by Daniel Reiver

All rights reserved

First Edition, December 2025

ISBN: 979-8-9936519-2-7

Cover Design & Photographs: Daniel Reiver

Maps: MapChart.net

Socials: @reiverwriter

For my Mom and Dad

如此多的错误,
仍然有更多的学习经验。

(Rúcǐ duō de cuòwù,
réngrán yǒu gèng duō de xuéxí jīngyàn.)

So many mistakes,
still so much more to have the experience of learning.

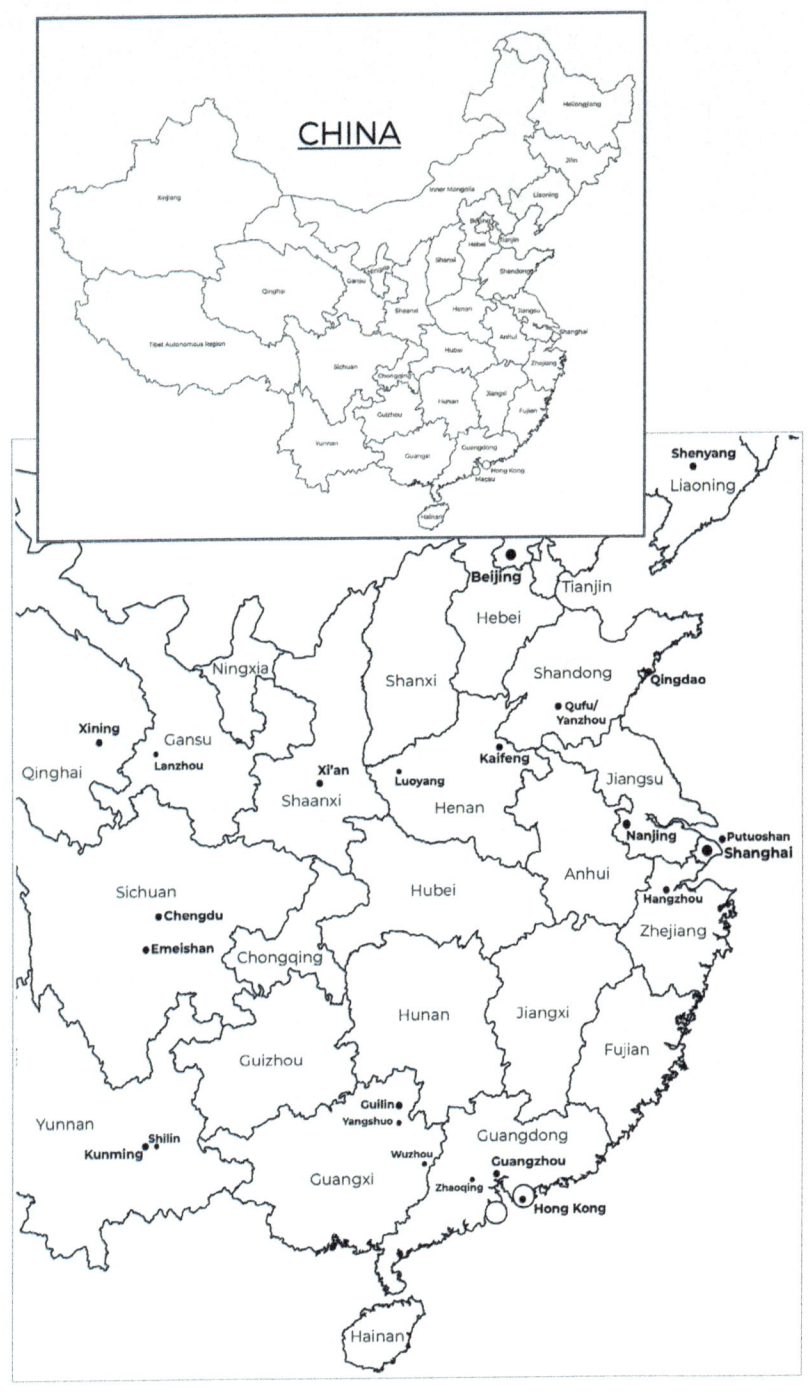

CONTENTS

	A Brief Language Note	i.
	Prologue	iii.
Day 1	San Francisco, Over the Pacific Ocean, Hong Kong	p.1
Day 2	Guǎngzhōu	p.8
Day 3	Guǎngzhōu, Xī River, Zhàoqìng, Wúzhōu, Guìlín	p.13
	Mandarin Language Pronunciation: Lesson 1	p.16
Day 4	Guìlín	p.17
Day 5	Guìlín, Yángshuò, Guìlín, Yángshuò	p.21
Day 6	Yángshuò	p.26
Day 7	Yángshuò, Guìlín, Yángshuò	p.31
Day 8	Yángshuò, Guìlín	p.34
	Signs Communism Was Over: Part 1	p.39
Day 9	Guìlín, Guǎngxī Province, Guìzhōu Province	p.40
Day 10	Yúnnán Province, Kūnmíng	p.43
Day 11	Kūnmíng	p.47
Day 12	Kūnmíng, Shílín, Kūnmíng	p.51
Day 13	Kūnmíng, Yunnan Province, Sìchuān Province	p.56
Day 14 &15	Sìchuān Province, Éméishān City, Bàoguó Village, Éméishān	p.63
	Mandarin Language Pronunciation: Lesson 2	p.71

Day 16	Bàoguó Village, Éméishān City, Sìchuān Province, Chéngdū	p.72
Day 17	Chéngdū	p.76
Day 18	Chéngdū, Sìchuān Province	p.80
Day 19	Gānsù Province, Lánzhōu, Gānsù Province Qīnghǎi Province, Xīníng	p.83
Day 20	Xīníng	p.88
	Mandarin Language Pronunciation: Lesson 3	p.95
Day 21	Qīnghǎi Province, Gānsù Province, Shaanxi Province, Xī'ān	p.96
Day 22	Xī'ān	p.101
Day 23	Xī'ān, Shaanxi Province, Xī'ān	p.105
Day 24	Zhèngzhōu, Hénán Province, Luòyáng	p.111
Day 25	Luòyáng	p.114
	Signs Communism Was Over: Part 2	p.125
Day 26	Luòyáng, Hénán Province, Běijīng	p.126
Day 27	Běijīng	p.133
Day 28	二	p.141
Day 29	川	p.146
Day 30	ㄨ	p.152
Day 31	岁	p.156
Day 32	六	p.159
	Mandarin Language Pronunciation: Lesson 4	p.163
Day 33	Běijīng	p.164

Day 34	Shāndōng Province, Qīngdǎo	p.166
Day 35	Qīngdǎo	p.169
Day 36	Shāndōng Province, Hénán Province, Kāifēng	p.171
Day 37	Kāifēng, Hénán Province	p.176
Day 38	Shāndōng Province, Yǎnzhōu, Qǔfù, Yǎnzhōu	p.181
	Signs Communism Was Over: Part 3	p.185
Day 39	Yǎnzhōu, Hénán Province, Jiāngsū Province, Nánjīng	p.186
Day 40	Nánjīng	p.193
	Mandarin Language Pronunciation: Lesson 5	p.198
Day 41	Nánjīng, Jiāngsū Province, Shànghǎi	p.199
Day 42	Shànghǎi	p.206
Day 43	ǁ	p.210
Day 44	ǁǁ	p.213
Day 45	Shànghǎi, Zhèjiāng Province, Hángzhōu	p.220
Day 46	Hángzhōu	p.223
Day 47	ǁ	p.227
Day 48	Hángzhōu, Zhèjiāng Province, Shànghǎi	p.231
Day 49	Shànghǎi	p.234
	Signs Communism Was Over: Part 4	p.237
Day 50	Shànghǎi, Pǔtuóshān	p.238
Day 51	Pǔtuóshān	p.244
Day 52	Shànghǎi	p.247
Day 53	患	p.252

Day 54	Shànghǎi, Hongqiao International Airport, Tokyo-Narita Airport, Over the Pacific Ocean, Sacramento Airport	p.260
	Epilogue	p.265
	Acknowledgements	p.269
	Glossary	p.271

A BRIEF LANGUAGE NOTE

Before I get going, I think it would be important to start with a note on the tonal modifier marks you'll see in this book. If you are already familiar with Mandarin pronunciation, please jump ahead; if not, please humor me for two pages.

Mandarin, the language I briefly studied in New Hampshire and mostly learned to speak while in China, is more commonly called "Standard Chinese" or, simply, "Chinese". All references in this book to Mandarin will be to that. It takes its name from the bureaucratic officials of the Chinese imperial courts of Nanjing and Běijīng, and, in one form or another, has for centuries been the language of Chinese national government and its authority. In the Mandarin language itself, the official name is actually "xiàndài biāozhǔn hànyǔ", meaning "modern standard Han language", which should tell you something about the dominance of the ethnic Han majority in China.

Colloquially, the language is called "pǔtōng huà": "the common language". Like every other phrase using the words "standard" or "common", these names reflect wishful thinking more than reality. Mandarin is far from the only spoken language in China, even now. Other widely spoken ones, often and incorrectly referred to as "dialects" and accounting for hundreds of millions of speakers, include Cantonese, the name derived from "Canton", the colonial name of the southeastern port city of Guǎngzhōu, near Hong Kong. Hokkien, spoken widely but primarily in the coastal Fujian province and Taiwan; and Shanghainese, the language which, in 1995 at least, was still widely spoken in and around the city of Shànghǎi, sometimes to the exclusion of Mandarin. These three languages are, respectively, of the Yue, Min, and Wu language groups, all of them tonal like Mandarin and each with different numbers of distinct tones than the

i

five Mandarin has.

Throughout the book, I have added tone modifier marks for Mandarin words and names transcribed into Pinyin (romanized Standard Chinese), but not for business names, such as hotels, and personal names when I don't know what mark should have been used. I hope that this does not become distracting, because I believe that I should at least try to represent the language as it would be said and, with the help of the brief explanation below, you will get a better sense of how things sounded as I traveled.

Mandarin's Five Tones

- ¯ ; called "yīnpíng", starts high and stays high
- ´ ; called "yángpíng", rises high, almost like asking a question, not quite like a Valley Girl
- ` ; called "qùshēng", is the opposite of yángpíng, starting high and ending low
- ˇ ; called "shàngshēng", starts high, dips the syllable, and ends high again
- ;The fifth tone, "qīngshēng", is no tone at all; it has no tone modifier mark and is spoken in a flat and neutral voice

As I traveled, I began to notice regional differences in pronunciation. The tones remained the same, but letters were dropped and/or added to each word. I have outlined those variations in the five "Mandarin Language Pronunciation" lessons listed in the Table of Contents.

PROLOGUE

Why was I going?

Even as I prepared to go, the question plagued me. Looking back, there were a lot of easy answers, all of which contained elements of truth, stories I told myself and convinced myself of as each in turn failed, but, like all easy answers, they were all lies. The honest truth, which I only really admitted to myself when it was too late to turn back, was that I was running away.

As escapes go, I could have chosen better, which is to say, I could have chosen easier. In going to China at this time, I would put myself in danger, I would get sick, I would have to learn a new language and customs virtually on the fly, and I would have to do so on what was, even then, a very small budget. It was, on the face of it, a terrible idea.

So, why? What was I running from and what led me there?

Well, to start, China wasn't just some place I found throwing a dart at a map. Six years earlier, when I was 17, I had signed up for a summer program to spend a month living with a family in Beijing. There, I would have learned to speak some Mandarin, I would have learned Chinese history and culture from their point of view, and, the big draw, I would have seen the Forbidden City, the Great Wall, and every other famous place we could go.

It would have been a great opportunity, but this was 1989. The Soviets were rapidly losing their grip on eastern Europe and central Asia, and pro-democracy movements were growing in authoritarian countries all around the world, including China. Weeks before we were due to go, student-led, non-violent protests in Běijīng's Tiān'ānmén Square were met with a brutal military crackdown that resulted in the deaths of hundreds, perhaps thousands, of protesters, putting an end to that movement and quite obviously cancelling my program's plans. Having already paid, we were offered an alternate route with group piggybacking through their other, active programs in Thailand and Indonesia, with a brief stop in Singapore in between. The experience proved to be challenging and humbling. What I saw in those countries sparked my interest in colonialism, which I then studied in college.

Studying colonialism in the early 90s was very different than it is now. You could take individual courses on it in history, sociology, or political science and build a major around it solely within one of those departments, but except for a few schools, that was it. I managed to build an independent, cross-disciplinary major at my school to study repeating patterns of behavior in colonial and post-colonial societies, specifically how those who overthrew colonizers mirrored the corruption and violence of the old regimes. As happy as I was with that, it made me virtually unemployable outside of a job in academia, which I very badly wanted to leave, or a job not requiring a college degree.

Somehow, I convinced myself journalism was an option. I was a quick study, I believed I could write well, and, with the end of the Cold War leading to civil wars and worse in former colonies and proxy states, I had what I believed was a valuable perspective on them. As I quickly learned, no one agreed. They wouldn't hire me for even the lowliest entry level position, not without a journalism degree. That was what they told me. Repeatedly. I could see why. Without a degree, they had no idea if I understood the basics of their industry or if I could write to their standard. If I really wanted to be a journalist, I'd have to take two years earning a degree and even then start small and local, far away from what I told myself I wanted to do with that degree, working my way up very slowly from the very bottom. And that was only if they were hiring, which they weren't.

Or, so it felt. My problem was that I was immature and impatient. I saw the world changing, I believed I understood the causes and how to communicate them, and I didn't want to have to take

Prologue

years sitting on the sidelines watching while the opportunity to share my insights passed me by. I had nothing against paying dues, I told myself, just against detours.

So, I hatched a plan: China.

I had never stopped wanting to go to China, to complete the journey I had started. This, I told myself, was the perfect opportunity. I resolved to travel to China, gain experience and a perspective that would be unique and attractive to potential employers, and return home to continue my wholly unrealistic, naive fantasy of becoming a professional journalist.

My first step in this delusional plan was to contact Mike Chinoy, then CNN bureau chief in Běijīng. I wrote to him and asked about an internship, believing that I could learn enough Mandarin before I arrived to get around and do my job. He wisely and politely turned me down. I was clearly ignorant of what that job would require and it was flatly ridiculous of me to believe I could handle it. I couldn't have.

Having failed that, I applied for a job teaching English at Shenyang Teachers College. Shěnyáng is a city northeast of Běijīng – north of North Korea, actually – in what was and still is China's rust belt. They offered me a job that might have been a great, life-changing experience, but it also would have kept me in Shěnyáng for about a year, including through its long, bitterly cold winter. Fearing that, and that the job would leave me little time to see the rest of the country, I turned it down.

What I realized in that moment, as the weight of that decision lifted, was what I really wanted, which was to explore, to see China on my own, paying my own way with no obligations and no schedule to keep. This was, of course, yet another naive fantasy sprinkled with just enough truth to keep me going. At this point, I was still denying my impatience and, to be brutally honest, my very clear need to escape the uncertainty of my post-college life. Without knowing what I wanted to do with that life, I was creating goals without understanding what they really were or what they would demand or what the consequences could be.

I did, at least, have some experience to fall back on. In the summer of 1993, with a Eurail Pass and an even smaller budget, I had backpacked through western and central Europe, taking a circuit around the continent starting and ending in Italy. I reasoned I could follow that same sort of route through China and, as I naively told myself, I'd only need to learn one language.

A year living at my parents' house after college allowed me to scrape together a budget of $5,000 from waiting tables and odd jobs. After I paid for my flight, that gave me about $20 to spend each day, including hotels and transportation. If that seems incredibly small now, it was, but back then it was enough to make a two month journey through China possible, if I was careful.

In June, I took the train up to New York to obtain a visa from the Chinese consulate. Until I had that, I didn't really have anything at all. It was a good test, or would have been had I never traveled by train before. The consulate was, and is, on the west side of Manhattan, facing the West Side Highway. It was a mission, a brief one. I submitted paperwork, I received a stamp, I was ready to go.

Except I wasn't. In July, I took what proved to be a necessary and essential ten-day Mandarin language immersion course up at Dartmouth's Rassias Foundation (now Center), named for the program's brilliant creator, John Rassias. Their teaching philosophy: Everyone roots for everyone else to succeed, and everyone helps teach each other. You help each other and quickly begin to trust each other to help. As I would find, one of the most valuable things it teaches is the comfort both in making mistakes and in asking for help to fix them, two skills that I would come to rely upon in China. Make a mistake, know that it's okay, and try again with the rest of your class until you all get it right. Learning this way, I left the course able to hold a simple conversation in Mandarin with accurate, tonal pronunciation. For both the process and the result, I can't recommend it more highly.

Was I ready then? In retrospect, no, but I had a good enough foundation in Mandarin to build on once I got there. I spent the rest of the summer preparing for the rest of it as best as I could. I bought supplies I believed I would need and practiced packing and repacking, a skill I wouldn't have expected to need, but which I would come to value the deeper I was in.

In August, I mapped out my planned route through China across the pages of my parents' big, blue National Geographic atlas, which I would leave spread open in their TV room so they could keep track of where I was, or at least where I was supposed to be on a given day.

As the summer of 1995 came to a close, we traveled out to San Francisco for the wedding of my oldest brother and sister-in-law. Whatever my reasons for going, I had committed to it and, for better or worse, I would have to make it work.

DAY 1

Saturday, September 2 – Monday, September 4
San Francisco, Over the Pacific Ocean, Hong Kong

•

First days are always long. It doesn't seem to matter what it's the first day of or how much you think you've prepared, there's so much to go through, so much to take in and understand. Something will change. Something will not work. Something will have been forgotten, or missed. Something you could not have foreseen will knock you down. Only when that happens can you understand what and how you have not prepared. And then you adjust. You have to. You're already in it.

This first day was especially long. I began it curled up in a bed in my brother and sister-in-law's house in San Francisco and ended it twenty-two hours and a full calendar day later curled up in a small bunk in a small, crowded cabin on a ferry docked in Hong Kong. Of course, I hadn't slept much the night before, maybe an hour altogether and I could barely call that sleep, so truthfully I would have to say my first day really began almost a full day earlier, Saturday morning, the second of September, 1995, the day my oldest brother and sister-in-law were married.

There are a few reasons to begin my tale here. The first is that San Francisco would bookend my journey. Like much of China at the time, it was rebuilding and reinventing itself, the city from the destruction caused by the 1989 Loma Prieta earthquake and the culture from the money flooding in from the rapidly growing tech industry. I would return to it almost eight weeks later, a very different person than when I left. The second reason is my lack of sleep, which started here and which would not improve in China. It was one of many things I should have foreseen on this journey but failed to, and I cannot understate its impact on me.

The third reason, though, may be the most important. It was what caused this first night's lack of sleep and set the course of my arrival in China: Drinking red wine gives me migraines. Nasty ones. Messy ones. Please bear with me as I explain this, because the pattern of how they develop is a pattern that will repeat in different ways, again and again, throughout this journey.

The reason red wine can trigger a migraine has to do with how chemicals present in it – quercetin, histamine, and tannins – build up in the body over time. They don't build up quickly. Over a week or so, a glass here, a couple of glasses there, not even getting drunk, body chemistry just reaches a tipping point. A lingering tightness in the jaw and neck builds to sinus pressure and a throbbing pain in the back of the head. Sudden nausea gives way to the telltale sensation of a knife corkscrewing along your left jaw, up the side of your head, and finally working its way down behind your left eye. Every sense is heightened. Light hurts. Sound hurts. And if it was because of something you ate or drank, your body wants to get rid of it, violently. I had experienced this several times before, but I wouldn't learn what was actually causing it until a few years after this, and only then after repeating through this same pattern enough times that I finally started to listen and understand.

The full attack started hours after the reception. I was sitting with everyone at dinner and quite sober. There were maybe twenty of us stretched out along a row of tables at the restaurant on Market Street. We had finished our appetizers and were waiting for the next course. I suddenly felt very, very sick. I fought it as best I could, drinking water, changing my breathing, checking my pulse, telling myself I had to stop it, but I couldn't. I tried to leave, but only got as far as the restaurant's bussing sink, where I'm still embarrassed to say I threw up. A lot. After that, the pain only got worse.

This would be the pattern I came to see on this journey, not oncoming illness, although there would be that, but small, seemingly inconsequential things adding to each other, building and compounding the effect of each other, failures of my own making combining with those of men and women who spent their days failing in their own self-defeating ways. I would see it in the lives of those men and

DAY 1: *San Francisco, Over the Pacific Ocean, Hong Kong* 3

women, too, how little, generational failures in their culture had led to ongoing misery and agony for everyone stuck in what was, at that time at least, a broken system.

    I could not have known this going in. I was only 23. I was still very young and in many ways still sheltered and dependent on others. This journey would test and often defeat that, as it should have. That should be the goal of a journey like this, gaining experience that removes the obstacles of inexperience and a sheltered life. It's a pity that kind of knowledge and self-awareness should have to be earned that way, but the lessons do last, if and when they finally take root.

    By the time the alarm on my watch went off Sunday morning, I still had a migraine and I was still a little green. It was a rough start, but a start it had to be. I had to go. I was already in it. I pulled myself together, stashed my wedding clothes to be collected on my return, said my farewells to my oldest brother and sister-in-law, and made my way down to the car where my parents and my brother, John, were waiting.

    We arrived at the airport only to find that the flight had been delayed two and a half hours, to 1:15 PM. I didn't know it then, but delays like this would be another recurring theme on my journey, one of those seemingly little things that built and compounded as I went on. This time, at least, I could wait it out at a comfortable airport.

    I was traveling with a large, gray two-piece L.L. Bean backpack, the same one I had taken through Europe two years earlier. It was already heavy and would get heavier once I started buying souvenirs, but I had done my best to keep things to a minimum. I had no idea how cold it might get in the north in September or the east in October, so I had packed a sweater, a pair of jeans, and one pair of thick, warm socks. Everything else was suitable for the heat and humidity I knew I'd face for at least the first two weeks.

    After I unzipped the smaller pack for the flight and checked the larger one, we all went to wait at the gate.[1] My dad thoughtfully dragged me over to change some cash for Hong Kong dollars so I'd have something for a taxi when I landed there. The woman at the counter exchanged a dollar less than I handed her, giving it back to

---

[1] It was a different time.

me with the rest of my change, I'll never know why. I noticed it but I didn't think much of it, not until after I arrived in Hong Kong, another one of those little, missed things that came back to bite me. My parents and John stayed with me as long as they could, but they had to get back for the post-wedding brunch. I was nervous and scared, which I figured they knew. I was also still in a lot of pain, but that I didn't want them to know. I didn't want them to worry, not more than they already were. I pushed the thought away, hugged them, and watched them go, and then I continued waiting, past 1:15, when I bought what airport food I could with the airline's $10 delay-voucher.

The flight finally left at 2 PM and was smooth. At thirteen hours, it was long enough to squeeze in another three, full, hot meals, which I ate while watching three full (well, edited for airline use) movies on one of the tiny, shared, 12-inch CRT TVs hanging from the ceiling that we all had to crane our necks to see. The sound came not through earphones or earbuds but uncomfortable, stereo tubes that plugged into the armrest and funneled the movies into your ears until they ached.[2] I couldn't sleep, though. I tried and I took as much Tylenol as I dared in one sitting, but the migraine lasted the whole flight, only ebbing as we neared our destination.

Finally, as the sun was setting over the western Pacific, we landed at Hong Kong's old Kai Tak airport, the one in the center of town with buildings whipping past the plane so close it looked like you could reach out the window and touch them. It was exciting and just a bit nerve-wracking, just like they always said, and I'm glad I got to see it before it was gone.

It was here that I forgot just about every word of Mandarin I had learned. I'd left my ten-day immersion course two months earlier able to hold a simple conversation with accurate tonal pronunciation, but I hadn't spoken with anyone in Mandarin since. One foot on soon to be Chinese soil and sure enough, I was useless. Even understanding that I was contending with a long flight, exhaustion, the shock of landing, the adrenalin that comes with the sudden pressure of having to perform in public, and a slowly fading migraine, opening my

---

[2] It was a very different time.

mouth and realizing that I couldn't find the first word was more nerve-wracking than the landing had been. It would pass. Thanks in no small part to that Rassias training, I would recover enough to get me where I needed to go, but it was a humbling entrance.

Mostly, I'm just glad I didn't get scammed when I arrived. I worried that I would. Exiting the terminal with my large, gray pack on my back, I entered a gauntlet of hawkers offering connections and rides to "guesthouses". What was at those guesthouses, I'll never know, not that I could have asked if I'd had to rely only on my conversational Mandarin because most of the hawkers not shouting in English seemed to be shouting in Cantonese, which in Hong Kong made perfect sense. My Mandarin would help me once I reached the mainland, but few in still-British Hong Kong should have been expected to speak it, let alone accept it spoken from a foreigner at that time[3].

It would be hard, and generous, to describe the hawkers outside the terminal as sincere in their welcome. Most just hung out along the sides of the exit ramp lazily waving and shouting their offers of "Guesthouse?", like beggars already thanking you before you've had a chance to turn down their overly rehearsed pleas for money. A few stepped out, blocking my path to make their own, overly rehearsed special offers just for me, but even they backed off with only a simple wave of my arm or firm shake of my head. There were so many of us leaving the airport, any effort to ingratiate themselves with any one passenger must've seemed pointless. For them, it was an hourly bounty of fresh meat, and my money was just as good as the next guy's.

As for me, I was just trying to get to the ferry to Guǎngzhōu, which my 1993 British guidebook still called "Canton". I made my way through the gauntlet and took a taxi across town to the ferry terminal, which was part of a shopping complex rather than the other way around. It was here, after frustrating some very kind and patient

---

[3] Cantonese is still the dominant language spoken in southeast China. The Hong Kong Cantonese dialect, which contains borrowed English words and other differences from Cantonese, has always carried a certain political weight, then as a rejection of the colonial British and now of the mainland Chinese government, which would prefer everyone speak the "common language" of China.

Guangxi University. It was in the guidebook as a thing to see, and in this case they weren't wrong. Even just the main gate was worth the effort. The gate led through a thick wall that had very old trees growing on top of it, some of them very large with long, spindly roots growing down over and through the wall.

The campus buildings were all old, pre-Revolution at the very least. It was quiet and mostly empty, not at all like the bustling campus of an American college in early September. I wandered and rested there for about half an hour before turning my attention to getting what would be my first train ticket in China.

A Hard Sleeper ticket to Kūnmíng, 600 miles and thirty-three slow hours away by train, would cost a reasonable ¥300, about $37, but it could only be purchased two days in advance, which meant I would have to make a round-trip up from Yángshuò on Saturday to buy it. My planning for the future complete, I found some more dān-dān noodles and called it a night.

DAY 5

Friday, September 8

Guìlín, Yángshuò, Guìlín, Yángshuò

•

In 1995, Yángshuò was still mostly a backpackers destination, a strip of hostels, open-air restaurants, and gift shops parked smack in the middle of a beautiful sea of rice paddies and the narrow hills made of karst, a kind of limestone, that rise like islands between them.

The best way to get there was and probably still is by boat from Guìlín down the Lí (Green) River. It's a nice way to travel, and the water really is as green as the steep hills rising on either side of the river. Suan, my self-appointed teenage tour guide, may have failed in his many entrepreneurial pursuits, shot down at every turn, but along the way he did get me a ticket for a boat ride down the Lí to Yángshuò that cost a lot less than the $45 that tourists were regularly charged in Guìlín. For that, I remain grateful.

I remember being in a rush to get out the door. It started with the shower. Getting the water a temperature that wasn't scalding or freezing was a challenge, with a lot of short-lived victories before things stabilized at lukewarm. That managed, next came the Chinese hotel soap, which was waxy and unusually hard. It demanded a lot of time and effort to release any lather. By the time I finished my shower, I was running late. Not really, not that I could have known because I hadn't made this trip before, but because I hadn't done it I didn't know how long it would take to get to the dock and I was afraid of missing the boat, so I dressed and packed quickly, checked out, and ran all the way over with my full pack.

It is here that I am reminded just how young and foolish I was, how careless I was, and how unprepared I was for what I was doing. I was making it up as I went along, reacting as much as anything, and not paying attention to the little things. "Xiăo xīn" (she-ow sheen) is the term I would learn. Literally, it means "small mind", but colloquially it means "be careful" or "focus". When it came to the camera I borrowed from my parents, I had been very careless. That included not testing it and also not checking the level of the batteries before I left. Those careless mistakes would in turn reveal another, unrelated yet equally careless one, which would waste almost all of an entire, valuable day of my journey.

We were two hours downriver from Guìlín, five hours upriver from Yángshuò. I had taken some pictures, one of them of a cormorant fisherman on his boat in the river as we went by.

The fishermen use a trained cormorant, partially bound so it is unable to swallow its prey, to dive into the river to hunt. When the bird returns to the boat, the fish is taken and, presumably, a swallowable reward given.

As I celebrated what I hoped would be a great photograph, the batteries in the camera died. I hadn't checked the battery levels because I, in my naive inexperience, simply knew that I had more batteries and I could replace them when I had to. No problem. I went to the big half of my backpack to get them and…Of course.

DAY 5: *Guìlín, Yángshuò, Guìlín, Yángshuò*

Before leaving the hotel, I had padlocked all of the zippers on the big half, a perfectly sensible thing to do if you're traveling alone on a boat and may have to leave your bag unattended for a moment. However, In my rush to make the boat, I had left all of the keys for all of the locks on all of the compartments in the hotel room back in Guìlín. Everything I needed for the rest of my journey except for the camera, the thermos, the guidebook, and the maps was in that big bag, including my passport and traveler's cheques. I cursed myself. I looked around at all of the Chinese tourists on the boat – I was, as I would be many places on this journey, the only non-Chinese tourist in sight – and I saw them all looking back at me. My panic must have been clear to everyone. The expression on my face could only have communicated one thing: How could I be such a complete fucking idiot?!

I sat and tried to think. I had no idea how to pick a lock, and I was too embarrassed to ask for help. I realized I'd have to go back to Guìlín and hope I got lucky. We still had almost five hours before we reached Yángshuò. I would then have to find a bus to take me one and a half hours back to Guìlín, followed by a five minute run back to the hotel. I resigned myself to it.

You might ask, Why not just break the lock? It was a thick one, actually well made. It would have been easier to break the zippers. Of course, if I did that, I wouldn't have been able to close the bag again. And even if they had a tool capable of cutting the padlock, they might have damaged the zippers, too. I considered my options and, sadly, going back was the best, first option I had.

I had nothing to lose at this point, so I reached into the bag by spreading the locked zippers apart as far as they'd go, and, after entertaining the crew and passengers for fifteen minutes, I got the batteries out, along with a pile of other things I then had to squeeze back in.

I had nothing to do then but change the batteries, take some more pictures, and wait. I went back up to the deck. I kicked myself. I cursed myself. I wouldn't even let myself enjoy the four course meal included with the cruise, and the meal was good. I think I only took one more picture from the boat, and I don't think it came out.

When we finally drifted round the bend to the docks at Yángshuò, it was overcast. Whatever pictures I could have taken then would have been too dark. That wasn't the worst of it, though. The worst of it was that I'd had so much time to think about it. I was furious with myself, and in that moment I didn't have the kindness or patience for others that I'd received so far from so many. I coldly shrugged off the vendors and other grabbers-on, which included, regrettably, a little girl who only seemed to want to practice her English. I brushed them all off, planted myself on one of the minibuses, waited while they dragged a few more customers on, and at long last was on my way back to Guìlín. The karst hills, shaded one behind another by the sunset, took my mind off the keys, at least for part of the ride. The hills, worn away by millennia of wind and rain, popped up through rice paddies like it was Monument Valley, but green. It was beautiful.

When we hit the main drag in Guìlín, I ran all the way back to the Overseas Mansion. The manager saw me coming and graciously held my keys out to me from behind the desk. The cleaning staff had saved them. More good luck for me, no matter how careless or rude I had been. That only hit me later, as I feasted on mǐ fěn from a street cart for ¥3. It was wonderful, the kind of cheap, wonderful meal that makes you think nothing in the world is wrong. It wasn't that the noodles were so great, just that I'd been lucky, and right or wrong that makes everything taste better, if only for a moment.

It was getting dark, so I went back over to where the minibuses lined up by the train station and sparked a bidding war, which was won by a woman offering the low, low price of ¥7.7. No sooner had she won me than she dragged me proudly onto her minibus. She had all the spirit in the world, but she was pretty lousy at getting passengers. I managed to convince an Israeli, Ayal, to take her minibus. He then joined me in drawing others. If we hadn't, we'd never have gotten out of there. On the road, she was better. She hung out the door hawking for potential customers. It seemed like anyone within her reach got scooped on board. Everybody's money was just as good; it didn't matter if you wanted to take the bus or not.

Leaning up against the window of her minibus, I finally started

DAY 5: *Guìlín, Yángshuò, Guìlín, Yángshuò*

to look at the city going by. Local businesses were set mostly in strip-mall type garages, open air until the gates were pulled down late at night. Being so, they were also living rooms for the families who ran them, with TV sets, mostly black & white it seemed, and card games in just about every one I saw from the road heading out of Guìlín.

After checking in at the Xiling Hotel in Yángshuò, I discovered my room had no light. They apologized and suggested I take a conveniently much more expensive room. I apologized, got my money back, and headed over to the Yangshuo Youth Hostel, where Ayal was staying. They put me in a shared room with two Austrians, Martin and Gerhard. The hostel had bike rentals and ticket assistance, too. I had everything I needed and all was good. Just another, normal, lucky day.

Xiǎo xīn.

DAY 6

Saturday, September 9
Yángshuò

•

The bicycle being central to Chinese national identity is something of a myth. When they were introduced to China and its neighbors in the late 19th century, cheap bicycles opened up transportation where few could afford draught animals or horses for riding long distances, let alone newly introduced cars. By 1995, that hadn't really changed. Outside of cities, few people owned cars. They still couldn't afford them. Buses, minibuses, and trucks were what you saw out on rural roads, those and modified tractors pulling wooden carts in place of horses, donkeys, and oxen.

What you didn't often see on rural roads were bikes. In cities, sure, because the roads were paved and flat and there were so many people and it really was convenient, but outside of them, with a comparatively sparse population and farther distances to travel and unpaved roads, not so much. Almost all of the people you saw riding bikes in places like Yángshuò were tourists, like me.

The most important lesson I learned riding bikes in China was that, despite the absence of cars, or perhaps because of it, no road in China was safe. Even with so few privately owned cars, road traffic at the time was chaotic with few widely accepted rules. In cities, riding a bike could jangle the nerves of even an experienced rider. Drivers rode their horns to keep anything that might get in their way out of it. Trucks and buses, if they could even see you, seemed to wait until they were almost upon you before blaring their horns. And other riders, as I would discover weeks from now, could be just as dangerous as any of them. Yángshuò, of course, is not a city and wasn't then, but the risks riding on the dirt roads nearby could be the same.

DAY 6: *Yángshuò*

Ironically, it wasn't a car or truck or reckless cyclist that nearly killed me. It was a tree.

I was about an hour into my ride out of Yángshuò. My legs had turned to jelly at some point, but I'd caught a second wind. The ride was filled with picture perfect vistas, smiles and waves from the side of the road, and even a chat with a local merchant when I stopped to buy water. This, I thought, was what I had come to China to see. It was what I wanted it to be. It was only when I decided to get off my bike that everything went wrong.

I had pulled off to the side of road to get some shade under a tree and take pictures of the rice paddies and karst hills stretching out all around me. The part of the road where I stopped was essentially the top of a wall that separated two rice paddies, each about ten feet or so below. The road was wide enough for a single car or truck to pass over safely if they drove slowly, in daylight. The tree was off by the left edge of the wall-road as I approached. It looked like it had taken root years earlier and had just been allowed to grow, like the trees on top of the walls around Guangxi University, possibly for the shade I now enjoyed or possibly because no one had ever bothered to take it down. Maybe they just thought it looked pretty? I did. I saw it and my first thought was to stop and take a picture of it.

So, having pulled up under the shade of the tree, I confidently planted my left foot at the edge of the dirt road and caught the toe of my right boot just a bit on the basket over the bike's rear wheel as I swung my leg over. I hopped on my left foot to steady myself, just a short one, maybe not even a full hop, and...I was lying on my back, covered in rice paddy mud, head to toe, ten feet down.

My arms and shoulders hurt from where I had tried to grab the top of the wall as I fell feet first. All I had managed to do was slam my upper arms down on the edge of the stone wall before bouncing off. I looked up at the wall rising high in front of me and I looked down at myself; I couldn't tell where I stopped and the rice paddy began. I had no thought of this, though, nor of the head-crushingly large rock just a few feet to the left of where I had impacted. I was thinking about the bike and my backpack in the bike's basket and the camera inside the backpack, all of them still high above me by the side of the road, or in it. I didn't know, I couldn't see them. There wasn't anyone around, for better and worse, but instinctively in that moment I was more concerned about not losing the camera than anything else.

I scrambled along the muddy bank to the dirt path leading down from the wall and ran up to the bike, which had fallen over, too. Mercifully, it and the small backpack holding my camera, which was somehow still in the bike's basket, hadn't followed me over the edge. I wiped my hands as best as I could and checked the camera. It was OK. Well, not OK. The fall seemed to have had no effect on the camera, but the problems I'd already been having with it remained. For the time being, though, I was just happy to find it in one piece. Relieved, I took the picture I'd meant to take when I stopped, of the paddy with a small shack at the far end and towering, green hills behind them as far as I could see. And then I took one of the new crater ten feet down, which failed when the shutter stuck. Sadly, the shots of the tree that caused this whole mess failed, too.

I looked down at the wall where my left foot had lost its grip. A chunk of it right at the top was now missing, no doubt buried in the mud down below. I don't know if it had been the tree's roots working their way into the stones over the years or the weight of my single hop that finally loosened it, probably both.

It didn't really matter, not then. I was in pain, and I was carrying I don't know how many pounds of rice paddy mud around with me. It was on me and it was inside my clothes. I had mud in places I didn't think I'd ever get clean. And my tires were low. So, I turned around and headed back. To add insult to my injuries, on my return, I managed to provide entertainment to the same locals who had smiled and waved to me on my way out, including the local merchant who had sold me water. They all got a good laugh out of it. I couldn't blame them. I earned it.

There was one good thing in all of this, just one: all of that mud ended up protecting me from the late summer heat and humidity, enough that I at least managed to enjoy a cool ride back to the hostel, stopping here and there to take shots of the endless hills and other, unblemished paddies.

I showered myself and my boots as best as I could with the hard hotel soap, sent my clothes to the hostel laundry, and went right back out again. With my arms, neck, and back sore, I moved slowly and stiffly like an old man, but I went out for the night scene anyway, just to see what it was.

Yángshuò was treating tourists to its Mid-Autumn Festival a little early. Mooncakes were being sold everywhere and firecrackers were set off on street corners long into the night. Proper celebrations would center around nearby Moon Hill later in the week. All of the tourists were out eating big on the cheap at Yángshuò's many cafes catering to western tourists. Among them were Mickey Mao's, Minnie Mao's, The Hard Rock Cafe, The Hard Seat Cafe (the name of which I did not yet appreciate), MC Blues Cafe, Planet Yángshuò, and The Rainbow Cafe. I was sincerely surprised not to find a Rick's Cafe Americain. I checked out all of the "antique" vendors for pricing's sake, but found nothing I wanted. After browsing here and there, and finding a lot of contemporary Chinese art that seemed heavily influenced by Gustav Klimt, I stopped in the "world famous" Lisa's Cafe to watch their movie of the night, a VHS tape of "Raiders of the Lost Ark" on a very small TV. A couple of lemonades later, the movie was over and I worked through my expenses for this comically dangerous day: $5, not including the laundry. For all that misadventure, I could've paid that money for a movie in a theater back home and saved myself the trouble. But trouble was why I was here, though, right? It was tempting to stay in Yángshuò, but I wanted to see the rest of this version of China before it disappeared completely. Or I did.

DAY 7

Sunday, September 10
Yángshuò, Guìlín, Yángshuò

•

Being the seventh day, I did what was good for me and rested, as much as I could. After the last two days, the less I did the better. My back and neck were more sore than they had been last night, and there was nothing to do about it except let them heal. Having wasted one day retrieving my forgotten keys and most of another recovering from a pratfall into a rice paddy, I now took the bus into Guìlín and picked up my Hard Sleeper ticket to Kūnmíng, along with some "kuài", slang for "money", meaning any kind of money, even dollars.

 I am sorry to say that, on my frequent trips back and forth to Guìlín, perhaps the best scenery I found in the region was viewed from a minibus moving at high speed. I never got off a clean shot. Most of the hills in the region appear to come in circular groups, formations described by locals as shaped something like the Big Dipper. They tend to slope away on the outside of the groups and have sharp faces on the inside, giving the impression that the entire area might be some sort of caldera, a thousand cones of a long dormant supervolcano worn away by wind and rain, but that isn't the case. Karst is a soft, sedimentary rock and these hills were no threat to anyone but the careless. Looking out at this scenery on the way back to Yángshuò, my neck and shoulders still felt tight, but they were showing signs of improvement.

 I spent what was left of the day sampling Yángshuò's cafés and trinket shopping. The one downside of the cafés was their placement on the main road running through town, which at the time was literally an open sewer. Cement grates covered the sluices, but the smell got ripe depending on the time of day and direction of the wind. I could not have known it then, but it was very much a preview of things to come[5]. After a pungent meal downwind at the Paris Cafe, I spent most of the afternoon upwind at the Sunny Side Cafe watching the movie "The Shadow" over a pot of green tea. After that, I took the very short walk down to the docks, where a Spanish tour group had just arrived. I didn't think they stood a chance in this country, not with the way they dove into the souvenir bazaar here. Of course, I did, too, and found myself with three pairs of jadeite chopsticks, one pair blue and green, which I would keep for myself, and two other pairs, green with veins of black and white, covered all over with white flecks. Those, I would give to my oldest brother and sister-in-law as part of their wedding gifts.

It was a few short steps back to the main drag, where I bumped into Ayal eating a late lunch at the Mei You Cafe. There are few things nicer than sitting and sharing a drink in the afternoon sun, and it was upwind of the sewers, so I joined him. A Brit named Richard stopped by with horror stories of how he and his friend had been robbed at the old train station in Guǎngzhōu shortly after their arrival and then again in Macao. By "shortly", I mean they hadn't lasted more than half an hour. They'd made the same mistake as me when I arrived in Guǎngzhōu, going straight to the train station to buy tickets; unlike me, they had gone inside, easy prey. I would end up going straight to the ticket windows in many of the places I visited, but I remembered their story at every single one and took care. As soon as his chips ran out, so did Richard. He moved fast, not fast enough to avoid getting robbed twice, but fast.

I mentioned to Ayal that I was from Philadelphia and he told me his friend was the lead trombonist of the Philadelphia Orchestra. It turned out Ayal was a classical composer, published and recorded. He and I then talked about film and music and the finer points of world travel until the daylight started to wane.

As night slowly crept in, I headed back to the stretch of carbon-copy souvenir shops near the docks. They seemed more impressive lit up in the growing darkness. After a bit of cross-bidding, I realized that I'd paid almost three times what I could have when I bought the jadeite chopsticks earlier. This, after I'd laughed at the poor Span-

---

[5] Day 13

DAY 7: *Yángshuò, Guìlín, Yángshuò* 33

iards. I'd have kicked myself more, but it wasn't actually that much of a difference in price, and the three pairs I bought ended up being the only ones I saw of their kind in the whole town while I was there, so it was a fair price.

For dinner, I watched "Indiana Jones and the Last Crusade" at Lisa's over a bowl of jiāozi soup, my first jiāozi in China. Jiāozi are wrapped dumplings, filled with meat and/or vegetables. I would make a point of trying them everywhere in China, both because they were cheap and because I wanted to see how the recipes changed in different regions. There doesn't seem to be a consensus on where the name "jiāozi" comes from. Like so many things in China, the name seems to have an origin too far back for anyone to know how it started. Some claim it has to do with the dumplings having a crescent or horn-like shape, as the fried versions often did; others claim it's because the dumplings can resemble lumps of gold, which the rounded, boiled versions often did. All of this is to say, they come in all shapes and sizes and at some point, as people will do, they just accepted what everybody around them said it was, in this case, a dumpling with meat and/or vegetable contents wrapped in a layer of dough.

Filled with wrapped-dough dumplings, I joined Ayal and his brother, a tài jí (tai chi) instructor for expats in Běijīng, at the Global Village Cafe for a discussion of free choice and Ingmar Bergman films over a pot or two of ginger tea. The main theme of Bergman's "Wild Strawberries" was prominent: It's never too late to make a change, and better not to live with regret. Trite? Maybe, but you know how sentimental Bergman could be.

DAY 8

Monday, September 11
Yángshuò, Guìlín

•

It was around midnight when I finally got back to my room. My Austrian roommates were packing, so we stayed up late talking about cities, violence, and football, American and other. Despite agreeing that the other guy's country was better so we could all get some sleep, they only managed a few hours, waking about 5 in the morning. They were leaving to find their own version of disappearing China, taking a Yangtze River cruise to see the river valley before the government completed construction of their Three Gorges Dam project and permanently submerged the valley and its villages under 300 meters of water. Looking back, I wish I had joined them. Sort of.

For my own day's journey, I stuck closer to home, choosing to climb Moon Hill, so named because of a large, crescent shaped open-

DAY 8: *Yángshuò, Guìlín* 35

ing just below the peak that creates a sort of natural arch. "Half-Moon Hill" might have been more accurate, but who wants to see that?

It was a muggy day. Yesterday's clear, blue skies had given way to a dull, pale haze. It took me a little more than half an hour to pedal down the road from Yángshuò. They were in the process of widening the road to allow for heavy two-way traffic, the kind of width you need for tour buses going to and from Wúzhōu and Guǎngzhōu. They'd also started building, in Yángshuò and along this road, the kind of resort stuff which would one day make this area too expensive for budget travel. That kind of construction required convoys of dump trucks, which in 1995 made up the bulk of the traffic on this road and which made it dangerous to look too much at the scenery. Soon, though, minibuses parked at the south end of Yángshuò would make biking to Moon Hill unnecessary. It's a shame, because riding out to climb to the top of it is something everyone should get to do, and something which should have as few distractions as possible.

The very top of Moon Hill is narrow and a little precarious, which fortunately keeps too many from making it up at once. More than three at a time, you were pushing your luck. I sat up top alone for nearly an hour. Having the view all to myself for that long was more than I could have asked for, and I knew it. At first, the haze had made me wish I'd come here yesterday, but by the end I knew that I couldn't have and satisfied myself with the view I'd been given.

36 AN INCREDIBLY FOOLISH AND DANGEROUS THING TO DO

One of the two old women holding shop on the shoulder below the peak passed me as I finally came down. She was climbing to set up shop on the peak itself, the heavy bag on her back full of bottled water and trinkets. Two tourists, German, I think, were on her heels. Down on the shoulder, I saw what the old woman had seen, a dozen tourists, dazed and exhausted by the climb, scattered on the rocks in the shade. They'd be thirsty and ready to spend when they reached her.

On my way up, I'd promised the other old woman that I'd buy a bottle of water from her on the way down, and she graciously stuck to the pre-rush price. Suddenly, people climbing past me started asking my advice, on Moon Hill, on bottled water prices, and on where the best deals were in Yángshuò. I had reached the top and, apparently, I spoke Chinese, so I was now an expert. I tried my best and moved on.

Halfway down the hill I came across an old man – to my young eyes, he looked maybe eighty or ninety – who had laid out his blanket of goods by one of the stone benches at a turn in the steps. He didn't have much to choose from, but I picked up a copy of the now-only-mandatory-for-tourists "Little Red Book", aka, "Questions from Chairman Mao Zedong".

DAY 8: Yángshuò, Guìlín 37

A mere ¥10 – about a buck and a quarter – it was in excellent condition, with a tissue plate leaf over Máo's picture and the original cardboard sleeve for the volume. Only 25 years earlier, in the darkest years of Máo's "Cultural Revolution", these books were carried by everyone as proof of loyalty to communism and especially to Máo Zédōng himself. Now, they couldn't sell them fast enough.

Back in town, I mailed my first postcards, picked up my mudfree laundry, and then repacked again. I would always be repacking on this journey, sometimes more than once in the same day. For dinner, I watched "Pulp Fiction" on the TV at Lisa's with an international audience over a bowl of jiāozi soup. All that remained for this perfect day was for the train to carry me off to Kūnmíng.

However...

While I had given myself over three and a half hours to get to Guìlín for the 1 AM train, I hadn't counted on the minibuses, usually parked at the north end of town, ending their daily runs at 8 PM. I should have thought of it – remember, "xiǎo xīn" – but I hadn't. Of course, without prior experience of missing the minibuses, I don't know how I could have known. There wasn't a schedule posted anywhere, and a cutoff time wasn't mentioned in the guidebook or by the drivers. It made sense that there'd be at least one minibus left, trawling for stragglers, but no.

By 10:30, I was still out there and as far as I knew there wouldn't be a bus of any kind until morning. I had to wait, nervous and then angry, as taxis offered to drive me the whole way for only hundreds of kuài, all of them laughing as they pulled away still empty.

Then, somehow, completely out of nowhere, a bus pulled in at 10:50. There wasn't a sign for it. There wasn't a schedule posted anywhere. You just had to know. Those taxis drivers had surely known. And so, too, had the men and women who had gathered to wait with me; they had all already sat on the curb long before I gave up and joined them. They'd done this enough times not to mind not knowing. It whad become normal to them. Maybe it always had been. They'd probably never considered not having a schedule strange. A bus showed up, eventually, and that was enough. It had been enough because it had to be. I wasn't there yet, and I wasn't sure I ever wanted to be.

The bus that showed up was huge, a full-size one built way back when Dwight D. Eisenhower was the evil, capitalist monster in Maoist children's stories. We waited on the curb, myself and the four locals, while the driver enjoyed a leisurely snack. The others, resigned to their fate, said he'd take no more than ten minutes.

We left a few "ten minutes" later, at 11:25. I had it in my head we weren't going to make it. I was convinced I'd have to eat the $36 train ticket, which on my budget would have been an extravagance, if not a disaster. I willed the driver to go faster and faster, but I couldn't tell how fast we were going. It was pitch black outside and the lights barely showed the dirt road in front of us. It felt fast. It felt like the bus was flying apart at every bump and coming back together just in time to hold every turn. Every time I saw lights coming towards us in the road, I worried we'd hit them, but they passed by, harmless and unharmed. This white knuckle terror lasted only a bit less than the usual hour and a half travel time to Guilín. In fact, the driver and his great, big, old bus got us into Guilín with fifteen minutes to spare before my train was due to leave. I was still shaking as I entered the station.

And, of course, I needn't have worried; the westbound train left Guilín thirty-five minutes late. Stuck high up in a top Hard Sleeper bunk, at least I could sleep.

SIGNS COMMUNISM WAS OVER

Part 1:

The Chinese Communist Party's hold on power is stronger than ever, in no small part due to their somewhat ironic embrace of capitalism following the death of Máo Zédōng. The strongest examples of this would come later in my journey, but so far I had seen the following:

#1: "Pabst Blue" everything; if it could be called a liquid, they bottled and canned it and sold it here. It was not the only American brand I would find here. Coca-Cola, McDonald's, Pizza Hut, and KFC already had a big and growing footprint in China and their influence on Chinese consumer culture was only growing.

#2: The American flag popped up on pens and other souvenirs at the shops in Yángshuò. It would appear just about everywhere I went in China, not perhaps as a symbol of aspirational freedom as much as "if you buy me, it means you already are free".

#3: The publishing downfall of Máo's Little Red Book. It hadn't even been 20 years since his death and he had been reduced for public consumption to something akin to a national mascot, like Mickey Mouse, who for Chinese consumers was far more popular.

DAY 9

Tuesday, September 12
Guìlín, Guǎngxī Province, Guìzhōu Province
•

Did I say, "sleep"?

If my rest atop Moon Hill had been an exercise in learning to accept what had been given, my day and two nights in Hard Sleeper would be one in learning to endure it.

Hard Sleeper, where I was trying to sleep, was the second lowest of the four classes of train travel. They were, in order of status: Soft Sleeper (First Class, sometimes in a private room; very expensive, at least compared to the others, and not available on all trains); Soft Seat (even more rare, due to the dearth of modern, soft seated trains in the country at the time); Hard Sleeper (a barely padded, narrow, wood plank bed in an open space with no privacy); and Hard Seat (just that, an unpadded wood plank bench covered with vinyl and/or cloth).

This was train #79 out of Shànghǎi, headed west, thirty-three long hours from Guìlín to Kūnmíng. The train, inside and out, seemed to have twice the grime that covered everything else in China at the time. I could attribute this to so many passengers being packed into so small a space, but that would only be a part of it. It hadn't been cleaned for some time. That has to be acceptible for that to happen, like people accepting that buses don't have or need schedules, and, for whatever reasons, the trains were filthy because it was.

It should come as no surprise, then, that the Chinese in 1995 were not the environmentalists even that Americans were, not that America's reputation for environmental progress at the time was deserved. Most of the polluting industrial technology and products American companies had "upgraded" from were simply sold abroad to "developing" countries, which at the time included China. Those styrofoam containers your fast food chain got rid of, they all ended up here, and on this train they ended up left on white trays along with the other garbage opposite each complement of six bunks. When those trays filled up, the attendants simply emptied them right out the windows of the moving train. This country, which made such economical use of its land, had not the respect for it that anyone outside of China might have thought. The only mystery was why the attendants waited for the trays to fill up rather than simply allowing passengers to chuck their own garbage out the windows themselves. But, no, nothing would be that simple, not here.

Everyone did save their bottles and jars, though: they used them for tea. Hot water was provided in a pair of thermal urns at the end of each car on the train, so every passenger I saw on the train filled their used jars and bottles with water and whatever tea they'd brought with them. Well, everyone except for the man sleeping on the bottom bunk below me. He made a tobacco bong out of his plastic bottle. An attendant found it and, yes, threw it out the window. I, of course, had my metal Eddie Bauer thermos, which I had bought in San Francisco before I left. Not for the last time, it drew a lot of attention, including a few admiring nods.

What was also provided free of charge was punishingly loud music. This was a Muzak-like medley of "Sound of Music" tunes tossed in with Běijīng Opera, Judge Bǎo serials[6], and some things that may have been on the soundtrack to "The Carebears Movie", stuff of sickening, pure evil. It didn't help that my bunk was at the top. It would have been cramped and uncomfortable even for a person shorter and thinner than I was, but it was also right next to the ceiling-mounted loudspeaker, which was very loud. It was excruciating.

Thankfully, during the day my bunkmates invited me to sit down below. That allowed me to see the countryside of Guìzhōu province, which, away from the tracks, seemed free of pollution. Guìzhōu was among the poorest of the provinces, almost entirely rural with little public transportation. That made it a difficult place to travel for a tourist, which was a pity, because from what I could see it was beautiful.

---

[6] Kung Pao sauce is named for Judge, or "Gōng", Bǎo.

Standing on this floor, even in a section where people were supposedly sleeping, required keeping your shoes on. In addition to garbage that missed the white trays, there was also the layers upon layers of stickiness that came from a pair of common hobbies in China: projectile sneezing and spit. Among the reasons for them were a combination of poor hydration, that despite all of the free hot water and tea, air pollution from the coal that powered factories, homes, and still some of the trains, and smoking, which they weren't supposed to do on the trains but weren't ever going to stop. Just ask the guy with the bong.

Sadly, there was also one other reason for the sneezing and spitting, which was what they spread: respiratory viruses. A lot of the passengers were simply sick with colds they couldn't shake, so they sneezed and spit on everything and everyone. Almost as prevalent as the soundtrack of Judge Bǎo and saccharine American show tunes were the sounds of snorting and hoicking that preceded sneezing and spitting as lightning precedes thunder.

I was told the train had a dining car, and it probably did somewhere ahead of Soft Sleeper class, but as I wasn't allowed out of my own class I don't think I'll ever know. The irony of class restrictions in "communist" China, even for food, never escaped me once. For Hard Sleeper class, stewards rolled through with styrofoam boxes of rice and a lump of dried meat. I opted to finish off the bag of digestive biscuits I bought back in Guǎngzhōu and get as much sleep as I could, loudspeakers and hoicking permitting. I made a mental note to remember to ask for a zhōng (middle) berth next time, meaning both a bunk in the middle row and also in the middle of the car. Middle berths had a view and headroom, and the middle of the car was as far from the loud muzak as you could get. As I saw it then, I would have seven or eight more of these train rides, and a soft sleeper for at least one of them. For the time being, though, I'd just have to wait for my next hotel to clean myself up. No sense doing it twice.

DAY 10

Wednesday, September 13

Yúnnán Province, Kūnmíng

•

We arrived in Kūnmíng ahead of schedule, about 9:30 AM. This would be an ongoing pattern with trains here, leaving late and arriving early. Sometimes, it would be the other way around. It surprised me less and less that they never had a printed schedule.

On the train, I had met Katsuo, a college student from Japan on his way to Tibet. He spoke only a little English, and I spoke no Japanese, so we communicated mostly in broken beginners' Mandarin. I remember him seeming so young, but he was really about the same age as me. In Kūnmíng, he was planning to stay at a hotel that had either been rebuilt or replaced since the guidebooks called it "cheap". Neither of us could afford a room in the new one, not even together, so I offered to share a double at the visibly cheaper Camellia Hotel. That hotel, now long gone, too, was on one of the old, tree lined boulevards of old, colonial Kūnmíng. Two floors of the Camellia somehow contained the consulates for two of China's southern neighbors, Laos and Cambodia. I could only imagine how they spied on each other. I still like to picture old, wooden hand drills comically opening holes through the floor or ceiling, big enough for comically oversized peeking eyes and listening ears as if they were in some old cartoon.

At the reception desk, they gave us the old "méi yǒu" (don't have) routine for the cheaper room, but Katsuo gave them the old "poor student, méi yǒu" (don't have money) reply and they gave us a decent double for the low, low price of just under $9 apiece. He was only staying one night in Kūnmíng, so I'd have to pay the full rate for the next two nights, but it was worth it.

While Katsuo returned to the train station to buy his ticket up to

Chéngdū, from which he would continue on to Tibet, I took the opportunity to wash as much of the train off of me as I could. Next, I had to eat, because I hadn't eaten much on the train, mostly digestive crackers. A couple of blocks down, I found an alley with a very active market. As I would discover, Kūnmíng was loaded with these, and they were all great. They had everything, from bananas and bottled water to piles of peppers and parts of animals we in the West still don't use. One lady specialized in goat hearts. Just goat hearts. About a block down, I found a little snack place that sold puffy, steamed bāozi, 3 kuài for a whole mess. A bāo in Mandarin is a purse or bag with a drawstring to close it; bāozi are named for them not only because they look this way but because the filling is literally stuffed down into the rice dough. It was a meat filling, probably pork, but maybe goat? Whatever it was, it tasted good.

The amount I spent for this meal was actually a lot compared to what I'd spend on most other meals in China. They would be closer to 1 kuài, which is to say, ¥1, about 12.5¢. Chinese currency broke down like this: 100 Fen were equal to 10 Jiao, which were equal to 1 Yuan (¥). You could literally scrape an entire meal together just pulling 1 and 2 Fen coins and bills off the sidewalk, because they were everywhere, actually litering the street. I noticed going back to Guǎngzhōu that not only did locals not pick them up, they actually seemed to make a point of not picking them up. It was as if they were diseased, which, given all of the spitting and projectile sneezing I'd seen since I arrived, might very well have been true. They would round prices down rather than chance you giving them an unwanted Fen. Many vendors and cashiers wouldn't even accept 10 Fen as 1 Jiao, and again, just 10 Jiao was the price of a bowl of dān-dān noodles or a yóutiáo, a long churro-like doughnut. The only place that would accept them? The bank.

Out on the town after lunch, I began to feel a little light-headed. My joints felt a little stiff, too. And then my sinuses confirmed it. I had caught something, although not from picking up loose currency. It was almost certainly from the big gobs of snot and spit that coated the inside of the train from Guìlín, or maybe from one of the minibuses going back and forth between Guìlín and Yángshuò. I'll

DAY 10: *Yúnnán Province, Kūnmíng* 45

never know. I had no choice but to go on and hope I could fight it.

I'd only just found a large planter to the side of the boulevard to rest on and was enjoying the shade and not moving when Katsuo found me. He was on his way to the Provincial Museum. I reasoned it was a short enough walk and even if walking didn't help my cold, there would be plenty of places to sit, so I joined him.

The museum had all sorts of archaeological treasures from the region inside, and dinosaurs. Or did they? Well, no. The dinosaur exhibits were closed off. They were redoing them, I think. In fact, most of the museum was closed except for two exhibits. The first had costumes of minorities from the southwest region. China's main ethnicity is Han, but the south and west are filled with dozens of other ethnicities, including Lisu and Lahu, who live throughout Southeast Asia, Uighurs, who live in the westernmost province of Xinjiang, and, of course, Tibetans, whose home was annexed by China in 1950.

In a cruel irony for Kastuo, the main exhibit was on the brutality of Japanese military occupiers in the region during World War II[7]. The 50th anniversary of Japan's surrender had been just weeks earlier. I couldn't read the text of the exhibit, which was in hànzì, but the pictures made the story quite clear. Katsuo, being Japanese, could of course read everything, the Chinese hànzì being mostly the same as Japanese kanji. I think he would rather have seen a dinosaur with the wrong head standing on its tail. I don't know what he'd been taught about Japan's atrocities in China during the 1930s and 40s, but it clearly hadn't been this. The pictures weren't especially graphic, but they told the story well enough. I didn't know what to say, or, frankly, how to say it. I told myself I could understand how he felt in that moment, but there was little I could do for him and I wasn't sure if going through the rest of the exhibit with him would help or hurt. I was tired and getting sicker by the minute, so I excused myself and caught my breath on the edge of an empty display upstairs while he made his way through the rest of it alone.

---

[7] As of 1995, the Japanese government's refusal to apologize for atrocities committed against the Chinese between 1931 and 1945 meant that they remained a palpable, present threat in the minds of many Chinese.

We split up for the rest of the day. While Katsuo went off to get a thermos like mine for his trip to Tibet, I went off to the Public Security Bureau (gōng'ān jú; aka, PSB) to see about the visa extension. There, I learned that the hànzì to English translation on my travel visa was a bit like some other translations I'd seen, such as the "Beware of Smoking" sign on the ferry from Hong Kong. It didn't say I had until September 22nd to renew my visa, it said that I had until September 22nd just to *enter* the country. I actually had thirteen more days beyond that remaining on my visa, until October 5th when I expected to be in Běijīng. There, I could extend it one month more to November 5th, which would be one week more in China than I had planned. If I wanted, I could spend a little more time here or there, just as long as I let my family know and it didn't get too expensive.

This good news was tempered by how sick I felt. It was still light out, but I was now fully congested and dehydrated to go with being tired, so I went back to the room early, picking up a piece of cake from a bakery on the way. It wasn't the best thing for me to eat under the circumstances, in fact, it probably made my cold worse, but it tasted so good. I took a short nap and stepped out for some noodles before returning to the room. When I got there, Katsuo was already asleep in his bed. The rest of the short night, I took some medicine and sipped a lot of tea while trying to work out the incredible logistical tangle that would get me to Běijīng by the 28th, just over two weeks away.

DAY 11

Thursday, September 14

Kūnmíng

•

There was a lot I liked about Kūnmíng. The tree-lined streets, the low, early 20th century architecture, and to a large extent the people all seemed untouched by the changes happening back east. Those chan-ges would come, sooner than later, and the feeling of having stepped back in time would change with them. For now, at least, I was allowed to enjoy the world around me. Well, as much as I could fighting off an already strong and still growing cold.

What I loved most about Kunming was watching meals made right in front of me. Last night, as I ate a bowl of dān-dān noodles, I got to watch the cook throw, pound, and whip more of the hand-pulled rice noodles against a table in the kitchen behind the stall. The longer he worked the rice dough, the longer it stretched until the gluteny, thin, white noodles suddenly freed themselves all at once, as if someone had clipped a string holding them together. That was a treat.

On the way to the station today, I watched at a street corner as my breakfast was made: a freshly cooked rice pancake coated with a chocolatey black bean sauce and wrapped around a fresh, warm yóu-tiáo. I know, I know, once again, maybe not something you want to eat when you have a cold, but it was good. It was so good, ingenious, even, and worth every bite. I wanted it to last forever.

Which brings me to that station, and the one thing that I abso-lutely hate about Kūnmíng even to this day: trying to leave.

This morning, Katsuo took the early train to Chéngdū. The line to Chéngdū wound its way north through the mountains of Yúnnán and Sìchuān provinces. It would take him 24 hours to get there. I wished him well and went right back to sleep. I had to get to the station, too, to buy my own ticket for the same train leaving in two days, but I had time to sleep in and badly needed it. When I finally did wake, I spent an extra hour or so sipping tea and trying to clear my sinuses before I headed out.

When people look back at China's history, they often talk about its bureaucracy, the smothering tendrils of the mandarins branching out from the centers of power in its various capitals to its farthest lying districts. It's true, going back to the beginning, China's emperors never had more than a tenuous hold on power. What held power was a combination of divine favor, which China's supposedly atheistic current rulers still call the "Mandate of Heaven", and a Confucian (and later Communist Party) culture that preaches respect for elders, authority, and, above all, the order of things. The Cultural Revolution was one of the few disruptions in this pattern, certainly for elders and order, but its short life and abrupt end only prove the point. What this always meant was that anyone clever enough to be a threat to that power was either conscripted into the bureaucracy, literally or figuratively shipped out to the desert, or killed as a traitor, that last one always in full view of public. China may be fully (state) capitalist now and the forms of serving the state may have changed, but this pattern was as true in 1995 as at any time in its history.

This is life under authoritarian rule. Efficiency for the state overwhelms efficiency for its people, which is to say, you don't question what doesn't work if the question offends more powerful people, and you certainly don't waste time drawing attention to it, let alone trying to fix it. For all of China's historic innovation, by 1995, centuries of bureaucratic authority had seemingly destroyed problem solving at the local level. China's transportation infrastructure was very local, and the culture was everything you ever heard anybody in any country ever complain about bureaucracies: lots of rules, nothing works, and people stop trying. If the fantasy of benign authoritarian rule appeals to you, beware: This is the broken world you get.

I arrived at the train station just as the ticket windows were opening. Over the next two hours, the lines and my frustration only grew and grew and grew. I was first told to go to line 12, where I waited in line for about half an hour. Reaching the window, I was then told to

DAY 11: Kūnmíng 49

go to line 14, where I was then told to go to line 10, which was just in time because I ended up near the front of a line that soon went five people wide going out the door. Forty-five minutes later, I reached the window and was immediately sent to line 4. It was here, at long last, that I realized what was going on. Well, no, nothing explained why I was sent to windows 12, 14, or 10, but window 4 was where they sold tickets for Soft Sleepers, the highest priced tickets, and they wanted me as a foreign tourist to spend ¥480 ($60) for a ticket to Éméishān City, the stop for Éméishān (Mt. Éméi), one of the four, holy Buddhist mountains in China. It was four hours south of Chéngdū, and my next destination.

A Burmese man who had also survived line 10 showed up behind me and the two of us noticed every foreigner from every other line eventually heading over to join us. Well, he wasn't going to pay for a Soft Sleeper, either. He was going all the way to Chéngdū, so he had a Chinese friend try to get him a Hard Sleeper instead. I don't remember what ticket Katsuo bought. I don't think I asked. I should have. As an American heading out of Kūnmíng, I was strictly not allowed to buy a Hard Sleeper bunk, so I settled for my only cheaper option, a $22 Hard Seat for the whole twenty hour ride. I might, with a hell of a lot of help, be able to upgrade on the train. This is what the man behind window 4 told me with a weak shrug. All this, and I had to fight for over two hours just to get it.

Now, I know what you must be thinking: the Soft Sleeper was just $38 more, so why not just spend the money? Well, I was on a very limited budget, $38 was a lot more money back then, I was young and therefore foolhardy enough to think I could stand one 20 hour trip on a wooden bench, and, I can't stress this enough, but when you add those things to the fact that I'd been spending less than $1 for just about every meal, $38 just seemed like an enormous amount of money that could and should be saved for something else, like food.

I was also an idiot.

Well, it was about midday now, too late to head out to the Western Hills, so I wandered around town trying to take urban landscape shots and cursing at my camera. I found a jiāozi stand in the northwest of the city where they pan-fried dumplings on flat, round pans that looked a lot like garbage can lids. For a little more than a dollar, I had twenty meat and vegetable jiāozi for lunch. I liked them so much, I went back for dinner. The cheerful stand owners certainly didn't mind the repeat business.

In between visits, I planted myself on a park bench by a lake they called Diānchí Pool. While looking up what to see and do in Běijīng, some overdressed locals laughed at me for wearing shorts. When they'd moved on, Yang Bangguo, a recent retiree of the electric company and something of a dandy himself, greeted me and then all but dragged me over to the park tea bar.

Yang was originally from Chóngqìng[8], at the time merely a very large city in the east of Sìchuān province. You may have heard it called "Chungking". We had a two hour conversation in both Mandarin and English – our Mandarin went better – hampered mostly because today, while I remembered to bring my camera, I forgot to bring my dictionary. I don't know why. Actually, yes, I do: I was careless, again. I lacked "xiǎo xīn", the focused mind. I could excuse it because of my cold, now in full swing, or because I was more tired from the challenge of backpacking across China than I had anticipated, but a lack of maturity, a major contributor to that lack of anticipation and discipline, was surely most of it.

The upside of not having a dictionary or phrasebook on me was that it forced me to talk, listen, and, best of all, engage. By the time our conversation ended, he had helped me with some Mandarin vocabulary and I had done my best to help him with English vocabulary and also idioms, which he had not been taught. For instance, in English, being "small minded" means something entirely different.

---

[8] In 1997, with a population larger than all but 50 countries, Chóngqìng was made a municipality separate from Sìchuān province, one of only four in China, the others being Běijīng, Tiānjīn, and Shànghǎi.

DAY 12

Friday, September 15
Kūnming, Shílín, Kūnming
•

Street-side yóutiáo wrap in hand, I got down to the train station early. I was there to find a cheap, quick bus to Shílín, literally, "the Stone Forest". It isn't an actual petrified forest, of course, that's just what people call it. Like the hills around Yángshuò, it was a limestone plain eroded by wind and water into hills, channels and caves as far as the eye could see.

I knew the deal from Guìlín and Yángshuò, so I hopped on a small bus that looked almost full and waited. I sat down across the aisle from a Chinese grannie with a big camera. Honestly, I have no idea if she was a grandmother, but I like to think of her that way, kind of like calling worn stones petrified trees. She was a small woman with a short, pixie haircut, maybe 60 or 70 years old. She spoke English and we talked while they drove around trying to fill the rest of the seats. She was funny. I'm sorry that I can't remember her name. I really wish I did. As we would all later see, you don't mess with a Chinese grannie with a big camera. At the time, though, she was just another passenger who couldn't understand why we were still circling the streets when the tour guide clearly told us we were leaving for Shílín. She being Chinese, I thought she'd be familiar with the concept of "face".

Face was today's lesson. Face is a part of that old, status-based Chinese culture that includes long fingernails and brand labels left on the cuffs of dress jackets. Rather than risk an embarrassing situation, a person may tell you something they think you want to hear, such as, "we're leaving right away", when they and probably you know they won't. We may like to think of this as "lying", it certainly feels like that when you're on the wrong end of it, but how many of us will say, "I'll get right back to you", and wait, or maybe never even follow up? We're all guilty of this to some degree. At best, you could call it "telling a white lie" or, if you want to be charitable, being "aspirational"; at worst, it's an insult, because you're saying the other person isn't important enough to be given an honest answer. Face tends to fall on the former, more charitable definition. It comes from embarrassment and trying to avoid it.

Ah, but what do you get when you normalize this sort of thing in your culture? Well, if you ask an average Chinese person on the street where something is and they don't know, they won't admit it. Instead, they'll point you in the direction you were already going and tell you, "Zǒu ah" ("walk"). Face isn't limited to Chinese or, broadly, East Asian culture. In the same situation, an Italian might point and say, "Dritto" (straight), and they'd do it for exactly the same reason, trying to avoid embarrassment. It's universal.

What you also get, as I and those with me on this bus would learn, is something that can be exploited and abused in very insulting ways. That was to come.

With the bus finally leaving, we all bought what we were told were tickets straight to Shílín. Of course, that wasn't true. When we made our first stop, we all knew right away it was not the Stone Forest. There was no Stone Forest anywhere near us or anything that looked like one. There was only a small gift shop, set off the side of the road like a vegetable stand with a storage shed. Here, it seemed, they grew only Shílín memorabilia along with the usual just-for-tourists trinkets. Actual Shílín, as we learned only after buying the tickets required to *enter* the gift shop, would be the next stop on our tour. They promised. After pressing our tour bus operators, we were told that we wouldn't get to actual Shílín until sometime after noon, hours after we'd boarded the bus that promised a quick trip straight there.

I was angry. I should add, I wasn't alone. The others were just as angry. Having a full-blown cold, though, and having dealt with hours of bureaucratic nonsense inside the Kūnmíng train station the day before, and perhaps not coming from a culture where you didn't complain, I wasn't just going to sit there and let these guys empty my pockets like I was an ATM. After all, Shílín's own overpriced entrance fee was still to come. Sure, what they were doing was and still is common in countries with foreign tourists all over the world, but that's no excuse. Shrugging and telling yourself "it happens all the time" is the surest way to make sure it does, and that it happens to you.

No. There is no excuse.

I held my temper as best I could and stopped short of calling the young woman who'd sold us all our first and second tickets a thief – "Xiǎo tōu!" (literally, "Small head!") – but I did make it clear, with some help from Grannie and a married couple, that we had all been misled, deliberately or otherwise, and we should get a refund for the gift shop entry tickets, at the very least. After all, we didn't even want to buy anything. The others backed me up and we each got a refund of ¥15. The young woman made a big show of contrition, "face", and we all naively put it behind us.

When we reached Shílín – actual Shílín – the young woman said something about departing at 2:30, but then, after seeing we were all confused, she assured us that we would leave at 4:00, just as she told us back in Kūnmíng. She held up four fingers and everything. Satisfied, we all went into the park.

The sign over the road leading to and from Shílín read, in English, "OFFICIAL CHINA TOURIST EXPLOTATION AREA" (sic). Really. And how was Shílín, the Stone Forest? They should have named it, "Stone Gardens". It was like a cross between Yosemite National Park and an amusement park. This, as I would find, was fairly common in China. Fortunately, the two parks were ticketed separately, so you could skip the rides if you wanted. If you must go to see the Stone Forest, and if you're in Yúnnán province you absolutely should, I recommend spending the night in a hotel at Shílín. It will cost you a lot more than Kūnmíng, but you'll be able to spend the whole next day wandering through Shílín, not the two rushed hours we had.

I only got to see a small section of the Stone Forest, and I wish I'd had a chance to see more. Up close, it isn't just tree-like totems, there are hills and gullies with rockfaces sticking out. It's a peaceful, restful place, especially once you get away from the amusement park.

When Grannie, the married couple, and I got back to the parking lot about a quarter to three, the bus was just one more sunny parking space. You might be thinking, ah, but didn't that dishonest young woman say something about 2:30? Yes, she did, but another couple, more distrusting than we were, went back before 2:30 and they said the bus hadn't even waited that long.

I thought about the refund we'd gotten. Had this been punishment for that? Had I handled it badly and lost face myself, somehow humiliating them and giving them an excuse to abandon us? Had we all lost face, those of us who had rebelled and demanded a refund for being ripped off? We hadn't been wrong, but if the bus driver and the ticket seller had been angry enough, or even just greedy enough, maybe they took advantage of the opportunity? All we knew was everyone on the bus had been ripped-off, even the few who hadn't asked for the refund. And except for me these were all Chinese. Those thieves had taken the return fares and run on Chinese customers. The others were even more shocked and angry than I was.

We waited, in vain. Close to 4pm, they still hadn't come back for us. Another driver, shocked by such a faceless gesture on another bus' part, but not enough to help us for free, drove us all back for ¥8

DAY 12: *Kūnmíng, Shílín, Kūnmíng* 55

each. Grannie really had to get them. She'd taken her camera into the park, but they left with her bag and everything else in it. Which brings us back to "Old World" western culture and why you don't humiliate people and allow them to save face: vendetta. That, too, is universal.

On the city limits, we caught them. They were parked outside of a garage. There wasn't anything wrong with the bus, they were just talking with friends, maybe about us, maybe not, it doesn't matter. Grannie took it from there. Perhaps they'd only seen her as a "grannie", too, some old lady too small and too weak to put up a fight. Their mistake. They swore they were just heading back that minute. Really! They promised! They swore! Honest! We had to believe them!

Grannie wasn't having any of it. She unloaded on them, possibly bringing back memories of their own enraged grandmothers. They let her back on the bus, she got her bag, checked to make sure they hadn't taken anything, and then lit into them again until they stopped pretending to care.

None of us got a refund for the return leg, but we didn't really expect one, not from them. They had exploited "face" the way grifters do the world over, relying on us to convince ourselves that they were sincere. There's no convincing them of their own wrongdoing. If there was, they wouldn't be doing it. They're probably still doing it now.

Back at the train station, I wished Grannie and the young couple better luck and turned the corner back towards the hotel. The woman I'd been buying my water from the past few days took one look at me and said it plain: "You really must eat something." She made me a bowl of dān-dān noodles from her cart and I ate it. It wasn't anything more or less than was offered, and being so it was easily the best part of my day.

DAY 13

Saturday, September 16

Kūnmíng, Yúnnán Province

•

I woke up in pain. It was fitting, because everywhere I looked out here and especially throughout this very long day, pain seemed to be a whole way of life. The pain I felt this morning, shooting and throbbing through my left, big toe, came from banging it on a chair leg just after 2 AM last night as I rushed through the dark because the hotel manager was pounding on my door.

There wasn't a fire, which had been my first, waking thought. He had come to ask me about a room slip he should have known I didn't have. When Katsuo and I had first arrived at the Camellia, we had told the woman checking us in that I would be staying until Saturday. I would be staying. I would. Just me. I had pointed at myself as I said it and convinced myself that her nodding, smiles, and repeated, "Duì, duì" (Correct, correct), meant she'd understood. She hadn't. As I understood answering the door, her "duì, duì" had been something more like a "zǒu ah", a face saving way to get me to stop talking. I'm confident I got the Mandarin right, but that clearly didn't matter. And now the hotel manager was banging on my door at two in the morning demanding that slip. I didn't have it because when Katsuo left for Tibet on Thursday, he'd brought it down with him to check out and had left it with whoever was working reception. Whoever that had been seemingly didn't tell anyone, so no one knew they already had the thing they were looking for. I'll never now why the hotel manager felt it was necessary to ask at 2 AM, pounding on the door like there was a fire, but there he was. I told him and he left, unsatisfied.

And now I was in pain. It was a good thing I'd already packed, because I barely slept before it was time for me to check out and hobble down to the station.

Along the way, I tried to find something to read other than my guidebook for the long train ride. At a newspaper kiosk, I picked up the latest copies of the International Herald-Tribune, which had news of the world that was already old before I left San Francisco, and China Daily, the country's official English language paper of record. They'd have to do, because for the next 20 hours I'd have them and nothing else. Today would be my ordeal by Hard Seat.

This was a Saturday in Kūnmíng, capital of and largest city in Yúnnán province, with only the one, coal-powered rail line connecting it to Chéngdū, an even larger city about 850km north and capital of Sìchuān province. This line, since replaced by multiple high-speed rail lines, had been dynamited through the hills and mountains that separate the provinces and was completed only in 1970, a mere twenty-five years earlier. Add that there was not yet convenient, affordable air travel between the two cities and, despite a travel time of 24 hours[9] between them, this was very a popular train.

For reference on what it was like boarding this train, I recommend watching the train boarding scene in the 1994 Jackie Chan comedy, "Drunken Master II" (Zuì Quán èr; Jui Kuen II, in Cantonese). It was exactly like that. Of course, I got stuck with a lousy seat, but it didn't start that way. I had a ticket for a window seat, first row on the left hand side of the car. This was a coup in Hard Seat, or so I thought, but an old couple were already there by the time I got through the throng and onto the train car. I wasn't about to ask an old couple to give me my seat, so I took the aisle seat and let them have the window. They, however, didn't want the window's soot, dust, and wind, just the air, so they switched with the men in the two seater opposite us. The trading done, I had to settle for the sole benefit of the aisle seat: extra leg room. That wasn't so bad, especially since I'd hurt my toe, but the seat with the legroom faced the front of the car next to the restroom, which on any train would be bad but here was almost unimaginably worse: not only did the latch on the sliding door fail to work but the glass in the forward door of the car was missing, possibly from someone's misguided attempt at "air-condi-

---

[9] It's estimated to be under 6 hours now with the new, high-speed trains.

tioning".

And so, for the next twenty hours – the time to my stop, Éméishān City – every time someone used the restroom I was one of the first to smell it. And the last, because this was a squat toilet, a simple hole in the floor which, not surprisingly on a moving and rocking train, a lot of people missed.

There were one hundred and eighteen people in each car, plus a few standing or sitting where they found room. There was no way I was going to get an upgrade to Soft Sleeper, not now. I would have paid for it. A few hours in, I would have paid just about anything. It explained so much about the station in Kūnmíng. With one rail line and this many people in the region, they could afford to stick it to foreigners. And of course, they did, but I should have had the sense to realize they were actually doing me a favor. If only they could have spelled it out this clearly. It was too late now.

While the line to Chéngdū had been completed around 1970, the train itself was much older, a hand-me-down from some city back east that had gotten a new train, then or more recently. That was the way technological change had worked in China for some time, the investment-rich eastern provinces passing their well used hand-me-downs to the poorer provinces out west. In 1995, that made traveling east to west and then west back east a bit like time travel.

So, this particular train probably dated back to the 1950s or earlier and, in all honesty, it looked like it hadn't been cleaned since. The floor was sticky with spit, because they all spit. They all did. They all projectile sneezed, too, because they all were congested, either from the very common cold or from the constant assault from burning coal. Or both. And when they had all spit or sneezed, they all then wiped it into the floor with the soles of their shoes, as if this somehow made it go away. A thin coating of dust had settled over years of spit and snot, sticking to it even after stewards came through with brooms. Add to that young mothers holding out their infants to pee on the floor, only some of them aiming their children away from the red carpet that ran down the center aisle, as if that could save it, and you had something you didn't even want to subject your shoes to. Garbage was on the floor; garbage was out the window: styro-

DAY 13: Kūnmíng, Yúnnán Province

foam, plastic, whatever. Grease covered the ceiling and the plumbing was so bad that the drain under the public sink across the aisle for the toilet had just six, one-inch tiles left, a shallow puddle filling out where the missing ones had been.

Oh, and they spit. I mentioned that, didn't I? Did I mention the man who hoisted what looked like a barely wrapped goat leg on top of my backpack that was on the rack above the windows? Did I mention the standard, overly cheery train music? It felt like evil torture under these conditions. Did I mention the people who just bumped you as they went by? One guy "just bumped" a baby in the head as he passed by. A baby! He just kept on going. Did I mention the smokers who were told not to smoke in the car, but did anyway because why did they even have those signs? Did I mention the people who came through the car and left that forward door open behind them, which, even when closed with just the void where the glass used to be whipped gale-force winds and dust storms through the car every time the train went through one of the hundreds of kilometers of mountain tunnels on this line? With the door open the winds were even worse, and they blew the garbage and the rotting red carpet off the floor and onto us and into us. You'd have thought all of the dried fluids would have sealed it to the floor by now, but no.

Did I mention the mindless, lost souls who, knowing how horrible the stench of the toilet was while they were inside with it, left the door to that rocking, rolling cesspit open when they were through? Open. Would the broken outer latch have failed eventually? Maybe. Probably. Not the point! Even a few seconds blocking that stench would have been welcome. Did I mention this was for twenty hours? Did I mention that? I had wondered what it would be like to see that time and it was here, every everlasting second of it.

Sitting across the aisle to my right were Mr. Hasim, the Burmese man from the station – a Muslim, as he had proudly introduced himself – and his stocky Chinese friend wearing an "Ernesto Zedillo, PRI"[10] cap, whose name I never did learn. Their slim hope of getting

---

[10] Ernesto Zedillo Ponce De León was President of Mexico in 1995. The Partido Revolucionario Institucional, abbreviated "PRI", was his political party. I don't think the man wearing the hat knew or cared.

Hard Sleeper berths had fallen short, too. Sharing my Hard Seat bench were the two men who had traded seats with the old couple at the start: a nondescript, silent man who seemed to hate everything about the window seat except that he could sleep against the frame, and an old army corporal, very quiet himself, who read his magazine and chain smoked.

On the rear-facing benches at front of the car were two, mismatched couples. On the left were another old couple who had replaced the earlier old couple a few hours in. They looked even older than the couple they had replaced. They still wore their blue Mao-suits and toted a canary swinging in its cage over their heads. The old woman was sick and frail. She had been carried onto the train by their burly, middle-aged son, who had solemnly paid his respects and left them to their journey. The old man was attentive to his wife's needs. He would spend most of the trip turned away from her, his legs over the side of the bench, his hands on his knees, propping her up against his back so she wouldn't have to sleep against the windowsill, which she had tried and found painful. With his hands firmly holding his knees, he was unable to cover his nose or mouth to keep from breathing the stench coming from the toilet; he was closest to it and never complained. He did this quietly, almost serenely, and probably not for the first time. Even at his age and with his own evident frailty, it seemed a duty and a privilege to him.

Doing this, the old man also had to endure a full, uninterrupted view of the couple across the aisle from him, on the other rear-facing bench, who might not have been out of their teens. Their infant son, the same one who was "just bumped" in the head, was also sick, a rash covering his face and mustard-yellow feces time and again covering the seat and floor before the exhausted, young mother could clean them up. While the old man's young counterpart left for extended smoking breaks with other young men in the space between the cars, the young mother remained alone in the seat to care for their sick child. "Ernesto Zedillo, PRI" tried to help her, explaining about the rash and what she could do to cure it, which I had to assume included no more travel on these trains.

The standards shone through, but from where did they come?

DAY 13: *Kūnmíng, Yúnnán Province*

Twenty-five years earlier, the elder couple might have traveled by bus, probably in a big, old one like the night bus that took me to Guìlín, and probably without a schedule, too. Given what I'd seen of the buses and roads so far, that would have been a slow and dangerous drive through mountain passes, even in 1995. However bad this train looked and smelled now, in 1970 it really had been technological progress, a luxury even. But not now. The young couple had probably only ever known trains just like this one, trains in which belligerent stewards cared more about how to stack a goat leg properly – that one on top of my pack – than about the piss on the carpet or whatever other foul, crusted things inhabited each car.

I may be judging the stewards too harshly. It's possible they cared at some point and gave up. It's possible. That, however, didn't change the conditions of this rolling toilet and their role in that. The southwest back then was such a poor region, but was that really all they had to set their standards to? Could they have aimed higher than whatever meager progress they'd achieved twenty-five years earlier?

Well, they could have, and they should have, but when has that ever been how things worked? People look at what they have, they ask themselves what they can hope to have, and then they ask themselves if they have the power to make that happen. Until people feel they have the power to effect change, they often fall into what many observers incorrectly call "apathy". There is no such thing. These people cared. Well, maybe not the young father, but everyone else seemed to. They, like old man with his hands on his knees, had settled on doing their best to endure what they could not change until the ride was over. So, yes, these people cared. I sat in the midst of all that filth and hopelessness, and I still believed that. I could see it. If your world is a rolling toilet, you're going to treat it like one. If they felt that they had something worth taking care of, something that felt like it truly belonged to them, that was truly theirs and not some rotting, depressing thing some government far away forced on them, I don't think they'd be throwing their apple peels on the floor and I don't think they'd be throwing their plastic and worse out of the windows. Like lies told to avoid embarrassment, it's universal.

Change takes time, a lot more time than any of us wants, and not unlike the time I spent waiting for this one train ride to end, it can feel like we'll never reach the destination. We become impatient for change, and not expecting it to happen we don't know what to do when it finally does. Give the people of 1995 Yúnnán province a new train and some would treat it like a new train. Others would still treat it like this train, like the only trains they'd ever known.

    I can't write objectively here. I'd known all sorts of trains in the 23 short years before I arrived in Kūnmíng. I'd crossed cities and continents on filthy trains and buses that this made feel like luxury. I had neither seen nor smelled nor touched nor felt nor imagined anything this terrible, this far below what had been my privileged, sheltered concept of standards. But I had seen it now, in a way I could not hope to ignore. I knew it was telling me something about myself, too, but I wasn't thinking about that. In the midst of this, I found myself turning inward, as I'm sure so many around me were. I was thinking about not wanting to think and failing. I was thinking about what I'd had to endure in my life, if anything had prepared me for this. Nothing really had, except for one thing, the thing that had made me so sickened by all of this: I knew I would get to leave. I knew I had that power, that privilege. I could, in a relatively short time, effect that change. For me, this misery had an end. I just had to get through it. I could and I did.

    Oh, I forgot to mention what I read in that China Daily I bought to read on the train. On the same day the government proclaimed that protecting the environment was their country's greatest concern and that they would redouble their efforts to fight pollution, they also proudly announced in a separate press conference that they had found the biggest coal field ever in Shaanxi province, with enough coal to provide energy for decades to come. It was a whole way of life.

DAYS 14 & 15

Sunday, September 17 – Monday, September 18
Sìchuān Province, Éméishān City, Bàoguó Village, Éméishān

•

I began this day on the worst train I would ever know and ended it at a monastery halfway up a mountain. In between, I would get lost and be grateful for it, climb where no one thought I could go and probably shouldn't have gone, and feast on freshly cooked eggplant in a shack with a valley view.

    The train crept into Éméishān City about 8 in the morning. The rain was so heavy, the drops hitting the roof of the train sounded like rolling drums. I took one last, quick look at the people around me, who still had hours to go, and I knew I was going to a better place, wherever it was. I threw on my blue rain poncho and heaved my heavy pack off the overhead rack – the goat leg and its owner had departed a few hours earlier – and rushed out into the rain. I really, really didn't want to miss this stop.

    I took the first taxi I saw to Bàoguó, the village below the mountain. The driver and his friend in the passenger seat were such helpful people that they stopped halfway to Bàoguó to make sure I was able to pay. They then suggested a hotel in town where I could stay. It was clean, they assured me, not too expensive, and, yes, it was owned by their good friends. As much as I hated to turn down such sincere hospitality, I did. They kept after me, though, assuring me in their own, special way that I wouldn't be able to find a better place and that they were just sure that they'd be seeing me again, but I paid and climbed back out into the rain. At last, they bid me good luck, laughing contentedly as I shut the door. Such nice, helpful people.

    Despite its previous failures, I decided to trust the guidebook and headed for the Hongzhushan Hotel. It was just up around the bend, and I only had to ask directions a few times. There, I could stash the larger half of my backpack and reserve a room for Monday night. A quick adventure with a hotel toilet – I had not used the train's – and I was off to the mountain.

The tourist map from the hotel store was typically vague and what signage there was at the bottom of the mountain was no help, so I took the first reasonable looking trail I saw. The rain was steady and hard, but these were clearly defined, carved stone steps, wide, flat, and solid. With that much effort put into making them, they had to go somewhere, didn't they?

I saw a great woodshed almost buried by the forest off the side of the trail and, remembering that I hadn't loaded my camera, lumbered over an overgrown path, ducking spiderwebs, and stood under the roof of the little shack to load up where it seemed mostly dry. I put the 36 shot cartridge in, threaded the spool, watched the film advance, closed the case, and was back to my spot on the trail to capture an image of the shack in the rain.

Up the trail, I passed an old woman who chided me both for not having a màozi (hat) in the rain – my thin, already rain-soaked poncho did have a hood, little good that it did – and, as I later learned, for heading up a trail not sanctioned for tourists. At the top of it, there was a temple under renovation. The foreman was giving someone else a tour and invited me along. The temple was to Samantabhadra, a Mahayana Buddhist bodhisattva. As sculpted here, he was very large, Indian-looking, and riding a six-tusked elephant. He was protected by four mean looking warriors, each about nine feet tall. Outside, some men were carving stone bases for the tree-trunk pillars that held up the roof. I wanted to keep going up the trail, but the foreman assured me that there wasn't a trail to climb, so I would have to go back down to the base of the mountain and find the real one.

The detour cost me about one and a half hours of rainlight, but I couldn't complain, not after seeing that temple. About noon, I started up what I hoped was the real trail. It was narrow and recently paved with asphalt. Not too far ahead, it branched off to a locked temple gate, a bridge, and then the first official temple for tourists, which

DAY 14 & 15: Sìchuān Province, Éméishān City, Bàoguó Village, Éméishān

seemed like a good sign. From there, the trail wound back through houses and small buildings and it was never quite clear which was a proper trail and which was a path up to someone's house. It was a long trail, going down as much as up. The rain had covered everything with a veneer of mud, making what would normally be slow going even slower, hesitant going. By the time I reached Qīngyīn Pavilion, a place I learned most tourists reached by bus in order to avoid the sloppy lower "trail", it was about 2:30 in the afternoon. Despite covering I don't know how many kilometers climbing up and down the various trails, I'd only gained about 200 meters in altitude. Somehow, my highest point before reaching Qīngyīn had actually been about 300 meters above it.

 I sat for a bit under the relatively dry cover of the Pavilion roof, watching and listening to the rain with a small troop of middle-aged Germans. It was almost hypnotic, a constant and calming patter, and if I'd had any sense I would've stayed right there the entire day until it stopped, but I didn't have any sense. I was too eager. I was too impatient. Fool that I was, I had a plan and I was determined to stick to it, or at least try. I had wanted to reach at least 1500m of this 3000m mountain before nightfall. Hóngchúnpíng Monastery, the next one up on the tourist map, was at 1120m, and like most of the monasteries on the mountain it also served as a registered, official hotel for climbers. If I reached it, I could stay there for the night. With my persistently running nose blending in with the rain, I'd told myself only that would make this trouble worth it.

 There were two possible trails leading up the mountain from the Pavilion, and neither had signs. The one on the left seemed to go down; the one on the right clearly went up. So, to be sure, I went to the two young monks sitting at the Pavilion monastery's guest registration desk – it was more of a short table with two chairs – and asked them which of the two trails I should take to Hóngchúnpíng. I pointed to Hóngchúnpíng on the map then pointed at the trails and asked, in Mandarin, "Hóngchúnpíng, left or right?" They told me to take the trail on the right, repeating, "Right". I asked them to clarify, and they pointed to the path to the right and motioned, "up, up".

So, up to the right I went, thinking that their snickering response to my "xiè xiè" (thanks) was to my poor accent. You see, "xiè xiè" spoken with the same down tones but written with different hànzì means "diarrhea". Context counts for a lot, and I knew that, but still.

It didn't really matter. The higher I climbed up that muddy, washed out excuse for a trail, the more likely it seemed that those snickering monks had expected me to give up and come back, like those friendly, oh so helpful taxi drivers had when I stepped out into the pouring rain. Those monks had been laughing because they'd sent me up the wrong trail. Nice monks, huh? Well, what I didn't yet know at this point was that there are Buddhist monks, who are devout and honest, and then there are "Buddhist monks", who wear the robes as a kind of work uniform and try to pry money from unsuspecting tourists. You can now see "monks" like them at tourist sites all over the world, showing you pictures of their decrepit temples and asking you for a few bucks to help rebuild them. I'm pretty sure these were the latter.

The trail went up, all right, and it was mostly mud. It was dangerous, a wrong step sending me off the side who knows how far down, but I figured that, it being a trail it was meant to be a trail and it would improve as the other trails had. Between that and a pig headed determination not to give those smirking monks any satisfaction, I wasn't going to give up. If it could be done, I would do it.

Idiot.

An hour later, still in the pouring rain, the trail had narrowed to little more than a foot in some spots. At the highest point, I looked back over the trail that had failed to kill me and forward at the trail that still could. Again: Idiot. At that point, I knew it, and yet I was filled with such a feeling of accomplishment. This had been a very difficult climb through the rain, and there I was, I don't know how far up. It was high. After all I'd gone through to get there, on the train, on this journey, maybe in my entire life, I had pushed my limits and I stood there alone. It's funny how doing something so foolhardy and stupid can make you feel so good about yourself. Of course, I hadn't been alone in my foolhardy stupidity. At least one other person had taken this route before me; they had left an empty cigarette pack as a memento.

I turned to look back and catch my breath and looked out into the valley. It was filled with a dense, white fog. I could only see the evergreens near me. Even as the thought came to me, a peak from across the narrow valley appeared through the fog. No sight from the summit could ever equal the pure, serene beauty of what I was seeing. There was just the peak, maybe two, then the lush, white fog, all framed by the evergreens. It looked just like paintings on scrolls and Chinese restaurant walls. Exactly like them. I'd always thought they looked fake before, stylized to make them look like something out of an old legend. Nope. Not only are those paintings realistic, they're practically photorealistic. I took three shots from my roll, because I wanted to have at least one come out right. With the rain and the climb and what may have been the single most beautiful thing I'd ever seen, I couldn't begin to tell you the emotions which held me there. The peaks dipped back into the fog and I stood there a little while longer. What I had done and what I had seen had been worth every misdirected, muddy step. More, actually. Much more.

I worked slowly down the trail a half-step at a time. With parts of the trail washed away, an inch's misstep would have sent me through the low brush down the steep mountainside. Really, I was just an idiot. I knew that after all I had done I could easily still not make it, and mercifully I wasn't so sure of myself that I was about to rush ahead.

Another hour later, I reached firm trail and another monastery. It wasn't, however, a monastery on the hotel's map. It was one of those other monasteries, and their "monks" made their own play for my money. I had seen another fork ahead and again asked which of these to take. This time, they sent me down. Again, the trail I'd been given had been washed away. I can't imagine that they'd taken the trouble to scout these bad trails. More likely, they just knew the right ones and sent tourists the wrong way, half to see them come back and half out of sadistic fun.

In some parts of this path a thoughtful person had dammed up the waterfalls, but other parts had, well, let's call them "gaps". I saw and it was going downhill, and the farther I went the less trail there was, just forest. Just a half hour after I'd left the second monastery, there I was, coming out of the brush onto a path zig-zagging its way across the stream on the valley floor. I'd heard the voices of tourists from I don't know how many feet above, and now here I was looking at them. Soaked from head to toe and dead tired, I was on the leisurely path which must have led down from Qīngyīn.

I followed it, winding my way up the valley to a cedar bridge and the little shack next to it, one of hundreds of gourmet restaurants dotting the mountain. Wet and tired, I stopped for a ¥10 dinner of tea, rice, and the best eggplant I will ever have the privilege of tasting. The family who owned the shack told me that Hóngchúnpíng was just "four minutes" walk up the trail. So, I looked out over the valley, ate, sipped my bottomless cup of tea, and told my day's story to the men who had spent their day in the torrential rain building a new roof for the bridge. When we were through laughing about it, they offered me some local liquor, which I declined. I nicknamed it "chòu jiǔ", pronounced "cho-jyo", which they all thought was funny. The rhyme means "foul smelling liquor". Ernesto Zedillo, PRI had taught me the word "chòu" on the train as we both briefly stretched our legs and took refuge upwind of the foul smell coming from the toilet. I bid them all good night, and made my way up to the comparatively dry refuge of Hóngchúnpíng.

When I reached the red-painted, wooden gate to the monastery, called a "páifāng", I rested and marveled at the gate's beauty. Up the remaining steps – or what remained of them; the rest had been demolished by a fallen tree – I stopped to look back at the gate and was caught by another beautiful scene: the glistening stone steps on the left led down to the gate, where its tiled roof rose at such an angle that it pointed up to the right, cutting through the tall, green trees and the field of dense, white fog beyond. It was composed perfectly for me. I never could have planned it. Still cold and wet, I took the shot and then climbed the remaining steps to the monastery and the promise of a warm, dry bed. I got myself a room looking out over the courtyard, laid out my wet things on a chair in the room, and curled up under the warm blankets to sleep, at long last, to sleep.

ise of a warm, dry bed. I got myself a room looking out over the courtyard, laid out my wet things on a chair in the room, and curled up under the warm blankets to sleep, at long last, to sleep.

I woke up a full twelve hours later. It was about 10 in the morning, and the monks and staff were watching "The Last Emperor" on TV. It had been dubbed into Mandarin, which felt strange, somehow. The rain hadn't stopped. It hadn't even slowed down. My clothes were still wet, so I put them back on. I didn't want to weigh myself down with a second wet set. I was still about 2000 meters from the summit, which was probably shrouded in fog, so I considered my health – not just the danger of taking a wrong trail but my still worsening cold – cut my losses, and returned down the trail I thought I knew. I'd had my adventure, one I never could have expected I'd have.

I stopped back at the shack for more eggplant and to see how they made it, took one last shot of the misty valley below, and once again said my goodbyes to everyone at the shack and the bridge crew. Back down through the valley, I took shots of the waterfalls and the spot where I came out of the mountains, which from the path looked just like the rest of the forest, and chose to hike the rest of the way down instead of taking the tour bus.

It ended up being a good idea. Halfway back along the roller coaster of a trail, I reached what I thought should have been the end of the roll of film, only there was no catch, no stop as the film ran out. It just kept going past number 36. And I knew. All of that beauty, the most wonderful shots I had ever taken, gone. Gone. Worse, they had never been. The film had slipped the spool after I closed the case, or maybe as I closed it. I have no idea. I'll never know. I had not 36 frames but 1, of every image I had captured laid one over another. The woodshed, the peaks hugged by the clouds, the gate at Hóngchúnpíng, the valley view from the shed where I ate the eggplant: all gone.

I cursed. I cried. There was nothing I could do. Even if I went back and took those same trails and risked my life all over again, I could never get those pictures back, or the moments I took them.

They were gone, too. I'll always have the memories, but I took those pictures to share. Sharing would have made them worth every stupid risk, every careless, naive, ignorant mistake. I can't ever describe, completely, the joy I felt taking them – thinking I was taking them – but I had those. I can see every lost picture before me now and I can describe them on these pages, but it isn't enough. I couldn't go back up, so I went back down. I passed the woodshed near the bottom. The rain had stopped, so the light was different, different and all wrong. Maybe it wasn't wrong, but it wasn't the same.

When I reached one of the lower temples, it hit me just how much I'd lost. I sat down and I cried again. The few people I could see just kept on going, trying to get out of the rain.

MANDARIN LANGUAGE PRONUNCIATION
Lesson 2:

In Pinyin transcription, the letter "C" is pronounced something like a "TS". In the wider region of western China around Sìchuān, the "T" part of that sound is dropped, as well as the "H" sound they drop all over the south. This makes things spelled "CH" in pinyin sound like a soft "Z".

Examples:

- "Sì chuān" ("four rivers", from which the province draws its name) becomes "Suh Zwān"

- "Chá" (tea) becomes "Zá"

- "Chī Fěn" (to eat) becomes "Zuh Fěn"

DAY 16

Tuesday, September 19

Bàoguó Village, Éméishān City, Sìchuān Province, Chéngdū

•

Yet again, I didn't get much sleep last night. I spent it fighting the cold I was now certain I had picked up from all of the spitting and projectile sneezing here. Have I described projectile sneezing? One nostril is pressed closed, the other aimed, sort of, the head cocked just a bit, and a glob of snot is shot as far as the wind will carry it. Mostly, it just ends up on the sidewalk, or a railing, or a doorknob, or the floor of a train, or...someone. Pollution, smoking, and dehydration may have been the roots of the congestion in China, but it was the habits of spitting and projectile sneezing that made colds so impossible to escape. They caught a cold and then spit and projectile sneezed everywhere. They caught a cold and then so did you and anyone else in range.

I spent most of the night at the Hongzhushan Hotel doing some spitting and sneezing of my own, into a cup or into the sink, and replacing the lost fluids with hot water. By morning, I could finally sleep, not that I had time. I had yet another train to take.

I took a taxi-van back to Éméishān City with seven or eight female monks. They were real this time, not uniformed professionals like on the mountain. We arrived at the station just before 9 AM, but the ticket office wouldn't open until 10, so I bought myself a zhàntái piào (platform ticket) at the information window. This would allow me to buy a regular ticket on the train. Some genuinely kind and helpful people showed me to the correct waiting room, which was a nice one for a Chinese station at the time, at least among the ones I'd seen so far. It wasn't Soft class, but it was clean and spacious with plenty of benches, all of them wider and more comfortable than what awaited me on the train.

DAY 16: Bàoguó Village, Éméishān City, Sìchuān Province, Chéngdū

Naturally, the train for Chéngdū left twenty-five minutes late. It was a tough ride, not as bad as the ride from Kūnmíng – nothing ever could be – but bad. One woman kept walking up and down the aisle hawking whole fried ducks that she carried in plastic buckets, calling out in a flat, disinterested voice, "Yāzi. Yāzi...Mai yāzi...Yāzi" (Duck. Duck...Buy duck...Duck)[11].

The passengers were friendly. Some traveling with "Nestle" and "Tang" jars for their tea were enthralled by my thermos. They said they hadn't seen one like it before and asked me where I got it. All I could think to say was, "At a store, at home", which, given the broadly generic nature of those words in Mandarin, could just as well have been replaced with a shrug. Their awkward smiles confirmed it.

And then I ran into a small problem. The entire ride to Chéngdū, no one had asked me to show my ticket, so I ended up not buying one. The problem was, I couldn't exit the station without presenting a train ticket. A much cheaper platform ticket didn't count. So, I decided to give sneaking out without paying a try. After all of the trouble I had been given trying to buy a ticket out of Kūnmíng and that entire, 20 hour ride up, I felt like I was owed. I entered the crowd leaving the train, and, with half that crowd bottlenecked behind me at the station exit, I pulled a little tug-and-puzzle and pretended I'd lost the ticket. If I'd learned one thing in two weeks' travel in China, it was that convenience overruled function and any trouble was more trouble than it was worth. The station ticket-takers rolled their eyes and waved me through. I don't think I really saved much on the four hour train ticket, a few dollars at most, but, man, did I feel good walking out of there.

I shopped around for a taxi and took one with a cheap fare. In Chéngdū, fares (with fine print) were posted on the taxi windows. I asked the driver to take me to the Jiaotong (Traffic) Hotel, a hostel, heaved my pack into the trunk, and was somehow surprised when he immediately tried to con me. And after all the trouble I'd gone through getting out of that train station! Yeah, that's karma for you.

---

[11] "Yāzi", pronounced "yad-zuh", is also slang for "male prostitute". I'm pretty sure she meant duck.

He took me very clearly in the wrong direction, then stopped to pick up a "friend" to intimidate me from the back seat: the Sìchuān Special. I chewed both of them out while pointing to my map, then perused the city map directory posted behind the driver, running my finger down the destinations listed in hànzì on the side to 公安局, "gōng'ān jú" (Public Security Bureau, aka, the cops), a good one to remember. A quick five minutes later, I was at the hotel, and he even gave me a discount. Swell guy.

At the Jiaotong, I took a bed in a triple with two Swiss who were headed to Mt. Éméi in the morning. I warned them about the trails and the fake monks then headed out to eat. I'd gotten used to eating less as I travelled, a bowl of noodles here, a plate of dumplings there, but I knew I had to eat more if I was going to beat this cold. I found a local tourist stand, the Rose Garden Cafe, and happily ate platefuls of some of the blandest food I'd have in China. After the previous few days, I really couldn't complain. I then bought a suspiciously cheap Soft Sleeper train ticket to Lánzhōu from the hotel's travel office. I had thought about flying to Lánzhōu because it was so far by train, but I had doubts about the safety of whatever short distance plane I might get in western China at the time, and I wasn't going to make the same Hard Seat mistake again, not if I could help it. Anyway, looking back, the route probably didn't require an expensive ticket. Lánzhōu wasn't exactly Chéngdū.

The currency exchange at the hotel claimed a service charge of 1.5%. OK, that's perfectly acceptable for hotel convenience, but *right after* I signed the traveler's cheques they then tacked on an additional 1%, making it 2.5%. Again, as I'd done warning the Swiss about the dangers on Mt. Éméi, I did my traveler's duty and told the man waiting behind me about the bait-and-switch surcharge. He exited so fast he practically left a cartoonish, man-shaped cloud of smoke behind. Some might tell you it's the same all over, that you're stuck in the system and you shouldn't complain and it's not really that much money anyway, but if it's such an acceptable thing to do, why wait until after the cheques have been signed? Why hide it? Why lie? No, if you've travelled even just a little, you know it's your money and that "everybody does it" line's a load of fèi huà. Buy into

DAY 16: *Bàoguó Village, Éméishān City,* 75
Sìchuān Province, Chéngdū

that, and you might as well accept price-gouging taxi drivers and broken down trains like the one I took from Kūnmíng. I retired at dusk to work on my lingering souvenir of Chinese train travel, the far too common cold. After the last three nights, sleep was all I could ask for. Well, sleep and an end to this cold.

DAY 17

Wednesday, September 20
Chéngdū

•

This was my 24th birthday.

Officially, there is a twelve-hour difference between Chéngdū and where I was born. Because all of China shares a single international time zone, being out west meant that time difference was actually more accurate than, say, the time given in Guǎngzhōu or Běijīng. Here, I was literally on the other side of the world. I'd have to wait until about 1 PM local time to celebrate the actual time I was born back home.

I wasn't sure how to feel about it back then. I'm not sure how I feel about it now. Part of me, the part I choose to listen to now, wants to remember that I was doing something brave and that I was pushing myself in ways that have helped me in my life since. Yes, I was also making stupid, foolish mistakes and I was often out of my depth, but that doesn't make it less true.

The other part of me, the part that had my ear this day, reminded me that I was alone, literally on the other side of the world, and isolated in ways few who did not live back then could fathom. I was sick and I was tired, and I was questioning my foolishness and stupidity in putting myself in a position where I would be alone if something bad actually did happen to me. That it was my birthday only made that feel more true.

On this day in 1995, I turned 24. I was in Chéngdū, China.

• • •

My Swiss roommates were up before light. Last night, they had been invited by locals to what they were told was the best restaurant in Chéngdū. It wasn't, and to make it worse their dinner hosts had stuck them with the $50 tab for their lousy meal. They were eager to get

DAY 17: Chéngdū

out of town. I can only imagine how they fared with the "monks" when they made it down to Mt. Éméi.

I didn't feel particularly special today. I was more concerned with my cold, my camera, where I would be going tonight, and what I would be doing until I left. Dropping the big half of my bag off in the hotel's Left Luggage closet, I tried the complementary "Western" breakfast that came with my room. It was served in a little side room off the lobby that looked like an afterthought, and it tasted like it.

I spent my meal worrying about my camera. Loading a roll of black and white film, I was afraid the film had slipped the spool again. Not yet knowing about the shutter issue which would actually ruin these shots, I wondered what I would do with a camera that wouldn't load film. I really couldn't afford to buy a camera here. Even a simple point-and-shoot camera would have cost as much as a week of travel, maybe more. Outside, I took a few shots to check the tension on the frame advance. It felt fine. I was guessing. It had felt fine on Mt. Éméi, too. After that, I had no confidence in my judgment as far as the camera.

At least I could enjoy wandering. Chéngdū wasn't like the other cities I would find out west. Kūnmíng had some modern comforts, but it still looked and felt more like one of its French colonial neighbors to the south. Lánzhōu and Xīníng, as I would soon find were little more than dusty trading posts on the frontier. Chéngdū was a large, modern city, with new, gleaming hotels and office towers, lots of new car traffic, and an affinity for corporate capitalism rivaling anything in the West. On my way to the city center, I passed a Mickey Mouse franchise store, packed with everything Mickey. People listened to Mickey here in China. They even painted his likeness on garbage cans, urging people not to litter. In a world where they no longer listened to Máo, they listened to Mickey, and Mickey was good.

Speaking of Máo, I passed a big, white statue of him in the city center, sandwiched between oversized billboards for Pabst Blue Ribbon beer. It looked like they were holding a free dental clinic in front of it. I guess you can't be capitalist about everything.

The center of Chéngdū was very interesting, mostly for the high walls. There were 10 foot high walls around the government administrative compound, where the cadres worked and lived. Given the glossy residential high-rises for the new money going up across the street with their own high-rise walls, these walls appeared to be less about government privacy than keeping the undesirables out. As a city, Chéngdū was truly representational of the changes going on in China, with a privileged few separating themselves from a many who weren't yet going anywhere. For a "classless" country, those high walls were a big red flag[12].

I went back to the Rose Garden Cafe for lunch, where a German named Christian invited me to join him. We had a good conversation about Chéngdū and its high walls, but I didn't mention that it was my birthday. I should have. It would have been good to celebrate it with someone. As we spoke, men across the river were climbing down one of the stepped, cement embankments to use it as an open-air urinal. It was as if they had no idea or care that everyone on our side of the river was watching. And we were. Just the most normal thing in the world. Based on the stains already there, they clearly weren't the first.

Not at all because we were all watching and joking about this public performance, I was late for my 2 o'clock appointment at the travel office to pick up my Soft Sleeper ticket for tonight's train to Lánzhōu. Still shellshocked from my first ride up north, I worried that they wouldn't hold it for me, thoughts of another long night and day in Hard Seat legitimately terrifying me. I needn't have worried; when I arrived, they held it out to me like my padlock keys at the hotel in Guìlín. Ticket in hand, I killed time sneezing around the neighborhood near the hotel before grabbing a new edition of the Herald-Tribune and a small piece of frosted cake to celebrate both the ticket and my birthday. Again, the cake can't have helped me with my cold, but how could I refuse? It was a fluffy, massive hit of sugar just when I needed it and I almost went back for more. I probably should have, but I talked myself down.

This was the one day I knew I had to make time to call home, so I went to a telephone exchange and placed a call. It was great to hear

---

[12] Communist pun intended.

DAY 17: *Chéngdū* 79

my parents' voices, as much as anything because I had an idea that I wouldn't get to speak to them for a while. Heading to the northwest, I had no idea if I'd be able to call them or anyone. Chéngdū was a big, modern city connected to the rest of the world; compared to it, Qīnghǎi province and the rest of China's northwest might as well have been on the moon. I told my parents they might have to wait a week or more for my next call. I didn't tell them about the cold, though, because I told myself I didn't want them to worry. Who was I kidding?

And then I waited to go. After a dinner of boiled dumplings so slippery I had to stab them with my chopsticks just to get them in my mouth, I enjoyed a hassle-free taxi ride to the north train station. Some intersections in Chéngdū already had the digital countdowns on traffic lights and crosswalks that we now take for granted in America, letting everyone know just how little time drivers, bicyclists, and pedestrians had to swerve across the intersections. The stay-out-of-my-way horns, naturally, persisted.

When I arrived at Chéngdū's old north train station, it was undergoing renovations to make it "world class". It has since been renovated again. The old Soft-class waiting room, locked from the inside to keep the undesirables out, was very nice in an Old World/Old West sort of way. It had caned armchairs, a TV, a stereo, newspapers, and its own snack bar. It even had a spittoon!

Being Soft-class, we boarded the train first – I had no idea they arrived so early! – and I made my way to my compartment. I had to wait to enter, though, as my arrival had interrupted a rendezvous between the conductor and a lady friend. When he came back for my ticket and saw that the other three Soft Sleeper bunks were still empty, he tried to get me to move to the next compartment. I declined. I didn't care what country I was in, I wasn't going to move just so the conductor could get his kicks playing "customs inspector". Soft-class problems.

DAY 18

Wednesday, September 20 – Thursday, September 21
Chéngdū, Sìchuān Province

•

Soft Sleeper class was an entirely different China. With the sole exception of the San Yu in Guǎngzhōu, a government run hotel for foreign VIPs, this Soft Sleeper compartment was cleaner than anywhere I'd slept in China so far. Not clean like the San Yu had been – the carpets showed ample remains of cigarette ash, food, and spilled tea, and the storage area above the door looked like it had never been cleaned, ever – but it was cleaner. It was the amenities, though, that set Soft Sleeper and those traveling in it apart: veneered wood paneling, padded bunks, factory lace sheets, two large hot water thermoses to be shared by only four people, tea bags, a fan that turned on and off, a light switch that turned on and off, a volume knob on the loudspeaker, a space on the door where (presumably) a mirror used to be, a Western, "sit down" toilet with plumbing and a door that both closed and locked for privacy, and a compartment door that locked for privacy, especially useful for both passengers and horny conductors.

The Chinese may claim not to have a word for "privacy", not in the Western sense, but you can't have a class system without it, and China has never been without an upper class. Even in the depths of the Cultural Revolution, Máo Zédōng's portrait hung above the gates to the famously private Forbidden City. Its history was his, its power was his, its class symbolism was his.

This train and everything on it were hand-me-downs from the east, built in the early years of Communist Party rule, so compartments like this one were a luxury perk for party officials and military officers when Máo Zédōng was at the height of his power. Compared to the masses traveling Hard Seat, the cadres "serving the people"

DAY 18: Chéngdū, Sìchuān Province

lived fat and did so traveling in trains like this and living behind high walls like the ones in Chéngdū. Most Chinese, certainly those out west in 1995, couldn't afford this kind of luxury and, I bet, had never even seen it. This perpetuated ignorance, a vestige of authoritative, centralized rule, pervaded Chinese history. The ruling class, whatever the political system, had always isolated itself in comparative luxury while telling the poor to endure. How many would have rioted knowing the truth? We've already seen. It's the other half of what they call, "The Mandate of Heaven"[13]. You rule until the gods decide you don't, or until the peasants rise up and take you down. I don't know if either of those things could happen in modern China, but I wouldn't want to get caught in Soft Sleeper if they did.

Before we left Chéngdū, I was joined by a soldier, who put her bags and parcels up in the storage area above the door with mine. I remember her peeling an apple with a pen-knife. She actually ate the skin as she peeled it, a first as far as I'd seen in the country. To a person, I had yet to see anyone eat an apple without peeling it and throwing the peel on the floor. I have to believe it had something to do with not-yet-banned-in-China pesticides, or bad memories of them. I can't imagine it was the just the flavor.

An hour of sleep later, we were both awakened by two boys in their late teens or early twenties who slammed the door open, turned on the lights, and complained loudly and at great length about not being given their coveted lower bunks. These were a new generation in China, and in many ways a new class. These two were spoiled, rude, loud, really into themselves, and wearing expensive but very ugly clothes, basically rich kids spending their parents' money, and they were easily two of the biggest assholes I have ever met. They chainsmoked in the "smoke-free" compartment, hoicked and spit loudly down from the top bunks, and if there had been a karaoke machine nearby, I'm sure they'd have abused us with it.

We were all shaken out of bed hours later by the engineer, who

---

[13] This was a term emperors used to justify their hold on power. They were divine. If they failed or were overthrown, it was god's (or gods') will. The Communist rulers picked up where the emperors and "republican" dictators left off, using the term to justify their power. President Jiāng Zémín actually used the term in a speech while I was in China.

had stopped very abruptly to let on more passengers. It was getting light out, so I wandered down to the Soft-class only dining car to see what they had for breakfast. It was empty except for the staff, which included the conductor's "friend" from when I boarded the train. I asked to see a càidān (menu), once, twice, maybe a dozen times, pantomiming, trying different pronunciations, trying anything. I got no response. They didn't seem to have a clue. I went back to my bunk, got my dictionary, showed them the characters, and they said, "Ohhhh, càidān", exactly as I had pronounced it the first time. Just some bored train staff having themselves a laugh, all in good fun. Maybe. It might also have had something to do with my spoiling the friend's good fun. Either way, the joke was on me. They pulled out a list of overpriced, prepackaged food and soft drinks just like you'd find on trains anywhere else in the world and I returned to my bunk.

I spent the rest of the day there, eating more digestive crackers and trying to drink as much tea as I could. I thought about returning to the dining car just to escape the loud, spoiled chain smokers in the upper bunks, but I needed to try to sleep, and beyond locking myself inside the toilet, facing the wall and pulling the covers over my head would be the most privacy I was going to get. Maybe Soft Sleeper wasn't so different, after all?

DAY 19

Friday, September 22
Gānsù Province, Lánzhōu, Gānsù Province, Qīnghǎi Province, Xīníng

•

The conductor, possibly still frustrated and bitter about my interruption when I boarded, woke us at 5:30 in the morning with all the subtlety, gentleness, and grace of the train's engineer. We had an hour to Lánzhōu, so the two princelings in the top bunks jumped down and pushed the soldier and me over so they could sit while they smoked cigarettes and brushed their teeth. Yes, they smoked *while* they brushed their teeth, and then smoked another cigarette when they were done. When we reached the station, they bolted, leaving me to claim their complementary noodle-dinner kits. The kits would prove helpful up in Xīníng, which I would find had little to offer at night beyond dust storms and sudden downpours. I wasn't tempted to thank them.

There wasn't a direct ticket from Chéngdū to Xīníng, at least not then, so on arrival in Lánzhōu I had to go straight back in line at the station. Lánzhōu station was a pit, wild dogs going after a bone. People would try to cut in front of the lines, pushing everyone stuck between the guide-rails back into each other. They would do this again and again until someone in line just didn't want to fight anymore and let them stay.

Back in Yángshuò, someone said the Chinese just wouldn't line up, as if it was something in them, like some kind of congenital Taoism run amok. That really wasn't it. It was people living in the same, broken system I'd seen at every station since Kūnmíng. I can only imagine the one in Guǎngzhōu, had I not wisely avoided it, would've been the same. The sole exception, so far, had been the station in Guìlín, calm, clean, and orderly, but I'm reminded, often, of the wait for the unscheduled bus that took me to it. People here weren't lazy or disorderly by nature, they adapted, like anywhere else. In this case, they had adapted to the laziness and disorder around them. Those standard guide-rails may have been intended to create order and straight lines, but what they actually did was corral people like livestock, crushing them into each other and demeaning them. Here in Lánzhōu, a security guard pushed people forward to make sure space wasn't being wasted. I can't see what was gained by it. Past a certain point, you were just pushing, or getting pushed, against a wall. What was lost, certainly for the person crushed in the pile, was any sense of dignity. Which raises the question: Isn't dignity something communism is supposed to champion?

To be fair, this wasn't communism's fault, not exactly. Given a generation or two, Fascist Benito Mussolini's trains wouldn't have run on time, either, if they ever did; we only ever had his word for it, a boast of Fascist efficiency and improvement over past failures. After all, who was timing them? Who was keeping track? Who was reporting to whom? Who was reporting at all? Under any authoritarian regime, they would have been said to run on time even if they were hours late because no other answer would have been acceptable. The truth of it is, failure is always acceptable in an authoritarian regime, just not the perception of it, so you adapt to it.

There is another, inherent flaw in communism, which is that the violent overthrow of the ruling class creates a power vacuum that is inevitably filled with people willing to use violence to get what they want, and those people tend to repeat the behavior of the people they replaced. For instance, they generally don't like hearing criticism or complaints, a standard that, as it works its way down the chain of authority to the men and women working at or near the bottom, creates a mindset of risk aversion and an expectation that nothing can or will be fixed, so people stop trying and nothing ever is. That form of communism in China reached its peak, or nadir, in the violent repression of the Cultural Revolution, and while that was safely in the past, those rock bottom expectations were still going strong out in the west of China in 1995.

So, yes, it was the government's fault for cultivating a system

DAY 19: Gānsù Province, Lánzhōu, Gānsù Province, Qīnghǎi Province, Xīníng

where everything broke and nothing got fixed, at least not out west, not yet, but, no, that wasn't communism, that was authoritarianism in general. The imperial and only-nominally republican governments the communists overthrew were very much the same. The inability to acknowledge problems is the cause of institutional failure and, as I was seeing day after day, it fostered an expectation that you, like me, were all alone, even if and maybe especially if you were crammed into a corral between two people just like you.

So, there I was at 7:30 in the morning, alone, about an hour into my wait, penned in between two other men who were also alone but, mercifully for them, not also wearing a heavy pack. It weighed about fifty pounds at this point and I considered taking it off, but squeezed in like I was it would have been very difficult, so I kept it on. Every push and jostle from the line cutters in front and the guard behind made it feel worse and worse.

As I neared the front of the line, the ticket seller decided that her shift had ended. There were no last few tickets, no replacement ticket seller, no warning, she just pulled the wooden shutter down. We were told by a guard to go to another window, seven corrals down. I had to wait for the line to clear behind me before I could back out and join the scrum. Running with my pack as best I could, I once again found myself at the back.

This line, though, moved quickly. It moved so quickly that it must have exhausted the poor woman working it, because by the time I was only third in line she decided to start her own fifteen minute break, this time with no replacement and no new line. We just had to stand there pushed up against each other and wait.

Of course, a sign over this particular window gave preference to soldiers, a little perk for service to the country. Not fifteen minutes later, I had been pushed back from third in line to about thirtieth and was starting to lose hope. Luckily for me and the dozen or so waiting behind me, the soldiers all made bulk orders, so they went fast. Well, not fast, but by now it was a different standard. You adapt. By 8:10, with some generous help from the guy behind me, I had my Hard Seat ticket to Xīníng, the only seat available but at the Chinese price, so I think I maybe saved a buck.

Time passed so slowly in Hard Seat. My 20 hours out of Kūnmíng might as well have been a week. My 32 hours in Soft Sleeper to Lánzhōu, by comparison, had been a blink of an eye, even with the obnoxious smoke-brushers, the lack of decent food, and my everpresent cold. This trip, a five hour local to Xīníng, was mostly uneventful. The worst moment came when the baby in the seat across from me woke a few hours in to piss on the floor and my right boot. Most of it managed to hit the floor, so I took the win. Again, it had become a different standard.

Of course, different, lower standards weren't only for passengers with limited options. On my way out of Xīníng station, I wondered how long the train ride from there to Xī'ān would be, so I asked at the station information window. I wasn't asking for an exact time, just an estimate, a best, experienced guess. They could have told me anything, really. The information clerk said he didn't know and sent me to ask at the ticket window. When I reached the front of the line and asked, the ticket seller indignantly sent me back to the information window. He genuinely seemed insulted by the question. Who did I think I was? Where did I think I was? Oh, right, I was at a train station. Where else was I supposed to ask? Who else was I supposed to ask? What could possibly be wrong with asking when a train *might* get where it's going? Was it a "face" thing? Was it something I shouldn't have asked? Had anyone ever asked? Had anyone ever thought to?

As old as the trains and infrastructure were out west, it's understandable that exact arrival times would be hard to come by, and that not knowing may have been a source of embarrassment, but at some point people just stop trying. That was their adaptation. Whether it was by design or, most likely, untold years of neglect, these men and women had become professionally stupid; that was their adaptation and they were taking everyone passing through down with them.

I wish I could put it a nicer way, but I don't know how. I'm embarrassed by it, yet somehow I have to get across the strain this broken system was putting on me. I was literally only passing through, living with it for the first time. I hadn't had to live with it like they

DAY 19: Gānsù Province, Lánzhōu, Gānsù Province, Qīnghǎi Province, Xīníng

had, as part of their whole life experience, but I also hadn't had time to normalize it. It added so much additional stress to everything, each instance, each avoidable failure compounding the previous ones. Out here in the land of technological hand-me-downs and limited contact with the outside world, that wasn't going to change.

I would learn, eventually, to adjust my expectations, to take the actual Taoist approach of letting go and letting things take their natural course, but not yet. I still had places I needed to be at certain times on certain days, and my expectations remained rooted in that as much as any travel experience I had before. I was also sick, and the strain of traveling with that for weeks filled even the smallest need with more urgency. That wasn't going to change, either, not until I got better.

DAY 20

Friday, September 22 – Saturday, September 23

Xīníng

•

My hotel room in Xīníng was a damp, rotten mess.

The guidebook had recommended the hotel – I don't remember the name – as "the best place to stay in town", but frankly there wasn't much else. It was located inside a shopping center, like the ferry terminal had been in Hong Kong, and like everything else in Xīníng it was both smaller and much, much dustier than anything I would see in the rest of China.

The Xīníng of 1995 bore little resemblance to the modern, skyscraper and hotel filled city of today. Back then, it was still very much isolated from most transportation and the tourism that comes with it. It was a place people passed through more than anything else. As such, it was a city locked in a much poorer, sparsely visited past. "Smaller and much, much dustier" truly described everything as far as the eye could see. Not that I saw much of anything my first day. That was cut short by dust storms that were only chased out by heavy rain.

I spent the night sneezing and coughing. Curled up on my bed with one of my noodle-dinner kits from Soft Sleeper, I watched the two broadcast channels available on the TV and ended up getting an insight into how the China I was visiting wanted to be seen by the rest of the world.

The first channel was a staticky haze. I could almost, just about make out a costume epic. The second channel, however, was quite clear. It was Beijing Television 2 (BTV2), a national network, and it was time for the evening news. The entire evening's program was dedicated to an overview of the United Nations' Fourth World Conference On Women, held in and around Běijīng, from the 4th to the

DAY 20: Xīníng

15th of September, so it had ended exactly a week before.

The broadcast began with testimonials from delegates, in English with hànzì subtitles, all extolling the "comfort" and "convenience" of the conference. They all praised the Chinese for making the experience as pleasant as possible. Said one Pakistani delegate: "They should be very proud of the work they have done." She wasn't speaking of China's efforts on civil rights for women but of China's efforts in pulling off a multinational conference. The women's testimonials were all taped during group visits to a section of the Great Wall that had been closed off to the public for the day so the delegates could have it all to themselves.

The second, shorter portion of the show returned to the studio, with clips of other, more prominent delegates and guests, including then-First Lady of the United States, Hillary Clinton, all of them praising the same successful efforts at hosting. Chinese commentators continued with testimonials of their own, again applauding the great success of the hosts.

Success. That was all anyone who watched coverage of the conference on Chinese television or read of it in a Chinese newspaper or magazine saw. Success, or rather the impression of it, seemed to have been the single, solitary goal of the conference. Could the Chinese government succeed in making delegates comfortable, feel important, and, most of all, impressed with how it and they had been handled? Evidently, some were. However, in their eagerness to play successful hosts, the government's messaging had missed, or perhaps just misplaced, the stated point of the conference. Nowhere in any of their coverage were the issues of the conference discussed, only the success of hosting one. What that lack of coverage of Women's Conference issues revealed was that the government, which controlled the media, did not consider them newsworthy. Only successful hosting was, which is a shame, because the fourth conference proved to be the last conference. After having one every five years, the UN never had one again..

The impression of success was and still is all there is. China's reputation and status among the powers of the world was and naturally remains of great concern to the leadership of the Chinese Communist Party. As with any government in power, and especially in a single party state, the Communists fear losing the power they hold. Coming out of a period it would like the rest of the world to forget, one in which its domestic and foreign policies cost China prestige and international prizes, such as the 2000 Olympics[14], the Party's hold on power at this time was at a crucial stage. China's burgeoning market capitalist economy was the fastest growing in the region, but rather than strengthening the party's hold on power, that success actually threatened to weaken it. With investment and fortunes growing noticeably faster in the eastern, coastal provinces than elsewhere in the country, the Communists risked losing the support of their population in the rest of the country.

As it was, immigrants from the poorer provinces were flooding the growing eastern cities looking for work; without enough to go around, crime in those cities was on the rise. The embrace of capitalism also made it more difficult to hide behind party doctrine the Party itself clearly no longer supported. Add to that other Pacific capitalist economies, in particular ones with sizable "Overseas Chinese" populations, gaining influence within China's borders and Party officials had to have wondered how long they could sustain their own influence along with their political monopoly. This had led to the Tiān'ānmén protests and crackdown, and had led to the ongoing, demonstrative challenges to Taiwan's legitimacy, which of course couldn't be resolved at a time they were dependent on Taiwanese investment. Toss in the potential of secessionist ethnic and religious minorities in the western provinces and China found itself in need of a public relations boost, both at home and abroad. Whether or not the majority of delegates agreed with BTV2's testimonials, the network fed the Chinese people what it believed they wanted, or at least needed, to hear: "Success is here, and it will reach you soon".

As for me, I had seen enough in three weeks not to take anything I saw at face value, pun intended.

It was foggy when I woke up. The dampness and dustiness of my room had done nothing but make my congestion and respiratory

---

[14] It had not yet been awarded the 2008 Summer Games.

problems worse. Out early to make a day trip to Qīnghǎi Hu (Lake), I asked the hall clerk if it was always foggy in the morning. She asked for help. It came in the form of an American woman who spoke fluent Mandarin. She re-asked my question for me and told me that the clerk said, "If it's sunny, then it isn't foggy, but if it's cloudy, then it might be foggy". Or maybe just the answers were? That was really what she said. The American, traveling with a friend, had been to Qīnghǎi Lake already and told me I wouldn't be missing anything if I skipped it.

Advice taken, I checked out of the hotel and crossed the bridge over the dried out river to the train station. With the dust everywhere, and familiar hills and canyons stretching out beyond the railroad tracks, it all looked like something out of a spaghetti western.

At the station, I waited in line at the eastbound window to buy a ticket on the next train to Xī'ān. That is, I waited until I realized that this long line was waiting for the ticket seller to return from her breakfast. The handwritten sign in the window said "9 o'clock", but that was hardly a guarantee, not out here in the wild west, so I dropped my bag off at Left Luggage and bought some breakfast for myself, a doughnut with soy milk porridge.

It was here, as I ate, that I first saw one of the old, Chinese army backpacks. An older man outside the station had one. It was maybe half the size of my big, gray pack, and made of dark green canvas with what looked like black, rubber lining on the top flap. It looked sturdy, and with all of the rain I'd seen lately, dry. In time, I would need another bag. My L.L. Bean backpack was old and it was already pretty full. I'd have to re-sew some of the seams before I even reached Běijīng, so finding a Chinese army backpack would become something of a quest.

By the time I finished eating, I'd lost only four places in line. That is, I'd lost only four if you didn't count the twenty or so line cutters and black marketeers crammed around the window, jumping over each other and propping themselves against walls and the guide-rails at other windows and against other people like a pack of Wall Street traders down in the pit. A brave policeman stepped in and dragged these animals away from the windows, one-by-one. They all came back the moment he left, of course. There's only so much any one person can do. At least he tried. The man at the front of the line turned and left the pile in front of the window with a huge smile that said, "I HAVE A TICKET. I AM FREE!" About 10:20. it was my turn, and my acquired skills to this point boiled it down to this: make it quick and get out of there. "Qǐng, lái huǒchē," I said. ("Please, the next train.") I paid through the teeth for a Soft Sleeper, but I had enough left over for that same, huge smile.

It was late now, too late to salvage a trip out to Ta'er Lamasery with its Buddhas carved out of yak butter. Yes, I really had been looking forward to seeing that, but sadly it was not to be. The two places I'd told myself I'd come all the way out here to see, the lake and the lamasery, I never even got close to.

DAY 20: Xīníng 93

Ah, but what I discovered wandering Xīníng's very dusty streets I never would have seen if I'd gone out to see the lake or the yaks. Xīníng proper was actually kind of beautiful in its own way. Take away the gaudy, glass buildings starting to dominate the skyline and the rest of it really did look a lot like a town in the old American southwest nestled down in a canyon to be near a supply of water. Take out the brutal, Eastern Bloc-style apartment house, and you could almost picture a steam train rolling in.

The sun had come out, drying last night's rain and releasing clouds of swirling dust, but it was chilly. Heading away from the train station, I noticed a pool table outside next to a small building under what looked like a carport. It was, naturally, covered in a thick layer of dust. It looked like no one had played on it for a while, but with fresh dust coating everything how could anyone know? I didn't think to ask any of the locals I met. I had become something of an attraction to them, like something carved out of yak butter. I guess not many foreigners wandered the back streets and alleyways like I was. I drew stares from children and adults alike. Some of the adults giggled right along with the children. They can be so cruel!

For lunch, I ate some flavorful yāzi (duck) dumplings – I'm not sure I should have taken that at face value – and then surveyed the street markets on my way to the Great Dongguan Mosque (Dōngguān Qīngzhēn sì). There were merchants selling pelts and fabrics, and entire streets of tables specializing in specific parts of goats. On one street they just sold goats' heads and hooves, nothing else. There were handmade, welded steel cooking utensils, too, big spoons to use in big woks. I bought one for my sister-in-law, a chef, just because we'd know how far it had been made from where she lived.

Closer to the mosque, there were shops selling bilingual, Chinese and Arabic Korans. The northwest of China has a large Muslim population. Even under Máo's "godless" communist rule, the religion persisted. The mosque itself was big and not very interesting. For such a supposedly old building, it looked fairly new. This was because it had recently been rebuilt. The impressive prayer hall, on the other hand, looked its age. With its wood-en columns and tiled roof curving up at the corners, it looked like any other centuries-old Chinese building. It looked like it could have been built for anything, like an official's office or a town hall, and maybe it had been. White tiles in the courtyard formed lines guiding visitors towards the entrance, like perspective grid lines on the floor of an Italian Renaissance church. When first built, it must have had a panoramic view of the entire valley. Not anymore. The view in 1995 was mostly more of that prefab, concrete slab, Eastern Bloc-style housing. I took a few shots of the prayer hall and the mosque's minarets and rushed back to the station to make sure I caught my train.

MANDARIN LANGUAGE PRONUNCIATION

Lesson 3:

In a way, pronunciation in Qīnghǎi province is the opposite of that in neighboring Sìchuān. Where Sìchuānese drop the "T" part of the "TS" sound, Qīnghǎinese keep the "T" and drop the "S". Both groups drop the "H" sound, making things spelled "CH" in pinyin sound like a breathy, hard "T".

Examples:

- "Chá" (tea) becomes "T'ha"

- "Huīchén" (dust, a very important word to know in the northwest of China) becomes "Hway-t'hén"

DAY 21

Saturday, September 23 – Sunday, September 24
Qīnghǎi Province, Gānsù Province, Shaanxi Province, Xī'ān

•

Again, I can't oversell the beauty of Qīnghǎi and Gānsù provinces. The terrain I saw as we passed through was stunning, a doppelganger for the American southwest right down to the "pueblo" farm houses. It rained just after we left, making the reds, yellows, and greens I saw from the train seem all the brighter, the "painted desert" of China. Beautiful.

And the train? The Qīngdǎo Liè (Line), named for the coastal resort city at its eastern end, was top class, making the Soft Sleeper I took out of Chéngdū seem exactly like the disheveled hand-me-down it was. This line connected the impoverished far west to the wealthier provinces of the north-central region and then to the even wealthier ones out east, so that shouldn't have come as a surprise. Yet, having spent a long, difficult week in the old-timey west, it did.

The wood paneling and lace curtains looked the same, but this train was clean. Oh, my god, was it *clean*. I was tempted to walk on the floor without shoes. No need. They provided slippers. The top bunks even folded away, so *special* travelers could have more space. And to think how long they'd had these. In China, this was obscene! My cabin-mates, three jovial businessmen aged 34, 65, and 68, tired themselves out talking business, so we all turned in about 9.

About 2 in the morning, I woke with a terrible sinus headache. I took the medicine I had, Tylenol and Sudafed, but two hours later the sinus pain was joined by a cold sweat and lower abdominal pain. This was food poisoning, most likely from the "yāzi" dumplings I had for lunch back in Xīníng. It had to be, because they were the only thing I ate after my doughnut and porridge breakfast except more digestives, and it couldn't be them.

DAY 21: Qīnghǎi Province, Gānsù Province, Shaanxi Province, Xī'ān 97

The great fear in this should have been that I was traveling on a train alone through a region with limited medical services, but, no, in this moment my greatest concern was the limited laundry services I'd seen so far and not soiling my clothes with "xiè xiè". About 4:30 or so, I climbed down to use the toilet and managed to use it without making a bigger mess than I could clean. I climbed back up to my bunk, retrieved pills, water, and the ratty, yellow wash rag I took from the hotel in Kūnmíng, and went out into the corridor to sit on a fold-out stool while I waited for the chills and stomach cramps to die down. An hour or so later, I finally went back to bed and was able to sleep until the conductor woke us from under our amazingly comfortable quilts maybe an an hour later, at 7 in the morning.

At quarter to 9, we rolled in, meat for the masses. As we waited to disembark, I had a proud moment. The 65 year old was from the south and spoke with a noticeable accent. I had gotten used to hearing the dropped "H"s, so as we all packed and got ready to go I found myself adjusting for it when he spoke and when I spoke to him. I still didn't catch half the words he said, but I had taken a significant step in understanding and speaking the language.

Anyway, the meat and the masses. There's very little that's hard to understand about people shouting "HELLO!" and tugging your arms. That was my greeting at the station in Xī'ān. One kind-looking woman pursued me, and I got into her taxi, only to have her tell me it would be ¥30 to my hotel. "No," I said. "OK, 20," she said. I got out and walked, heavy pack and all. Still sick with a cold and still recovering from last night, I just wasn't in the mood to haggle. Xī'ān was much bigger than I imagined. I guess staying in smaller towns and cities had tricked me into forgetting just how big a city can be, even one still surrounded by a medieval wall.

Two miles along, I gave up and flagged down another taxi which took me to the Renmin Dasha Gongyu for only ¥8, standard outside of the station area. The Flats, as they were called in English, were another guidebook hotel recommendation. The staff here weren't surly at all, they were mean. I took my lousy room and liked it. Once in, I took a shower in the red-knob cold water then used the hotel's laundry, which mercifully cost a lot less than I'd feared it would on the train. Handing it over, I understood then just how precious each piece of clothing was, and then my greatest concern became making sure I got them back.

I made it out to the street at noon. I wandered through some side streets and back alleys until I found a bench to rest on. My stomach had settled enough to drink a bottle of water and eat some digestive crackers, but my cold persisted, I was tired, and, for this day at least, I was wary of local food. Two young girls peaked out from one of the alleys and started hanging around, saying "Hello" in that shy, giggly way kids do. I guess they lived nearby. I may have been one of the first non-Chinese tourists they'd ever seen, maybe even the very first. I took out the camera and they ran. I teased them with it for a while, then tried to coax them into a picture.

As a tourist, I didn't usually take pictures of people; they moved, they were awkward, and they often seemed to be in the way more than anything else. These kids, however, were naturals. After retreating back into the alley a few times, they sacrificially pushed out a little boy who might have been one of the girls' little brother. He was a toddler, two years old at most.

I took a couple of pictures of him and, seeing it was safe, the girls pushed him aside and hammed it up for the camera.

DAY 21: Qīnghǎi Province, Gānsù Province, Shaanxi Province, Xī'ān

They couldn't get enough. They even dragged friends in, literally dragging them from down the block, just one more picture, one more, again and again until they ran out of friends. I was fading, though, my cold and general exhaustion catching up with me, so I thanked them and begged permission to go.

I stopped by the bus station to see what kind of tours were offered and cashed two more travelers cheques before taking a moto-taxi all the way back to the hotel for another ¥8. My day was done at 3 in the afternoon. I slept, wheezed, coughed, sneezed, and did some creative sinus plumbing for the next six hours.

When my sinuses were clear enough to go out, I stopped by the hotel's painting shop. They had a price sheet on the counter, there for tourists in the hope they'd see it and not bargain. I looked around to see what they had. There was a scroll painting I liked. It was of a woman walking under the branch of a tree with red petals falling around her. It wasn't the greatest painting of all time, but I liked it.

I then made my way across the street to "Mum's Home Cooking", which, naturally, was next to a place called "Dad's". "Mum" was actually younger than I was, and she actually was a mother, of a girl about the same age as the boy in my afternoon pictures. Mum's restaurant was a kitchen with a bunch of tables out front where all of the other backpackers in the area seemed to hang out. It was also a bike rental and an ad-hoc concierge service for whatever else a backpacker might need, such as train tickets. It was all above board, so you paid a price for convenience, but I would find it was all worth it. I was cold and not yet hungry enough to stay, so I promised Mum I'd return in the morning, got some bottled water, which I badly needed, and went back to the room to tally my spending and sleep.

Not five minutes later, as I sat on my bed, the lightbulb above it exploded. The room went black. I had no idea how much glass was in my hair or on my clothes. I felt my way to the door and made my way to the front desk. It took ten minutes to get someone to come to my room to check it out. She stuck her head into the dark room and said she couldn't clean it then, but would come back at 7 the next morning. "NO!" I insisted. I was firm on that. The owner, or manager, then popped in and told her to get a new lightbulb. He surveyed the scene, she gave him the bulb, he carefully replaced the first bulb, the light went on, he looked around again, then turned to me and asked, "OK?"

"NO," I repeated. "NOT OKAY."

What followed was a half-hour of haranguing, arm-twisting, and neck-wringing. They wanted me to sleep in the glass on the bed and walk on the glass on the floor for the rest of the night, and maybe the rest of my stay. I wasn't sleeping on broken glass, and I certainly wasn't paying them for the privilege. They could clean it or they could give me a new room. It wasn't easy, I had to shame them into it. They took the standard, performative offense at being made to lose face, but only held it the standard amount of time. I'm not sure if they were thinking about the money or just tired of arguing, but they finally gave me the room across the hall. It was, and how could I have doubted it, a far better room in every way: cleaner, quieter, more comfortable, and with a better bathroom.

And the light over the bed didn't explode. Not once.

DAY 22

Monday, September 25

Xī'ān

•

I was out early for breakfast. I wasn't sure, but I felt confident enough to try Mum's muesli. I was finally starting to feel better, like I might finally kick this cold, and with that came the feeling I had to make up for all the time I'd lost recovering. When I finished eating, I rented an old Flying Pigeon bike from Mum for ¥4 and was off.

In Xī'ān in 1995, the only thing you had to worry about when riding a bike was other riders. Never mind the cars, buses, and spit that could and would fly at you from all directions. One girl on a bike flew around a corner and almost sandwiched me into a car, in traffic; she just kept on going. The good news was that there weren't many cars in Xī'ān, not yet and not compared to other major cities in China at the time. The air was more breathable then, too. That's not to say you wouldn't have the standard, black coal stripe down your finger when you wiped your nose, but it was nothing like the toxic stew in Guǎngzhōu and, from what I hear, far, far better than it is now.

I reached Dong Dajie (East Avenue) in the city center and immediately couldn't find a place to park my bike. An American teacher, Carla, was passing on her bike and saw me standing there, confused. It turned out the main avenues in Xī'ān were the only place in the city you couldn't park a bike. She led me just a block over to an underground, public bike lot. With Carla's help, I was free of the bike for only 5 Jiāo (¥.50, about 6 cents). How nice was Carla? She owned a non-profit restaurant down by the Big Goose Pagoda called "The Rose Garden Café". Like its namesake in Chéngdū, it served a Western menu, and all of Carla's profits went to help Xī'ān's needy children. And, yes, in communist China, there were.

I promised Carla I'd pay her a visit later and walked from the bike lot to the Bell Tower, positioned at the center of the intersection of four avenues. In the west, we think of a bell tower as something tall and slender, like the Leaning Tower of Pisa. Here and elsewhere in China, they look like temples built on top of short castles. The Bell Tower in Xī'ān used to ring the hour, but that stopped when traffic noise started to drown it out. It was a museum by the time I arrived, reachable by braving the traffic or an underpass. I was feeling very tired by the time I climbed the steps to the top, the last three weeks' sickness, poor diet, and poor sleep catching up with me as they would until I rebuilt my strength, so I sat for a while and enjoyed the views.

From the Bell Tower, I walked over to the Drum Tower. The big cities all had both. It marked the beginning of the Muslim Quarter and a gauntlet of souvenir tables. One lady actually scolded me for not coming to a complete stop in front of her booth. Really, she shook her finger and everything. At first I thought I had done something wrong but then she started showing me the souvenirs and I realized I was free to go. I wandered around in circles until some people, and then some more people, pointed me to the Great Mosque. It was great, yes, and pricey to get into, but these places around Xī'ān were well cared for and it paid for upkeep. I looked for jiāozi and only found a place where they didn't know what meat was in it. I named every kind of meat I could and only got shrugs. I wasn't hungry anyway.

I retrieved my bike and rode all the way down to Dà Yàn Tǎ, the Big Goose Pagoda. That's what the guidebook called it. Officially, it's the "Great Wild Goose Pagoda" or, literally, "Big Wild Goose Pagoda". It's a beautiful, elegant building, over 1,300 years old now, set in the middle of a park, and one of those things that make journeys, even ones like this, so necessary. It actually looks like what we in the west would call a bell tower, each of the seven levels narrower than the one below it. I sat a while just staring up at it, taking it in. Among the many things I had neglected while dealing with my illness and the constant stress of travel here was this, taking it in, experiencing where I was instead of focusing on getting where I needed to be. Yes, I had had moments, but not enough, not as I should have or could have had I been healthy and wealthy, or even just a little bit of that other thing. Despite my hopes at breakfast, I was still sick and still tired, so taking some more time just sitting there was worth it. Maybe that was wisdom finally starting to reach me?

From there, I searched in vain for Carla's restaurant, circling around the park on my bike and trying to remember if she told me more about where it was. I never did find it.

On my way back to the hotel, I took a detour through the park atop the city's medieval walls. I had no idea there was a park, and it was great. Quiet and comparatively unpolluted, the park had trees, boulders, and benches, and was filled with locals reading poetry, debating, playing xiàngqí (Chinese chess), making out, and strolling, park stuff with breathtaking views. A bike path wound its way through the park and the whole place would have been worth a day's visit just to unwind and forget about the rest of the trip. I should have taken more time up on that wall. I should have come back and spent an entire day just sitting and taking it all in like I had at the Pagoda. If I had known what lay ahead for me in Luoyang, I'd have done exactly that. But I didn't know and I didn't stay. If this beautiful, quiet moment was the universe trying to tell me to slow down and take care of myself, I wasn't yet ready to hear it. Maybe I needed to fail just a bit more for that wisdom to sink in?

Between the park and the hotel, the dusk air suddenly turned into a cloud of gnats. We're talking biblical plague stuff, it was that thick. Safely back at the hotel, I picked the bugs out of my teeth, picked up my laundry and checked to make sure every valuable piece of clothing was there, chucked it all onto the bed, and dove into the shower to wash the rest of the bugs off. I put clean clothes on and, man, did I finally have an appetite. I felt good for the first time in weeks, almost euphoric in that way you feel after you've been sick. I had a huge meal at the German-language table over at Mum's. I didn't speak German, but they were friendly and I enjoyed the company. It was the most I'd eaten in one sitting since Chéngdū, which had only been five days ago but felt so much longer.

I should point out here that in this long day of recovery that ended so well, I did not call home. I should have. Really, I should have called yesterday right after I arrived, but I still felt very sick and exhausted, both from the way too common cold and the "yāzi", and all I could think about was clean drinking water and sleep. Today, though, I had no excuse. I had been out of touch five days at this point, which I'm sure I told myself wasn't a lot, but to my parents, half a world away, me traveling five days alone through the remote northwest of China wasn't just a lot, it was terrifying. However bad my cold and food poisoning might have felt, it could have been much worse. But I wasn't thinking about that. In the state I was in, I was thinking how good it felt not to feel so bad. I was thinking about the here and now, not about things or people that felt very far away. I wouldn't call tomorrow, either, or the day after. I would pay for this selfish, short-sighted thinking, not yet, but soon. Until then, was just happy to be where I was, at Mum's, safe and secure.

It didn't take long before I was joined at Mum's by another American, who called himself Larry. I had met him briefly at Mum's last night. He stood out from everyone else, in that he was a middle-aged man in properly laundered clothes that no backpacker would ever wear. He was affable, though. Very friendly. He said he was from New York City and was in China on business, staying at a proper nearby hotel that no backpacker could afford. New markets were opening up, he told me, and he wanted to see the country. He asked a lot of questions. Over dinner, he asked me all about where I'd been in China and then what to see and do when he visited Philadelphia, where I was from. He said he'd be going there soon. He seemed oddly excited by the idea.

The lights, strung out in strands over the table area, blew out, and until they brought some candles the only light we had was from headlights breaking through the trees and the dust the traffic was whipping up off the streets. It was pretty surreal.

For dessert, I ordered a Hard Sleeper ticket to Luòyáng through Mum and went to bed.

DAY 23

Tuesday, September 26
Xī'ān, Shaanxi Province, Xī'ān

•

It was day of the tour, the day of Qín Shǐ Huáng, the day of so many people and names and faces.

I was taking a night train, so I had to pack and check out. Despite our issues with the lightbulb and the room change, I trusted the Renmin Dasha Gongyu enough to leave my heavy pack in their storage room for the day. Well, it was them or take it all the way over to Left Luggage at the train station and make it back in time for the tour, so maybe I was just trusting their convenience. I took the chance.

I ate breakfast over at Mum's with a Finnish couple, Katherine-Marie and Marco, two Italians, and an Israeli. The Finns, the Israeli, and I were all going on the same tour to see the tomb of Qín Shǐ Huáng, founder of the Qín Dynasty and the emperor who gave the country its most well known name, and his army of terracotta warriors, buried nearby for over 2,000 years and discovered in 1974, only twenty-one years earlier, by farmers, just like Pompeii.

The bus to see them was leaving at 8:30. This was a proper bus, not one of those tiny minibus vans like the ones trawling outside the train stations in Guìlín and Kūnmíng. It was small, seating only 13 plus the driver and the tour organizer in a front passenger seat, but it had a center aisle and an accordion side door, the sight of which was oddly reassuring. We were told to wait for the organizer, who was off recruiting more people for the tour, which was run through the hotel. Although I had doubts about anything run through this particular hotel, Mum had suggested it and I trusted her.

When they finally let us on board, they found that they now had one too many in the tour group – me – and stopped. I explained what I had been told back at the hotel and the others took my case. The organizer relented and let me sit over the engine access console located between the front seats, with a ¥5 discount for the heat. Given this start and the staff at the hotel, I didn't really have much hope for the tour. Whatever else happened, I would at least get to see the terracotta warriors. Well, I hoped.

We were all foreigners: two Finns, the Israeli, two Dutch, two Irish, a Dane, a Japanese, three Germans, and the two Americans, myself and Larry. Everyone had a great sense of humor. Most had come down from Běijīng, although I don't believe any were involved with the Conference On Women. They all had horror stories of how China had changed from our flawed mutual guidebook, especially Běijīng. They offered advice on where to stay and go, which would help me. I did the same for where I had been, including Thailand for a few on the tour who were going there next.

We arrived at the tomb. It felt like a big deal pulling up, but getting off the bus it was just a large mound off the side of the road. Wide steps led up the side of the mound to a flat top. It had a nice view of the plateau around us, but that was it, just a place to stand and nothing else. There were actually more vendors than tourists. I couldn't help but think of the bus to Shílín and entrance fee for the roadside gift shop. This, at least, really was Qín's tomb. I'm sure it's been built up since then, with better signs and better vendors, but standing there, none of us were sure. We all had to laugh.

When we reached the terracotta warriors, the tour operators told us we had an hour less than the two and a half hours they'd promised. A riot just about broke out. I again remembered Shílín and, speaking more Mandarin than most of the others, I made a clear, reasoned case that may have helped to change the driver's mind. Of course, the crowd of angry tourists right behind me may have done the rest. Still, I remembered what the drivers in Shílín had said to save face right before ditching us and prepared myself for the worst. I certainly wasn't going to leave anything on the bus.

Janet and Antonette, the Irish women, helpfully offered to buy a ticket for me with the "student" ID cards they'd bought in Xī'ān. The cards gave them a discount of ¥40 each. The only problem was they checked IDs at the gate, and I and my so-called "student" ticket were

DAY 23: Xī'ān, Shaanxi Province, Xī'ān 107

escorted across the way to the office. The first woman in the office scolded me and ordered me to pay ¥75 on top of the ¥20 student price. She left suddenly, while I was still trying to explain my way out of it, and was replaced by another woman who just as suddenly asked me to pay only the original ¥40 discount I shouldn't have had. All paid, she gave me a souvenir coin and sent me on my way. I caught up with the group, told them how they'd tortured me, showed them my shiny new coin, and we all went in to see the soldiers.

They had built what looked like an extra large airplane hangar over the dig site. You couldn't really see all of the soldiers, though, just the few front rows, and they ushered you through like they were the Crown Jewels ("No pictures, please. Move along, move along, so the next in line can see."). As we left the first building, I bumped into the Israeli, who had wandered off and bumped into an Israeli tour group. They had all then strayed into one of the outside "museums", which had cost them plenty for, well, nothing. The second building had whole warriors and a whole horse, up close. There, we didn't have to rush. It was definitely the highlight. The third building showed evidence that everything had originally been painted to resemble the models, like Greco-Roman statues of the same era. All told, it was well worth the full price of admission.

The Irish, the Finns, and I found our bus still parked where we left it at 12:30. The others had gotten back earlier, not wanting to tempt fate. The only straggler was Larry, who returned twenty minutes later. He said he'd gotten lost.

On the way back, we stopped at Banpo Neolithic Village. This was a fun place, only not for what we paid to see, which was the boring museum. The rest of the grounds were dedicated to a kind of "Banpoland", a theme park with a motif of naked, big breasted women having sex with and/or killing naked men and animals. Honestly. The site map showed places like "Food Street" and the "Merrymaking Pavilion".

Before leaving, we all stopped to photograph the entrance to the Banpo Matriarchal Clan Village and Cultural Center. The naked, big breasted torso and legs of a woman formed the outer wall, with the entrance to the cultural center right *THERE*. I can't imagine why they told us not to go in.

I also can't imagine they took anyone from the World Conference On Women to see it.

When we got back, most of us – everyone but Larry – commandeered Mum's and ate lunch. I'd just paid ¥40 more than the "student" card holders for a single entrance fee, and a lot more since Yángshuò, when I had passed on buying one. Now that I knew they worked, I asked Janet and Antonette where they got theirs. For ¥35, I was now a student of Chinese art history, up from the southern island province of Hǎinán. I paid ¥5 more than they had, but it was a seller's market.

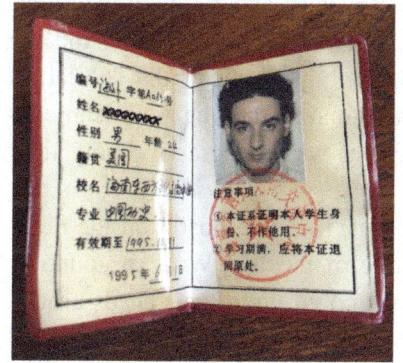

I had time to kill before Mum delivered my train ticket, so I went back to the hotel's art gallery to see about that scroll painting I liked, the one of the woman under the tree branch with red petals falling around her. I walked in just as the shopkeeper was finishing up with the Germans from the tour.

They had purchased an 18 inch scroll and a set of four small Four Seasons scrolls for ¥350. I checked this against the counter price sheet and it looked like the Germans hadn't bargained. I would. Some gentle bargaining later, I had the price of my one meter wide scroll down from ¥600 to ¥220, about $27. Not bad at all.

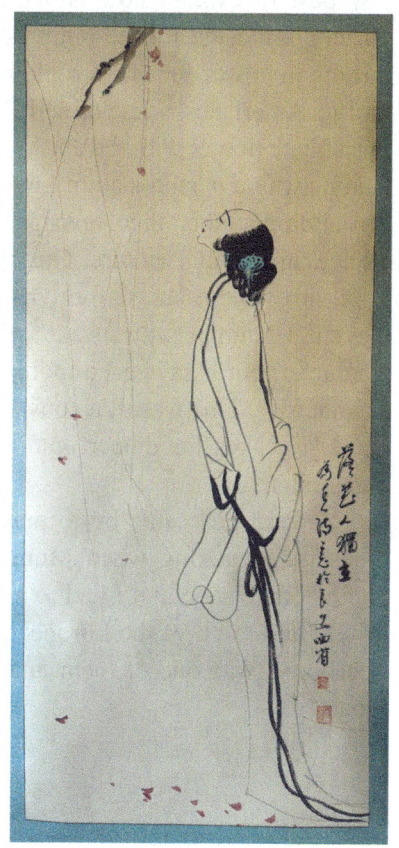

The shopkeeper provided a translation of the text inscribed down the lower right side of the painting. It was a painting of the Sòng dynasty poet, Lǐ Qīngzhào, who was born about 1000 years ago. She was considered to be a patriotic poet, perhaps most famous for the line: "In life be a hero among men, In death, a champion among ghosts". The red petals might have been from crabapple flowers, the subject of one of her poems. I would mail it home from Běijīng.

Over a dinner of banana pancakes and chocolate milk I discussed American politics, education, and "Revenge Theory" with the Finns, the Irish women, and a Belgian named Jean-Louis. What did the Finns think of their president? "He's a big, fat meatball! The fattest one we've ever had!!" They were all amazed that the American educational system could be as bad as it was, geography being their common example.

"Revenge Theory", as I dubbed it, focused mostly on the death penalty, the United States being one of the few Western countries still using it. None of the Europeans could wrap their heads around such a barbaric practice. I agreed with them, then and now, but I did my best to explain how Americans justify the death penalty as a means of closure for the families of victims and, even more so, as a means to power for those wielding the blade, and how both are central to Americans' sense of self. We equate justice with closure, and we equate power with the ability to force closure, but having already taken away a person's ability to cause harm, it's impossible to see it as anything other than revenge. Revenge plays an outsize part in American popular culture. Our heroes, in movies, music, and literature, are violent and unforgiving. That's no accident. That we still have the death penalty speaks volumes about American morality and character, but it says even more about our collective selfishness and immaturity. This wasn't a conversation I expected to have eating banana pancakes for dinner outdoors in Xī'ān, but I hadn't expected that, either.

A local girl came by to practice her English, and we had only just started talking when Mum arrived with my ticket. The train would leave soon and I had to go. I said my goodbyes to the girl, to Mum, and to all of the Europeans, who were all great and made me feel like I was one of them and who I miss to this day, and I was gone.

DAY 24

Wednesday, September 27

Zhèngzhōu, Hénán Province, Luòyáng

•

Yet again, China's train schedules proved aspirational, at best. A trip that was supposed to take over eight hours didn't even last seven. Six hours in, the conductor woke me to return my ticket. I looked at my watch and, thinking I had two full hours to go, I thought I had one more to sleep. Nope.

Less than an hour later, at 4:54 AM, I was forced out of my bed by the next occupant. We had just left Luòyáng. No one, meaning no one who worked on the train, had checked to make sure I was gone. Sure, I had been woken prior to the arrival of the train, but that had been almost an hour before, it was a sleeper car, it was still dark, and we were seventy-five whole minutes early. Seventy-five!

And now you know why everyone in Xīníng was so terrified of giving estimates. I had been a fool for even asking.

I should have taken this as a sign from the universe to skip Luòyáng and go straight on to Běijīng. I'd have been early by a day, but it was Běijīng and I'm sure I could have found some thing to do. But no, again, like my decision to trudge up the muddy, hillside trails of Éméishān through the pouring rain because I had committed to reaching that temple, here I was determined to complete what I had started no matter how much I suffered for it. I had come all this way to see the world famous Longmen Caves and I was going to see them, and that was that.

I talked my way into staying on until we reached Zhèngzhōu, the next major stop, two hours down the line. They had wanted to put me off at the next stop. I shouldn't, after all, be riding for free, not with this kind of service. At Zhèngzhōu, a friendly platform attendant pointed me to the track for the next train back to Luòyáng. Just after

7, a brand new double-decker train pulled in. Some nice men helped me plead my case, and I was able to avoid paying an additional ¥11. This conductor told me, "We arrive at Luòyáng at 9:45." I think she was teasing me. I think. The train was new and mostly clean. Later on, an attendant sweeping the aisle became outraged to see people treating the car like the old, garbage dump, Hard Seat class. "This is NOT a TOILET!!", she scolded them.

Seated with me as we left Zhèngzhōu were a middle-aged couple from Guǎngzhōu and a male Běijīng university student who came from Wǔhàn. I could sometimes understand the couple better than the student because, as I was proud to recognize, he spoke with a mix of northern and southern accents. He thought he was speaking strictly Běijīng-hua, the dialect and pronunciation from the region around Běijīng, but sometimes he would drop his "H"s as I imagined he would back home in Wǔhàn.

My failure to get off the train at Luòyáng meant that I now wouldn't be able to see it and the nearby Longmen Caves in one day, which had been my plan. I did get one good thing out of it, though; if I hadn't been on this train coming from Zhèngzhōu, I wouldn't have seen the sharp cliffs and narrow valleys of the Hénán countryside east of Luòyáng, into which farmers had carved and expanded caves to use as homes. Every flat piece of land all around, including over the caves, was used for farming.

We arrived about 10 o'clock and I took a double with shower at the Tianxiang Hotel, because taking the much cheaper single would have meant using the public showers. I needed to change money for Běijīng, so I set out to find the bank recommended by the increasingly discredited two year-old guidebook. Two very confused taxi drivers later, I got to the bank, which, of course, no longer exchanged traveler's cheques. They sent me to another bank on the other side of town.

On the way, I stopped for some jiāozi at an outdoor stand, where I saw a family of five: a mother, a father, one daughter, and two sons. At the time, China still officially followed the "One Child" population restriction it had implemented in 1979, so either this family was bucking that system or that policy wasn't so strictly enforced

DAY 24: *Zhèngzhōu, Hénán Province, Luòyáng* 113

here. While eating, I also saw a man with one of those Chinese army backpacks. The men who had them all seemed older. They were probably veterans. I'd have to find an army surplus store to buy one of my own.

After lunch, I stopped to take some pictures of odd things in and around the street traffic, like sculptures over bus stops advertising toothpaste and body lotion, and beach-ball shaped garbage cans.

I had locals spotting for me to make sure I didn't get hit by a car or a bus. We all had a lot of fun. On the shot of the giant tube of toothpaste, a minibus pulled into the frame and stopped, waiting for me to take their picture. The driver and passengers were just clowning.

When I finally reached the address the first bank had given me, a man in a suit showed up, asked if I had business inside, shook my hand, and kissed my check. Then he discovered that I didn't want insurance and sent me to the actual right place, which had moved around the corner. Money safely in pouch under shirt, I walked through town back to my hotel. Luòyáng was awfully big for being small and in the condition I was in, I was exhausted by the time I got back. There was nothing on TV but four channels of the same brightly colored soap-opera, so I poured myself a cup of tea and laid back for a quick nap.

DAY 25

Thursday, September 28

Luòyáng

•

Fourteen hours later, I woke up. It was 6 AM. Everything I had meant to do last night, like calling home and calling my mother's childhood friend with whom I'd be staying in Běijīng, would have to wait until I got there. They didn't have to wait, not really, and shouldn't have waited, but where my head was at this point in my journey, it was exactly the kind of poor decision I was capable of making. I just wasn't thinking straight. I had been sick for weeks, I was exhausted, I was dehydrated, I had been navigating a transportation and tourist system riddled with institutional failures, and I was determined, in reaction to all of that, to fight my way through and complete what I had started.

And so it would be here, in this place and on this day, that all of this got the better of me.

Having failed to meet my obligations and then having failed to fix that mistake, I got up to take a shower. There was no hot water. I went down to ask about it; I was asked to wait. Nothing. I packed up and went to reception to demand a refund down to the single room, no shower price. They told me that there was hot water, but it only ran between the hours of 8 PM and 10 PM. I persisted. I hadn't been told. I could, of course, have asked when I checked in. I probably should have asked, but up to that point each hotel with limited hours for hot water had told me when I checked in, without needing to be asked. Here, I hadn't asked and no one had thought to tell me, so plenty of blame to go around, I guess. Still, I held my breath long enough and I got my refund. If I was wrong here, I certainly paid for it later.

At the train station, wearing my full pack, I hopped from line to

DAY 25: *Luòyáng* 115

line until I found the right one, for train #76 to Běijīng. Yesterday, I had been told to come back today for a Hard Seat ticket, all that was available leaving Luòyáng, this despite the man kicking me out of my bunk when the train had stopped at this same station only hours earlier. Maybe it was just trains heading to Běijīng that had no beds? No problem. It took a while to get to the window, but it was made quicker by a railroad employee who, at great pains, physically removed the mob from around the window and kept it away, like the policeman had in Xīníng. Keepers of Line Integrity, I salute you.

Once at the window, I asked nicely in Mandarin, "Please, train #76, today, Hard Seat ticket." The woman gave me a ticket and I thanked her, but as I was leaving the window I noticed something wrong with the ticket: It had no seat number. I remembered the scrum leaving Kūnmíng and how meaningless a seat number in Hard Seat could be, but my ticket then at least had a number. I asked someone in line. She had given me a "zhàn piào", a Standing Ticket. A standing ticket meant that I would either have to stand the entire fourteen hours to Běijīng or sacrifice my pack by laying it on the sticky, soiled Hard Seat floor and using it for a seat. So, having a seat number might not guarantee getting that seat, but it guaranteed getting a seat, and that was what mattered.

I turned right back around, catching sight of the ticket given to the Chinese man who had been behind me in line: Train #76, seat number 35. The man who had told me about the standing ticket let me cut back in line and I again asked the woman for a "yìng zuò piào", a Hard Seat ticket. I had asked for one in the first place, hadn't I? I was told that there were no more seats on train #76. I told her that I had seen the other man's ticket, that when I had asked there had been at least one. How could he be able to get one and not me? It was a stupid question with an obvious answer, but it was the kind of question that needs asking.

She walked away and spoke to a man who then came over to the window. He apologized in English and said there were "no more tickets for seats on train #76". I repeated, in English since he spoke it, that I had specifically asked for a seat and that she had understood me well enough to tell me there wasn't one when I came back. He offered me a seat on train #232, leaving three hours later, at 8:12 PM, and arriving in Běijīng at or near or in the vicinity of 10:20 in the morning. I took it, seeing that it was the best I would get. I didn't forget the other man's ticket. I don't think the man in the window believed I did, either, he just didn't want a scene. You know, "face". He knew what she had done and we both knew why: There had been a ticket for a seat on that train, just not for someone like me.

Some of you reading this know all too well what this experience feels like, and many of you who know that feeling have experienced it in your own home country. That I was experiencing it in someone else's country doesn't make it much easier to take, not repeatedly, not when you've been sick and tired and frustrated about so many other things. I took my Hard Seat ticket and left.

Leaving the station, I was seething with anger, about the shower at the hotel, about the standing ticket, about the train arriving so early yesterday and all of the bullshit I had been putting up with since I arrived in Kūnmíng. I was angry that I was still sick and angry that I had gotten sick and how and why I had gotten sick. I was angry and I was distracted and I wasn't thinking. Whatever "xiǎo xīn" meant, I had forgotten it. Whatever camaraderie and inclusion I had felt in Xī'ān just two days ago, I felt completely alone now. This journey was getting to me.

Anyway, I left the station with three extra hours to kill; three hours eating up time I should have been spending in Běijīng, three distracted hours I would manage to waste, not calling anyone as I should, not planning as I should. I stopped by the clock-tower outside the station to clean my camera lens, something I told my self I could control. A young German traveler sat down next to me and asked my thoughts on Xī'ān and Chéngdū, where he would be going next. I told him what I knew, briefly, then set off to find a bike for the day. The first place I found, just up the street from the Tianxiang Hotel and the suspicious bike-rental they had recommended yesterday, were very nice people. They rented me a sorry looking thing but asked only ¥6 for the day.

I wound through the streets to the road that led out of town, south, to the Longmen Caves. It was a long ride out and, as I realized

DAY 25: *Luòyáng* 117

on the way back, slightly up hill. There was a bridge crossing a wide, marshy river. Southeast of it, they were building some Disneyland-looking thing in an area that had been farmland. As I got close to the caves, I needed to ask directions. "Zǒu ah, zǒu ah", they all said. The last one, I asked three times. Three times he waved his finger off in the distance, over there, somewhere, thereabouts. I stopped asking and just kept going. After an hour of riding, I finally made it to the caves, and it was there that everything fell apart.

When I pedaled in, I parked my bike by the souvenir shop for a small fee. The shopkeeper, an old woman sitting out front on an aluminum beach chair and knitting, was friendly and polite. She took my money, nodded with a small smile, and returned to her knitting. So far, so good.

And then I crossed to the ticket window.

The first ticket had a picture of the caves, the second, a gate in the shape of a dragon's head. I was given no choice of which ticket to buy. I had to buy both. No, no student discount. No, no separate tickets for the park and the amusement park, as there had been at Shílín and for the terracotta soldiers in Xī'ān. I had to buy both or nothing. I tried to explain that I didn't want the second ticket. The ticket seller told me that everyone had to buy both. Everyone. I persisted. I only want to see the caves, I said. No, she said. I had to buy both. Some Chinese teenagers came along and bought tickets for both at the local price. I wondered if maybe there were two sets of caves. The ticket seller wouldn't say and wouldn't give in. She said, yet again, that everyone had to buy both tickets, so I gave in and bought the second ticket, which cost as much as the first, tourist price.

At the entrance to the caves, I asked the ticket takers if there were more caves to see with the dragon's head ticket. They seemed amused by my question. No, they said. Well, what is it? I asked. You'll see, they said. They actually said just that: "Nǐ huì kàn dào de."

What I saw in cave after cave was that there wasn't much of anything to see at all. There were a few larger caves with their statues mostly intact, reliefs of guardians snarling at visitors that somehow escaped damage, but most of the statues in the rest of the caves had been removed to Western museums during the colonial era. Some of the ones left were missing their heads. The smaller cavelets carved into the rock were almost entirely empty.

DAY 25: *Luòyáng*

A hawker selling cheap souvenirs followed me around, harassing me as I tried to take pictures of the few remaining statues. I put up with it, trying to be polite, until she grabbed my arm while I was taking a picture and pulled me towards her. You can hawk all you want, but you do not touch. You do not grab, you most certainly do not pull. I shouted at her and chased her off. I don't like doing that, anywhere. I understand there are cultural gaps and hawkers grabbing at you isn't remotely limited to China, but anyone would feel threatened by someone grabbing and pulling them like that, and it had been common enough so far in China that there was going to be a limit. This day, with everything I had endured in addition to being pawed and cursed at by a souvenir peddler, was the day I would reach it.

Quickly through with the caves, I bumped into the German again, down by the ice cream stand. He had beaten me to the park and told me he'd only bought the first ticket. He spoke no Chinese of any kind, and had held out with that same ticket seller until she gave in. It seemed I'd arrived one person and a few words of Mandarin too late. And then I saw the dragon head from the second ticket over the entrance to a crappy amusement park with basic carnival rides and junk food. It explained why the teenagers had bought both. They probably never even looked at the caves.

I'd had enough. I walked the short path back to the caves entrance, where the ticket takers saw the expression on my face and knew I'd "seen it", and then back to the ticket window. I had been clear about not wanting to buy it and now I knew that I had never had to, that I had been made to out of spite for what the German had done, or worse, for being a tourist who wouldn't bully her back. I only wanted my money back for the second ticket. This had been my only goal walking back. It was when I reached the ticket window that I realized it had been the latter, that to her I was just an easy mark, not for money, just someone she could push around. It was this that made me angry. I won't say angry, though. It was more enraged.

You see, when she saw me coming, she started laughing. At me.

She was dealing with a small group of Chinese tourists. She gave them their tickets and quickly brushed them to the side to make room for me. She was cocky, enjoying her power. I waited, I'd like to say patiently but my expression must have given me away. We both knew she had lied to me. I had been respectful and had asked for just the one ticket in clear enough Mandarin that she knew to say, "No, you have to buy both". I firmly demanded a refund for the unused amusement park ticket. She didn't say a word. Instead, she smugly shook her head and laughed again and pointed to a sheet of white paper taped to the inside of the window: 不予退款. I didn't know the hànzì characters, not then, but I understood: NO REFUND. With so many statues taken by museums and collectors before the Communists took over, there were bound to be dissatisfied customers, so they had made that sign. That sign lent her authority. It was something she could point to and hide behind. I was not going to get a refund. She just leaned back, smiled, shook her head, and, once again, laughed straight at me. She was enjoying this. This had made her day.

It was this that pushed me past my limit. She had done this to me and had been able to do this to me because of who I was and the expected language barrier, and because of the fact that she was in a position to exploit it. It was also because I had been alone. Had I been with a group, as I had been in Shílín and Xī'ān, none of this might have happened. Alone, though, I was vulnerable.

What she was doing was a petty abuse of power, one enjoyed by petty people the world over, and she was really enjoying it. The amount of money I'd been made to pay was only ¥10, hardly more than a dollar, so, maybe you could argue that I was the one being petty. But it wasn't that. It never is. I knew how little it was and how useless arguing over it was, and still I could not walk away. I could not wake up and live my life with any amount of dignity having walked away, not from that laughter and not from the reasons for it.

That, at least, was how I felt in that moment. The trains, the hotels, all of the official government policies that attack that dignity, those I could stomach. It may have taken a lot of patience, but I was willing to accept the line on subsidies and taxes. Even the tourist prices I could stomach. This was different, though. This had gone beyond money, beyond any "policy" before I ever approached that window. I could have been any non-Chinese tourist, she would have done this and hid behind that sign. I can't imagine I was her first or last. Whether it was because of what the German had done or because of what so many other tourists had already done or just because she was having her own bad day or bad life, nothing could excuse it. This was about power, about her taking it from me or some other tourist unfortunate enough to have been here today in Luòyáng. That's where that smugness came in.

What I did next I regret, mostly because it brought me down to her level but also because it was something that I knew could have no result in getting what I really wanted to say across. Even before I thought of doing it, she was already pulling the roll of tickets away from the window. I don't even know if I would have thought of it if I hadn't seen her starting to pull them away. It was a reflex. She didn't want me to take them, so that was what I did. This was about power. It was also plainly stupid. If I'd had the self-awareness I liked to think I had, I'd have remembered what I'd just said in Xī'ān about revenge and the American character, about the selfishness and immaturity of it. What I'd just done wasn't about getting any kind of justice, not real, lasting justice, it was just about making me feel good in that moment. For just that moment. It was revenge, and it didn't work. It didn't make me feel better, not even for a second.

No, all it did was this: I took the roll of tickets to that amusement park and that brought a commotion, which brought a crowd, which in turn brought a policeman. My thoughtless, stupid decision had led to this, and this very well could have ended much worse than it did.

As angry as I was, what little Mandarin I knew to speak just about left me. I froze. Standing there holding a roll of those stupid tickets, I was facing a policeman and a crowd of Chinese locals and I couldn't find the words I knew that I knew. I could understand the lies the ticket seller was telling the policeman, though. She told him I had bought the two tickets, used both, and wanted an impossible refund. "What can I do?" she asked with an exaggerated shrug.

The policeman then asked my side. After many tries, first with him, then with the help of the shopkeeper who had been knitting across the way, I tried to explain that I had only wanted one ticket but she, the ticket seller, had told me that it was either both or nothing. It took the shopkeeper telling me, "You shouldn't buy the second ticket if you don't want it", for me to realize that I wasn't making sense and that she and the policeman both thought I hadn't even bought any tickets yet.

As I calmed down, my vocabulary came back. Finding the right words, I explained how I had only wanted a ticket to the caves, how the ticket seller had told me that I had to pay for both tickets, that I had paid as I was told to, and that I had not used both. I showed the shopkeeper the unused dragon ticket and told her that I had never wanted it. I shook my head and waved my hands, probably too much, but I wanted to be understood.

The shopkeeper listened and nodded, then went to the window and began scolding the ticket seller, shaming her in front of everyone, because the ticket seller had clearly been lying and, maybe, because she saw how the ticket seller had been laughing at me before I snapped. She came back to me and told me I could have my money back if I returned the roll of tickets. I guess the ticket seller had stopped enjoying it. I thanked the shopkeeper and the policeman, who was satisfied with the shopkeeper's solution, retrieved my money and then my bike, and left that foul place behind me.

I don't know if anybody in that crowd ever understood me or what they had been watching. To them, they had been confronted with something ugly, and we turn away from ugly things. They must have understood when the shopkeeper shamed the ticket seller, but only then. In a culture in which public shaming is such an extreme step, that much must have gotten through, but what if she hadn't been there? Would the policeman have helped me the same way? He hadn't seen the ticket seller taunting me, I don't think. My inability to express myself to the crowd probably left them with the impression that I only wanted the money, just another spoiled foreigner, rich enough to travel so far and still throwing a tantrum over a mere ¥10. That was easy enough to believe.

It wasn't about that to me, but how could they know what I was thinking? I hadn't told anyone what I was thinking. I'm not sure I had the words to. Of course, if I could have expressed myself in

DAY 25: *Luòyáng*   123

Mandarin with the amount of clarity I have writing this, I probably wouldn't have gotten into this fight in the first place. It had been the very things that were my weaknesses in China that the ticket seller had preyed upon. I have to believe the shopkeeper understood that, too. That was why she defended me. That was why she shamed the ticket seller.

But here's the thing. If this whole story sounds unpleasantly familiar, obvious even, odds are, like the bitter, apathetic railway employees I met in western China, and the passengers habitually destroying their trains, you have been living with this your whole life, on one side or the other. When you have people who are ignorant and resentful of outsiders, people whose job is their life and who hate their job and the customers who remind them of that, that is what you will have. They seek a target, an other to be made small so they don't have to be, and twice this day, I got to be on the receiving end of that. That both ticket sellers felt they had to lie to do it should tell you all you need to know about their awareness of right and wrong. That one of them felt justified in adding petty insult to petty injury, well, to that all I can say is I'd like to think she's still stuck in that same hateful, dead end job, stuck with those giggling fools taking tickets to empty caves. If that sounds petty, especially after all of these years, I accept that. She was a bully then and she's probably still a bully to this day.

I'm not breaking new ground here. I understand that to them I had money. It didn't matter how little money I actually had, I had the kind of wealth that gave me the ability to travel to China and to spend my way through it. I had the ability to leave, too, to get on a plane and go home. That was its own kind of wealth. The ability to leave a place is a luxury, maybe the biggest luxury of all, one that be controlled and denied. I had it and these two women didn't, and that, I think, was what they saw in me. To them, it meant I should pay more, accept less, and know my place. This wasn't the first time someone here had seen and treated me that way, and it certainly wouldn't be the last.

It's a shame, really, because when I returned to the city and returned the bike, do you know what the old couple I rented it from did? They offered me some of their tea. For them, that simple act of generosity was the most natural thing in the world. They were kind people. Their kindness made me all the more ashamed of how I had behaved, and at how sheltered I had been in my life before this. The man who had explained my train ticket and let me cut in line to fix it, the shopkeeper, the policeman, this sweet old couple, they were how most people are, in China and everywhere. They were how I needed to be. I shouldn't have needed to remember that.

SIGNS COMMUNISM WAS OVER
Part 2:

#4: "Gone With The Wind" VHS tapes were sold at train stations.

#5: The businessmen on the train to Xī'ān drank Pabst Blue Ribbon beer and used Johnson's Baby Oil for lip balm.

#6: A sex shop, gadgets on full, storefront window display, had opened a block down from the train station in Xī'ān. Maybe this was common in China before the rise of Dèng Xiǎopíng's "socialist market economy", but it sure looked new.

#7: A TV commercial for Chinese apple juice used a cowboy and an American flag to sell its product.

#8: Ads on the new, double-decker trains used American flags, too.

DAY 26

Friday, September 29

Luòyáng, Hénán Province, Běijīng

•

What can I say? The train was packed to twice its capacity. Boarding the train in Luòyáng once again confirmed one of the worst stereotypes about Hard Seat travel[1]. It seemed like they would crush even the smallest child and throw aside even the frailest old woman just to be first to get on the train. Watching the crush at the train doors, I really could imagine the old women stepping over the children and the children shoving the old women right under the train. It was that ugly, all the more so because only some of them had seat numbers on their tickets.

Down in Kūnmíng, there had been plenty of seats for everyone, so there hadn't been a melee getting on the train. There had been a comedic scrum at the doors, yes, of course, but nothing approaching actual violence. Add another carful of people to each car, though, and even the real estate of the filthy, sticky, mucus and urine soaked floor was carved out between haves and have nots. They weren't just fighting to get on the train, they were fighting to have a seat on a bench, or the edge of one, and if they couldn't have that they wanted one on the floor. Wherever they were going, standing for hours was not an option.

Viewing the melee from the rear, my genuine fear was my hard won seat number going out the window with the rest of the garbage. In an ordered, organized world, holding ticket 17 should have put me on bench 15-16-17, on the aisle a few rows back from the front. Having a numbered ticket, I could at least point to it if my seat was taken, hoping the other person cared. I still might not get my seat,

---

[15] Again, I encourage you to watch Jackie Chan's "Drunken Master II".

DAY 26: Luòyáng, Hénán Province, Běijīng

but I had a chance. I certainly couldn't without one, not without a fight. As the mob squeezed in ahead of me, I had every expectation that my seat would be occupied by whoever had been cutthroat enough to seize it before I got to it and I would be sitting down in the muck.

Somehow, it didn't work out that way. I was first to my seat. I don't know what went wrong, I hadn't rushed. I couldn't have if I'd wanted to, not with my heavy pack and all of those children and old women clawing at each other in front of me. No matter, because there I was with my choice of seats. Wanting air, I sat by the window; my memories of the ripe stench from the ride up to Éméishān were still strong. They're still strong now. In theory, it would also give me a place to rest my head when I slept, if, in theory, I could sleep. The ticket holders of seats 15 and 16 arrived looking at their tickets, greeted me, sat in seats 16 and 17 without complaint, and it was done. Whatever guilt I felt about taking their window seat faded quickly as I noticed the bargaining at the other benches around us. People were trading sides, changing sections. It was normal, just like the scrum outside. And then it got even more strange. For all of the cutthroat brutality of getting to the seats, once the horsetrading was done and the train got going, possession seemed to be settled law. Wherever you were, it was yours for the duration. Get up to stretch your legs or use the toilet and the guy who took your seat for a moment of relative comfort returned to his spot on the floor when you came back, thanking you for the opportunity in the most civilized manner possible. Whatever expectations I had come to have about train travel in China, I couldn't have predicted any of it.

As for our car's standard squat toilet, about two hours in, I joined some others who were waiting to get in. It was unoccupied, but the door was locked, maybe to keep it from sliding open like the Éméishān train's had. We could see the steward trying to sleep in his tiny office next door. One of the Chinese passengers knocked politely on the grimy window. He knocked some more. The steward looked up; we pointed and pantomimed, "We need to unlock the door." He rolled away from us. We all knocked a little more. Finally, he got up. He got up, came out with his keys, locked the office door behind him, and went off to find some far corner of the train where he could sleep without anyone bothering him about doing his job. We could only stand and watch as he disappeared into the next car. We followed him, not that he meant us to, and climbed over the piles of people sitting in the aisle to use their toilet, which was unlocked and somehow not sliding open.

I spent the rest of the night trying to sleep, but mostly getting filthy. I appreciated the legroom heading up from Kūnmíng, that and nothing else, but I had no idea how cramped a window seat would be, let alone at double capacity. I had room for one leg. What I did with the other one I'm not sure I can explain. It was contorted in a way that made it difficult to sit, let alone sleep. Fifteen and a half hours later, an hour and a half late, we trundled into the station in Běijīng. I was finally there.

And then we had to wait.

Two conductors came onto the train to check tickets and passports. No foreigners could leave the train until they had. And then came the punchline. It seemed the ticket sellers at Luòyáng station, the ones with the seat-no-seat-shuffle, had left a parting gift for me and two other equally foreign gentlemen in my car, both of whom who had spent their fifteen and a half hours on the floor with Standing tickets. According to the conductors, Luòyáng had "forgotten" to charge us the tourist price, which was more than the tourist price we all thought we had paid. It felt like some scam dreamed up at the Běijīng end, another "tax", another "surcharge", another abuse of petty power to line someone's pockets, but I was just as happy to place the blame on Luòyáng. It was fair to blame them. They'd earned it. The fine (or bonus or gratuity or entry fee or whatever) came to an extra ¥70 each. They gave us a choice: either we paid the shakedown or they wouldn't return our passports. It was a fitting cap to my misadventure in Luòyáng. Ah, but it wasn't over. I then paid ¥30 more to get to my hotel and ¥150 more for the cheapest one-star double in the city. All told, that was about $30 of my estimated $20 per day budget, and I'd only just arrived.

To remove the stench of the train (and Luòyáng), I improvised a hot and cold shower, the hot water supplied by my thermos. I scrubbed down my boots with the complementary hotel toothbrush. That done, I was off to Jiànguómén Wài Dàjiē to find a phone exchange and some Tylenol. I found both, but didn't buy the Tylenol, which at the "Friendship" Store was prohibitively expensive.

Now, as you may remember, on my second day in Xī'ān, September 25th, I neglected to call home. Before I arrived in China, I told myself I took that responsibility very seriously. After my first lapse, for which I was rightfully scolded by my mother, I'd made an effort at each stop to seek out a telephone exchange and at least try to call home. During the next two weeks, I mostly succeeded, but, as the strain of being ill and the stress of a sometimes hostile and dangerous tourism system took their toll, I had thought about it less and less. I'd adapted to changing conditions, just not in the way I should.

It had now been nine full days since I last spoke to my parents from Chéngdū. Between then and that second day in Xī'ān, I had either been incapacitated or unable to reach a phone. From the 25th to my arrival in Běijīng, I had no excuse, at least no good one. There had been phones in Xī'ān and Luòyáng. Yes, I had been distracted by illness, exhaustion, and frustration at how I was being treated, but I had allowed myself become distracted. I had not practiced "xiǎo xīn", as I knew I needed to. It didn't matter that I had warned my parents that I would be out of touch, not from their point of view, waiting for me on the other side of the planet. For all they knew, I was missing, or worse, and who could blame them?

At 3 o'clock, I finally called my mother's friend, Jacki Eyman, at her apartment in the Kempinski Hotel, which was in the then-new Lufthansa Center complex in the northeast of the city (it is now called the Yansha Center). I should at least have called Jacki before I got to Běijīng. My Luòyáng detour had left me a day late by my own schedule, the one I had given my parents and they had given Jacki. As Jacki told me, my parents had been panic-stricken, not just for that one day but for over a week, the kind of panic parents feel when their child is missing, which in my thoughtless lack of contact I had been.

My parents had, in fact, contacted the United States Department of State while I was still out in Qīnghǎi, only four days after my last call. If your child is traveling alone and possibly in danger half a world away, why wait? A woman from the State Department had assured them not to worry, telling them that the State Department was in contact with the Chinese and that the Chinese were tracking me and knew where I was at all times. Considering I didn't know where I was at certain points, this was an obvious lie, one my parents hadn't bought for a second.

Looking back, it occurs to me that the State Department might actually have tracked me down in Xī'ān. Yes, "Larry", the much older businessman palling around with young backpackers, asking so many questions about Philadelphia, and disappearing from the tour group at the museum. I could be imagining it, but the timing lined up. It's entirely possible that they knew who I was and were waiting to see what I was doing before they relayed my whereabouts back to my family. If so, they never did tell my parents that they'd found me. The first my parents heard anything was from Jacki, days after I left Xī'ān, when she phoned them immediately after finally hearing from me. That the State Department ultimately never reported anything to my parents is troubling, and I'm only guessing about "Larry", but however they may have failed, the blame for this remains entirely on me. I could have saved everyone a lot of trouble and my family a lot of pain, but I didn't. For that, to this day, I remain very sorry.

When my taxi pulled up at Jacki's, I was unrecognizable. She and her husband, Jack, had met me at my parents' house back in May, just four months earlier, and she was shocked at what she saw approaching her in front of her building. Bearded and overly thin from the strain of travel and two weeks of illness, I think I confirmed a few of their worst fears. She would later tell my parents after I returned home that what I had done was "incredibly dangerous". Her words. I can't disagree. To them, I would add "foolish", although from what Jacki said that may have been implied. I hadn't even thought of how I looked or how I must have smelled despite my attempt at a shower – more unintentional adaptations to my environment. It wasn't until we were up in the apartment and I saw myself in a living room mirror that I saw what she had seen from her point of view.

It was humbling. I had once held the absurd fantasy of arriving in Běijīng and heading over to CNN's offices to meet Bureau Chief Mike Chinoy, who months ago had so politely and wisely discouraged me from applying for a job there. I could only imagine what he would have made of the haggard, sickly mess I saw looking back at me. Not only wouldn't he have hired me, he would have had me sent home for my own good, and he wouldn't have been wrong.

Jacki doted on me and, rightfully, let me know exactly how much trouble I'd caused. After she fed me a bit of just about everything she had to build up my strength, I called home from their apartment phone, the only one I'd found so far that accepted my international calling card. My parents were upset, worried, and groggy, because it was almost 5 in the morning for them and they'd been up since Jacki's call an hour earlier. They held back on their anger, but I could hear it in their relief, and I could also tell I'd scared them in a way I never had and never wanted to ever again.

A cup of jasmine tea later, Jack arrived. He worked in another part of the Lufthansa Center. They insisted that I stay with them in their extra room, and also use their maps, their guides, and their driver. A driver! I thanked them and accepted, but I told them I'd have to go back to my hotel for the one night because I'd already paid. It was as believable as what the State Department had told my parents, but I felt ashamed and eager to leave. Like my parents, I'm sure they saw through it, but they allowed me to save face.

On the way back to my hotel, I stopped for a burger at some overpriced, American-style gastropub across from the Lufthansa Center. I'd actually dreamt about McDonald's coming in on the train, with the train pulling up to the drive-thru window. I hardly ever even ate McDonald's back home, but I knew there would be one in Běijīng and there's something comforting about things from home, even fast food you'd swear you never eat. This burger wasn't any good, not even as good as McDonald's, but I needed it. The restaurant had ginger ale, too. Surprisingly, of all things, a soft drink made with ginger wasn't popular in China, which made it hard to find. For a couple of hours, I sat there watching foreign business people coming in for bland bar food and loving it.

Finally, as it began to get dark, I had enough, so I worked up the courage to try the taxis. I had to go back to my hotel, the Jing Tai, down in the south of the city. That's the Jing Tai, in the south. Jing. Tai. South. No one could find it. Two drivers and more than two hours later, I was able to walk the last block myself. The first driver gave up. The second one, bless his heart, was even worse. He was a genuinely nice, well-intentioned person, and not once did I believe he was trying to cheat me as other taxi drivers had and would. That said, he'd receive clear directions I could understand from people on the street, get lost, drive a few blocks running up the meter, stop, get out, ask directions again, and repeat the process.

The thing to remember here is that Běijīng is surrounded by ring roads – what we might call a "belt parkway" – meaning they'll take you to any side of the city. I knew this even after one afternoon, and the directions I heard him receive were to take one of the ring roads from the northeast to the south, turn off at the south exit, and drive three blocks further south. One person sent us to an upscale hotel to get a translator. We met a small party of businesspeople who tried, in vain, to help. One of them, a young woman, told me that these drivers were all peasants from the countryside, illiterate and far more ignorant of the city than even I was, so I should be patient. I tried to explain that I'd been trying for almost an hour and a half at that point. She wished me luck, but again advised patience. I tried. I did try. After two hours, this particular ordeal was finally over. Walking the last block, I wasn't sure how much more of it I could take. However I felt about traveling when I first arrived in China, I just didn't like it anymore. Patience. I would try.

DAY 27

Saturday, September 30
Běijīng

•

I barely slept. I spent the whole night thinking about what I had put my parents through and my rage in Luòyáng and my frustration with everything and everyone everywhere I went. I felt certain I'd started this trip as thoughtful and considerate as anyone, an experienced traveler with all the patience anyone could have, but somewhere along the way I'd gotten as lost as last night's taxis.

I know that the incident with the ticket seller at the Longmen Caves was different. She was intentionally abusive and took pleasure in it, but I had reacted without thinking, rightfully defending myself but then doing something I should rightfully be ashamed of. Somebody hit her, she hit me, I hit back, and we were all hitting somebody else down the line, or tempted to. I found myself on trains and in the back of taxis struggling to hold my temper and, worse, I found myself selfishly ignoring my obligations to people I loved.

And that was all I could think about that whole night. I had to find a way to get back to who I was when I started this journey, before I had to keep telling myself to be patient. I couldn't go on isolating myself, alternately defensive and lashing out. No one deserved to be around someone like that. I'd rather I wasn't either.

• • •

As is China, no sooner did I believe I understood something than something came along and changed it. This morning, it was taxis. My ride back to the Eyman's apartment took only twenty short minutes, half as long as the shortest of my four taxi rides yesterday, and this driver was direct, friendly, and knew exactly where he was going. He didn't overcharge me, either. Just a man doing his job.

Jacki again greeted me out front and I followed her upstairs to drop off my heavy pack. We then turned around and went right back down to meet Wang, their driver, waiting in a Toyota 4Runner. Waiting for me in the back seat was a picnic basket Jacki had packed for me. After all I had been through getting to Běijīng, the idea of being driven around in the back of what was for that time and place a luxury car was a lot to take in. It wasn't mine, obviously, but passing all of the older, Chinese-made cars, buses, and trucks on the highway it made me feel uncomfortably rich.

Wang and I got to the Mùtiányù section of the Great Wall early and I finally got to see if my "student" ID card would work. It did. I paid all of ¥9 to enter, about $1.10. At the time, Mùtiányù was the second most popular part of the Great Wall around Běijīng, fully equipped with gondola service for those not looking to make the short climb up the steps. For foreigners, student or not, taking the gondola cost $10. I chose the steps.

Up on the Wall, the view is everything, even with the morning fog slow to give way. From the middle of the wall section, I made my way up to a high tower, all the while thinking, as one does, "I'M ON THE GREAT WALL!! I'M ON THE GREAT WALL!!" I really did think that, and if you go, you will, too. It was genuinely exciting. With everything I'd been through, I'd forgotten how excited I'd be to see it. The only negative thing about the experience I can think of, beyond the food wrappers, cigarette butts, and other garbage strewn everywhere, was the Chinese bubble-gum pop blaring from speakers perched high up like the ones in Hard Sleeper train cars. Funny, how none of the TV interviews I saw of World Conference On Women delegates touring the Great Wall had any music. Maybe those particular delegates had been on a different, music-free section of the Great Wall? Or, you know, they just turned it off for them. Success.

By the gondola dock next to the tower they had Internation-al Direct Dial telephone service. It had been installed for the conference and kept. Soon enough, cell phones would make it less of a big deal, but the idea that you could call your jealous friends from atop the Great Wall of China and brag about it was certainly big back then.

The views from the top of the tower were certainly something to brag about. Most of my pictures from there didn't come out – heart-breaking shutter issues, again – but thanks to the internet you and I can now see that view any time we want. The only photograph that did come out of that roll was from the interior of the tower, scratched out hànzì graffiti covering the stones, much of it probably done by tourists who came to visit before anyone conceived of a tour bus. Some of them, like graffiti carved into Greek and Roman ruins around the Mediterranean and the bell towers of Medieval and Renaissance churches all over Europe, had to have been from tourists and guards and others who passed through centuries ago.

I took it all in for over an hour, wandering up past the tower, seeing how far I could go before I exhausted myself, giddily stopping to catch my breath and marveling again and again that I was on The Great Wall of China. It really has that effect.

Thinking I had more than just memories to take home, I headed back where I climbed up. From the base of the tower, I saw them arriving, crowds of tourists and more crowds coming up behind them. They had come and they would keep coming until there were so many they blocked out any sight of the stones beneath their feet. By the time I made my way through them back down the steps, the tour buses from Běijīng had filled the parking lot and there was barely room to walk. I noticed a sign over one the shops at the edge of the parking lot: "ICE CRAM". I didn't go in.

As Wang drove me to the Míng Tombs all the way on the other side of Běijīng, I dove into Jacki's picnic basket. I offered some to him, but he would have none of it. Not his thing, sandwiches. We wound our way through villages and hills and quickly arrived at the Tombs. I switched over to black & white film, because, on Jacki's advice, we were skipping the official tourists attractions and heading for the "ruins". Black & white just seemed right for ruined tombs. These photographs, mercifully, all did come out.

The first tomb I saw, of Emperor Jǐng Líng, wasn't that ruined. Yes, much of the marble was gone, but mostly the place was just unkempt. And just like on the Great Wall, there was litter everywhere. In addition to cigarette butts and food wrappers, other visitors had left styrofoam containers, plastic bottles, at least one, sad banana peel, and boxes from film rolls. I don't think the boxes were from anyone actually taking pictures of tombs, though. Most likely, they were from the ones taking pictures of themselves with oh-so-serious expressions and just enough of a tomb in the shot to let people know where they'd been. I cleaned it up as best I could wherever I took a picture, but since there wasn't anywhere to put it, like a garbage can, I mostly just piled it up out of view.

The second tomb, of the Emperor Yǒng Líng, was closed, although I managed to squeeze off a shot through the gate.

The third tomb, though, of the Emperor Dé Líng, was the find of the day. It wasn't a ruin, it was a wreck. Marble was strewn everywhere, even more than garbage. It was only four hundred years old, the last of the tombs to be completed, but it might as well have been have been the Roman Forum.

If not for the litter and other other tourists picnicking on the grounds, it would have been easy to believe no one had been here since Dé Líng's funeral. The ne-gative that was neglect had become a positive that remained untouched. An Australian family eating near the gate said how wonderful it was to get away from all of the noise pol-

lution, and tourism of the city. I had to agree. The lack of blaring bubble-gum pop only made it better.

I took my time at this tomb. Behind it, there was a large mound, maybe twenty feet high, in the center of a clearing. I don't know what it was for. It looked like someone had burrowed a narrow trench through it up to the top. It could have been erosion. Around the edges of the clearing, young couples sat under trees enjoying what was to them just an overgrown park.

As Wang drove me back along the highways, we passed a man in a dirty suit carrying a large pistol. He was just walking along the edge of the road. There's some kind of story there. Further down we passed a life-size, painted, clearly cement policeman, filling a gap between the real policemen who watched over the traffic. I can't imagine it fooled anyone, but I suppose in the back of drivers' heads, maybe it did. The man in the suit? Maybe not.

Wang dropped me off and I returned to the apartment to clean up. Jacki was busy making spaghetti and meatballs. Her friend, Lee, would be joining her, Jack, and me for dinner, along with Lee's mother, Elaine, and son, Ari. At dinner, I told them all about my journey, as much as I thought I understood, including my run-in with the ticket seller in Luòyáng. It was good to talk about it, just as it's been good to write about it here. It was still raw back then, but it gave me a chance to go back through what happened and see how the pieces fit together, and to better understand my role in it.

When I finished with my story, Lee stated that she didn't believe racism existed in China the way it did in the United States or Europe, and it would be a mistake for me to frame Chinese behavior based on our country's history. She also thought I might have overreacted to the ticket seller in Luòyáng, that in my lack of experience in China I might have misunderstood a typical "nervous" Chinese laugh.

I have to say that, although Lee was otherwise very nice, I did not appreciate the condescension in her response. Yes, she had lived in China for sixteen years, but despite that what she said made her seem as sheltered and naive as I had been before I arrived. It made me wonder how often and how recently she had left comfortable Běijīng, and where she might have gone if she had. Had she been out west? Had she endured the ticketing pens of Kūnmíng, Lánzhōu, or Xīníng? Had she even seen Hard Seat, let alone taken it? Or had she been protected from seeing such things by her employers and/or her Chinese hosts, spending those sixteen years in comfortable places like the Kempinski Hotel? I didn't ask. I didn't want to be rude and embarrass my generous hosts. I can't help but ask now.

However skeptical she was and may still be of my story and the idea that a Chinese person could be racist or abusive to others just because they look different, I can only say this: the Chinese are people, just like you and me, and just like us they are as capable of prejudice and abuse as anyone. They are just as susceptible to the same stresses, the same vices, and have all the same weaknesses as any other human. And I'm pretty sure a nervous laugh doesn't include pointing at the person who made you nervous and gloating at their powerlessness.

Lee did tell us some very interesting stories about life in China during the Tiān'ānmén protests and crackdown in June of 1989. Holed up in their home with dozens of people, she and others started a 10,000 piece jigsaw puzzle to pass the time. They needed to focus their minds on something else, something with low stakes, a problem they could solve but not too quickly. They finally escaped the house and the mainland, but they never did complete the puzzle. They found it put away by the cleaning staff when they returned. As far as they'd gotten with it, for all it had done to keep them sane and bonded them during the crisis, for as much as they'd hoped to finish it, it would take another crackdown to get them to try it again.

It was a perspective on that time I never would have considered. Like her suggestions on my experience in Luòyáng, it didn't change my understanding of what anyone did or why, but it did give me a broader understanding of the world in which it took place.

DAY 28

Sunday, October 1

Běijīng

•

Ahhhhhh, the day I'd been waiting for, the 1st of October. This was the anniversary of the founding of Communist China, in my mind some kind of combination of May Day and the Fourth of July. I'd imagined a parade in Tiān'ānmén Square, maybe even fireworks that night. I didn't care what it would be, I wanted to see it all.

Of course, looking out the window as I ate a light breakfast, I could barely see Běijīng through the morning fog. I wondered if I'd get to see anything at all. Then Jacki came in and made me eat some more. I'd gotten so used to eating so little as I travelled, I'd forgotten I could and should eat more. Yet one more poor adaptation. As I ate a second breakfast, she and Jack told me this was normal Běijīng weather. I could wait for it to go away if I wanted, but that could take hours or months.

At 10:30, pretty late for my days here, I was out and tooling around on Jack's mountain bike, which flew on Běijīng's flat streets. I quickly reached the center of town, past the elegant hotels built to impress foreign dignitaries in Máo's time and the newer, glossier ones built to impress the delegates to the World Conference On Women (and anyone connected to the International Olympic Committee who might be passing through). I parked the bike and wandered around the area to the east of the Forbidden City, which included the Jiànguómén Wài Embassy District and the Wángfǔjǐng shopping district.

Wángfǔjǐng was overrated even by guidebook standards. There was absolutely nothing to see, unless you counted countless people. At the end of it, on the corner of Jiànguómén Wài Dajie, was the first McDonald's in China. Before you snicker, this historically important site was as essential to see and experience as the Summer Palace. International capitalist commercialism was and still is seen by many as a form of imperialism, and to see it in action in post-colonial, post-communist – yes, *post*-communist – China was something. Inside, the place was packed. A wandering waiter filled out orders on a form. From there, you fought your way past some of the nicest people ever to stick an elbow in your face and muscled your tray back through and over the crowd. Then, you got to look for a seat. Here, again, I benefitted from kind locals. Long after an older couple and their son had invited me to take their free seat, I could see others still wandering around with their trays and eating standing up.

Oh, and again, remember those Styrofoam food containers we in America were all so proud we stopped using back in the early 1990s? They had all found their way over to China. They, along with pull-tab cans, engines that used leaded gas, and just about anything pumping ozone depleting CFCs into the air, were being made and used in China and other "developing" economies. Why dismantle and destroy expensive machinery when you can sell it down the industrial food chain for profit and destroy somebody else's environment? That their environment was and still is connected to our environment was just one of those inconvenient truths we were and somehow still are too happy to ignore. By now, the Chinese have developed sufficiently to ban much of it themselves, and they have no doubt sold much of that same machinery to unregulated, developing countries as far down the food chain from them as they had been when they bought it from us.

Anyway, back to the day they were all supposed to be so proud of. My next stop was Qiánmén Lu, directly south of Tiān'ānmén Square. On this day of all days-off, the street was packed, wall to wall. Cars had trouble moving through a sea of people who didn't yet seem to expect them. Cars weren't new to Běijīng, but the number had increased drastically in the previous few years and this was a shopping district where people had always walked.

I found an army-surplus store, at last, but they only sold dress greens and buttons. The Chinese army backpacks I'd seen in Xīníng and Luòyáng – weatherproofed canvas on the outside, lined with rubber on the inside, and built for any kind of abuse – were nowhere to be found. The store had new bags, all of which looked cheaply made and suspiciously civilian, lacking waterproofing and rubber, nothing a soldier would want to be seen with let alone carry into battle. I'd have to find one of the real ones somewhere else.

Except for a few people wandering around, Tiān'ānmén Square was empty. No parade. No speeches. Nothing.

The skies were completely overcast. It looked and felt like it was about to rain. I took a few pictures of guards standing in traffic in front of the Forbidden City, presumably to keep people from getting hit by the cars whizzing past, and fled the scene. The blurs in these photos were courtesy of my wonky camera shutter.

I made my way through the alleys to Liúlíchǎng, the famous "antiques" district southwest of Tiān'ānmén Square. It was really two short alleyways, with most of the vendors selling the same stuff, all of them asking post-World Conference On Women exaggerated prices. I was looking for unusual things, and I could see why they would cost more, but this was ridiculous. One shop had a big bin filled with all sorts of old junk. There was an old, wooden meditation ball on top. It wasn't even a sphere anymore, it had been warped by years of use, one side worn down, which made it more attractive to me. I asked the woman behind the counter how much it would be for the set. She shrugged and said she couldn't say since there was only one. She'd clearly given up trying to find the second ball or anything else. I'd seen new sets going for ¥40 or so, so I rooted around to see if I could find the other one. When I finally did, she asked ¥400 for the pair, this after I'd gone to the trouble of finding the second ball for her. She went from having nothing to sell to asking a price no one would pay. I actually laughed. She was serious. I guess she expected me to bargain, but for what? I dropped each one back exactly where I found it, buried treasures for some other lucky traveler to find, and left without another word.

In another shop I met Keith Culvert, who bought antiques such as hair-crystal and sold them in Los Angeles. I tried to bargain for an old, metal tea pot. The teapot was low, wide, and elegant, and it still had its tea leaf strainer basket, but the vendors had scraped the brown tarnish, or patina, from the lid and side to see what metal they had underneath. The scrapes revealed a shiny, bright copper, and they ruined the teapot. For tourists like me and dealers like Keith, the tarnish and patina was the true selling points. They meant something had age even if it wasn't that old, it meant something had been used even if it hadn't. Unfortunately, as Keith explained to me, most vendors did this. Some actually scraped off everything, making them shiny, but ruining the smooth finish or engraved designed of the original item. Many potentially valuable antiques were thus reduced to garbage. They could and did still ask the same prices, though, and here, as with the well-used meditation balls at the other place, the prices were out of hand. Keith agreed that the Conference had something to do with it. In Guìlín and Xī'ān, vendors had asked as much as five times the price they accepted, but notions of supply and demand in Běijīng were getting ridiculous. Their expectations may

DAY 28: *Běijīng* 145

point where, with the flood of wealthy, expense account tourists gone, they would hardly sell a thing. Then again, there were always more tourists, and by now the prices for even the worst, scraped junk must be higher than ever.

Keith had to rush to meet his wife, a Chinese woman with a joint-venture textile factory in China. He told me that the government-run shops inside the Liúlíchǎng market building, closed today for the holiday, would have better prices. If I really wanted something good, I'd have to get it there.

By the time I returned to Tiān'ānmén Square, it had started to drizzle and crowds were gathering. These were not huge crowds, at least not by the standards of the square, which is massive. Guards stood along the edge of the street to keep people from jaywalking into speeding traffic, which too many seemed eager to do.

At 6 o'clock, they lowered the flag, folded it, and marched it across the street and disappeared through Tiān'ānmén (the Heavenly Peace Gate), the outer gate of the Forbidden City with the massive portrait of Máo Zédōng hanging above it. Was this the great celebration of the foundation of the People's Republic? No. They were just lowering the flag. They did it everyday.

Riding back to the Lufthansa Center in the dark with the rain coming down, I stopped to take some unexpected shots of enormous balloons lit by the streetlights. One long day out and my photographs of them and rain-soaked traffic guards might have been the only things I had to show for it. So much for People's Republic Day. No big parades, no tanks, no missiles, no nothing. Not even a firecracker. I had seen China, but maybe Tiān'ānmén Square wasn't the right place to look.

DAY 29

Monday, October 2

Běijīng

•

I was at Rìtán (Temple of the Sun) Park early this morning, just after 7, taking shots of lily-pads and reflections of buildings and trees off the water in the pond. Elderly Chinese were going through their tài jí, fencing, stretching, and something that looked like a Chinese version of Country & Western line dancing, all in silence except for the music. As I strolled through watching them, a funny thing happened: They all suddenly stopped. I looked at my watch: 7:30 AM, seconds past. No sound, no warning, they just stopped as if they'd been cued or programmed. They broke up and walked away, and pretty soon there was hardly anybody left in the park.

Walking to a bench, I passed two men. One stood motionless,

eyes closed, while the other centered his Qì, the life force within each of us, by drawing it down through his body with movements of his fingers. As I sat contemplating how peaceful it all was, another man came up and joined me. This being Rìtán Park, smack in the center of the Jiànguómén Wài Embassy District, he had come to find an English speaker to help him translate what looked like a receipt. We worked on it for a while before I realized that "PAID" was actually "PATD", as in "patented", with the rest of the numbers patent codes. I didn't know how to explain patent law in English, let alone Mandarin, so I apologized and wrote what I thought I understood in English on his paper so the next person might be able to help him.

I then rode Jack's bike down to the Forbidden City. I found a good parking spot just before the morning rush and was in by 9 AM at the student price. The area between Tiān'ānmén and Duānmén (the Upright Gate), the first of the inner gates, was filled with the official souvenir and vending stands. It was sad. And ugly. Best not to think about it. The tour began by Wǔmén (the Meridian Gate), the next gate in and the official entrance to the Forbidden City.

Here is where it got surreal. You see, the ticket included an audio

148   AN INCREDIBLY FOOLISH AND DANGEROUS THING TO DO

tour, and whose voice did I hear guiding me through the Forbidden City, the vast palace compound of the Míng and Qīng emperors? Whose voice do you think? Roger Moore. That's right: James Bond, 007, fictional hero of the imperialist, neo-colonialist British Secret Service. Weirder still, it was a very good tape. Very good. I might have missed it if Jacki hadn't recommended it, although she did neglect to mention the Roger Moore part. Maybe she hadn't wanted to ruin the surprise. The tape was informative, it drew your attention towards small things you might have missed – as well as away from the other tourists, which was a real trick – and Sir Roger's voice was pretty relaxing, again considering the sea of mostly Chinese tourists wandering through with me, most of them pushing and shoving and blocking views to most of what I had come to see.

At one point, as I was in the middle of taking a picture, I felt someone tugging on my arm. "Duì bu qǐ, duì bu qǐ" (Dway boo chee), a woman said. The words usually meant "I'm sorry" or, more literally, "I am not correctly together", but here, especially after my experience at the Longmen Caves, my first thought was a hawker was grabbing for my arm. I turned and was happy to see I was wrong. Instead, it was two young, Chinese women who wanted to have their pictures taken with me. I was, it seemed, something of a tourist attraction myself. I was tall with curly, brown hair, I had grown a full beard by then, both of which were uncommon in China, and, as the women kept saying to each other, "Dà Bízi" (Dah Beedzuh). Compared to the average Chinese, I had a "big nose". I finished taking my own shot and then posed with each of them. Twice more this day, I would be drafted into pictures, and not one time did anyone ask my name. They just wanted pictures with "Dà Bízi". It was a strange sort of celebrity, if you could call it that.

I ended up going through the Forbidden City in only two hours, much less time than I thought it would take. At first, I was disappointed at how quickly it went, but then I realized that I had seen what I had seen in the time it took to see it. It had taken just that long and no longer. Jacki said that you used to be able to see much more of the palace, but they had been shutting off more and more areas to the public. Maybe if they hadn't kept so much of it forbidden?

I exited through Shénwǔmén (the Gate of Divine Prowess), the north gate, and crossed to Jǐngshān (Prospect Hill) Park, where you could climb to Wanchun (Ten Thousand Spring) Pavilion at the top of the hill to look out over the Forbidden City and the then still-undeveloped hútòng neighborhoods all around it. It was a nice place, if you didn't mind rude people. One guy shoved me out of his way and nearly sent me down the steps. I'm not exaggerating. Like the girl in Xī'ān who almost pancaked me into a car with her bike, he didn't even look back.

There was also an open-air karaoke booth.

I ran for cover and escaped down to Běihǎi (North Sea) Park, a big lake to the west of Jǐngshān Park and the Forbidden City with an island in the middle of it. It was as crowded as it was beautiful, and it was very beautiful. I didn't go up to the White Pagoda, though; it didn't look like they could squeeze anybody else in. At the Kentucky Fried Chicken restaurant inside the park, the statue of "Colonel Sanders" by the entrance had Asian features. At one point, Harland Sanders was a real, human man; now, he had become just another, malleable Ronald McDonald.

From Běihǎi Park, I walked back to Tiān'ānmén Square, where a crowd had gathered to watch the fountains flowing. In contrast to the drizzly 1st of October, today there wasn't a cloud in the sky. After another picture with some "Dà Bízi" fans and a few of my own, I headed down past MR. BEEF SEAFOOD RESTAURANT LTD to the shops at Liúlíchǎng that had been closed for the government holiday. At one shop, I saw an old, lacquer picnic set. With six round, stacking boxes, each maybe 13 or 14 cm wide, lacquered on the inside, caned on the outside, they might have made a nice gift once, but they weren't in any kind of shape now. Yes, it was old lacquer, but I sincerely doubted it was from the "Sòng dynasty" (960 –1279 AD), as the vendor insisted. For such a priceless antique, he was asking ¥2000, about $250. I admit, I didn't know pricing as far as these went, not at this point, but I did know enough to thank him, no, and start walking. "¥500?" he called after me. I kept walking.

I saw a lot of nice instruments I might have bought for my brother, John, a musician, but they were all inlaid with ivory, which I was not going to buy. Even if they thought they were improving their chances of a sale by lying about it being ivory, which was a possibility, it was better to walk away. At the last shop I found a great-looking, small táogǔ, a kind of pellet drum venders used to draw attention, until I realized that the facing drum-bases were really skull caps of a some kind of animal, which I was also not going to buy.

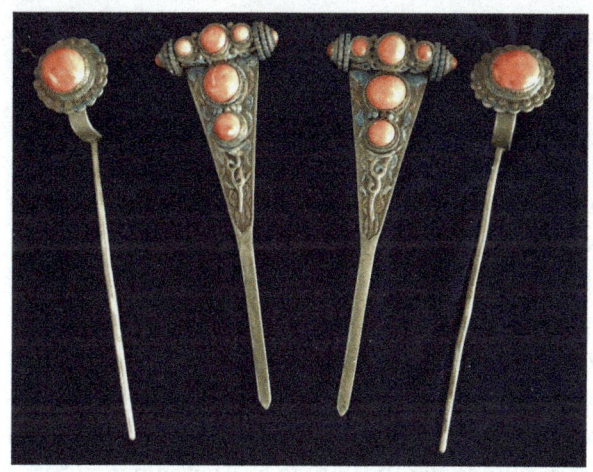

The shop did have a couple of things I wanted: a set of well used silver, coral, and enamel hairpins, which I guessed were probably late Qīng dynasty (1644 – 1912) by how much hair you'd need to wear them, and a slightly younger, wooden pocket sundial with a built-in compass and paper instructions pasted on the bottom. I would buy them for my parents. The bargaining was slow, more than two hours coaxing the prices down to where I didn't feel like too much of a chump. I still paid a lot, especially for the hairpins, but both of them seemed rare, certainly in my price range.

I had a bit of buyer's remorse about the hairpins by the time I returned to the Eymans' apartment, but Jacki told me that whatever I had paid, I had to weigh it against never seeing something like them again. It was good advice. I never did anything like them the rest of my time in China and the sundial, by far the cheaper of the two, may have been my favorite thing I brought home.

DAY 30

Tuesday, October 3

Běijīng

•

In Kūnmíng, I had been told to renew my visa within three days of its expiration. It was time.

I overslept a bit, but I was able to get out on the road and down to the Public Security Bureau office outside of the Forbidden City's east wall before 9:30. Jack said he thought government offices might be closed for a couple of days due to the national holiday, but he was wrong. Sort of. All of the other government offices were open, just not this one. I went around to the PSB office by Tiān'ānmén, where I hoped I could get some help, if not answers. They asked me to come back on the 5th, which would mean holding my passport past my visa expiration. I'd wake on the 6th with no proof I belonged here. Sure, they gave me slips of paper saying this and that, but a hassle in a foreign country could take who knows how long to clear up, even with well-connected Americans on hand to help me out. I didn't dare risk that, and a helpful student from Singapore made sure I didn't have to, acting as intermediary between me and the guards. Finally, after some sort of conference, a compromise was made and I was assured that I could take care of everything tomorrow. That settled, or postponed, I went out to Yíhéyuán, the great Summer Palace.

It was a good thing I stopped for something to eat first, because this little jaunt on the map turned into the longest little trip it could be. You see, in 1995, there were sections of Běijīng that literally did not have street signs, not in hànzì and certainly not in English or anything else. As you headed further out into the mostly residential northwestern edge of the city, intersection after intersection had nothing to tell you where you were. This may not have been a challenge for locals, but that may have been the point.

At the time, Běijīng had plenty of street signs in areas they expected, or preferred, a non-local or foreigner to want to go, such as the areas around the Forbidden City and Tiān'ānmén Square, the embassy district, and the Lufthansa Center.[16] For destinations beyond the ring roads, such as the Great Wall and the Summer Palace, they could be reached by chauffeured company 4Runner or a tour bus or something else driven by locals who knew the area and could make their way around without getting lost. So, the government clearly expected and welcomed visitors, but had they wished to encourage actual free movement, it seems like they would have had street signs in hànzì everywhere.

What good then was a map without street names or landmarks when they were the only way you could find anything? The one I had was from the Board of Tourism, and it might as well have come with crayons and a children's menu. I had more than an hour of backtracking, and at one point I was over a kilometer *west* of Yíhéyuán, with the entrance to the park over on the east side. Fortunately, it was sunny and the sun held.

It was past one in the afternoon when I finally got there. I used my student card and paid ¥2, the Chinese price. The foreigners' price? ¥35, which included tickets to everything you'd never want to see at the Summer Palace and one for the few you would. Without the card, I'd have had no choice, no matter how much Mandarin I could muster. It added some further perspective to my misadventure in Luòyáng. Here, though, there were signs in multiple languages making it clear that there was one price whether you used the extra tickets or not, not just one in hànzì saying, "No refunds". And here, everyone selling the tickets seemed genuinely nice.

Inside the gate, the view opened wide. A bridge to the left of the entrance crossed to an island in the middle of the great lake. The design was impressive. I could see why an emperor would want to call

---

[16] The area around the centrally located Beijing Hotel, in particular, not only had street signs, it was still plastered with electronic signs and murals welcoming the International Olympic Committee delegation as part of China's bid to host the 2000 Summer Olympics, which had been awarded to Sydney, Australia in 1993. At the time, though, the 2008 games, which Běijīng would host, were still in play.

this place home.

I let myself wander and took some pictures. I did not, however,

take any inside Fó Xiāng Gé (the Tower of Buddhist Incense, above), where there was a sign asking people not to. There weren't any fake Buddhist monks begging for money here, or venders selling the usual tourist junk. They weren't even selling postcards of the multi-armed and multi-headed Buddha inside, so it boiled down to this: House of Worship. I don't subscribe to any organized religion, but I at least respect that others do and I try to abide by their wishes in their holy places. Many other tourists here, Chinese and foreign, did not. The sight and sound of their flashes were constant.

Of course, taking a look around the famous Marble Boat, forever berthed by the lake, I found it hard to nitpick about photographs at a temple. Looking at it, it was hard to imagine that this boat-shaped, double-decker gazebo had the reputation it once had. It was now crammed with tourists and giving way to what euphemistically could be called "the elements". They did have ice cream, though, "Bud's Ice Cream of San Francisco", so I made the best of it and bought myself a cup of green tea flavor. I sat back under Cháng Láng (the Long Gallery) and watched a crowd gather to watch a tall sprinkler watering the grass. Yes, it was literally just a sprinkler and, yes, they really were just watching it. It was sort of like a fountain, I guess, if the fountain had no design concept beyond just looking and functioning like a big sprinkler. It was about 3:30 now, and the sun, though still high, looked as if it was about to dive behind the western hills. The sky was beautiful over the lake.

I completed my circuit of the city by bike, returning to the apartment at 5 o'clock. A month into my journey, I was starting to feel a whole lot better.

DAY 31

Wednesday, October 4

Běijīng

•

"Xiǎo Xīn"

As far as I'd come in the past month, geographically and mentally, those two words and my failure to embrace them continued to plague me. I had been having a great time riding around Běijīng and I was feeling healthier than I had since I arrived in China, so, naturally, when I set out this morning to buy my train ticket to Qīngdǎo, I forgot my passport, my money, and everything else I needed back in my room. A few days of comfort, it seemed, was all it took for me to get sloppy.

It was 9:30 in the morning and I had ridden all the way down to the train station before I noticed. Mercifully, it had been a short ride. Běijīng being on a plateau, I managed to face a strong headwind coming down, riding south then west, and then again coming back, riding east then north. Having also forgotten my building and apartment keys – seriously, I was some kind of idiot today – I was lucky to catch Jacki before she left. It all reminded me a lot of my earlier, careless mistakes back in Guìlín, the other time I'd let my previous luck and comfort cloud my thinking. It wasn't nearly as stressful as that had been, but that was in no small part because of the support I knew I had here, support that I very clearly still needed.

The shortness of the return ride was good, because it took me a long half-hour just trying to figure out how to get into the station once I got back. The Foreigners' Ticket Office was inside, but security prevented anyone without a ticket from getting in past the barriers. Yes. At long last, I went back to ask passport in hand, and they simply waved me through. Of course, they did.

And then came the lines. There were three lines at the Foreigners' Ticket Office: the first, for reservations in advance of six days, precisely; the second, for five days or less; and the third, for when they took your money. The whole process took about an hour. I spoke with some other foreigners waiting in line. Some, residents of Běijīng, complained about the price hikes which followed the increase in tourism, and all, resident or not, agreed that this system of forms to get forms and lines to get to lines wasn't merely bureaucratic, it was institutional torture.

By the time I escaped with my ticket, the Public Security Bureau office where I needed to renew my visa was closed for lunch, so I spent mine going shop to shop, collecting official posters from the United Nations' Fourth World Conference On Women. I thought it would be polite to offer to pay for the posters, but with the exception of one shop they were all too happy to get rid of them, no charge. Most simply hadn't bothered to throw them out after the conference ended. The government, not the shopkeepers, had put the posters up, so all except that one shop were happy to see them go. That one shop wanted to keep their posters because they covered up the shiny columns on the sides of the door, which they didn't like. Unfortunately, I couldn't find all of the variations, and some of the best that I saw elsewhere eluded me. You'd have thought, with all their attention to interna-

tional opinion, the Chinese would have had the posters on sale at tourist sights, but they didn't. If they had been during the conference, they weren't anymore.

Posters in my little, gray bag, I went back to renew my visa. I had to fill out the form twice because I used red ink the first time and, I swear, the ~~bureaucrat~~ woman behind the counter told me only they got to use red ink. Still, it was done. I'd have to leave my passport with them, but I would have my new visa before I left for Qīngdǎo.

Tooling around on the bike, I came across a street east of the Forbidden City lined with antique and souvenir booths. In one booth, I found an old, ratty, torn stamp inside the cover of a Russian language Little Red Book. I shouldn't have shown it to the shopkeeper, because the second he saw it he wouldn't let me buy anything, even though we'd already agreed on a price for the book, which I had foolishly assumed meant it and anything found inside. Nope. The wiry, little miser hadn't ever thought to look for anything inside of them, and now he wanted to spend the rest of the day going through everything else in the shop to make sure he hadn't missed anything. He was already flipping through the pages of another book as I left. So I didn't buy anything and he didn't sell anything. That'll show me. I did see two more sets of wooden meditation balls, one offered for a mind boggling ¥800 and another, which actually looked like they'd been used, offered for only ¥85. I didn't buy either, but that last price, from a very nice, old lady, put a lot of Běijīng's new pricing in perspective.

At the south end of the street, to the east side of Tiān'ānmén Square, there was a huge, digital clock counting down, to the second, the time until July 1, 1997, the date Hong Kong would rejoin the motherland. I had missed it my first two times passing through the square. I must not have been paying attention.

DAY 32

Wednesday, October 4 – Thursday, October 5

Běijīng

•

Last night, Jacki and I had something of a fruitless discussion on where China might be, where it might be going, and why. Our conversation followed much the same course as the one over dinner with her friend, Lee, the other night. She had insights as a foreigner living in China for years and I had insights as a foreigner traveling through China for the very first time, and neither could convince the other which perspective was best, or why one of them should be.

From my experience so far, mostly spent in the south and west where most Chinese remained stuck in the impoverished past, I believed I saw gaps growing, walls literally and figuratively going up between classes, and that the Chinese were going to have problems when only a relative few had money while the rest remained where and what they were. Jacki warned me not to judge the country too quickly. She reminded me that I hadn't, after all, been in the country that long, and she pointed out that the Chinese were so diverse and complex that they didn't even understand each other.

Jacki's point was a good one, certainly about how much of the country and its people I still had to see. It would be something to keep in mind as I spent another three weeks traveling the country's north and east. As much as I had seen and would see, there were things I had missed, too, and places I had skipped, as well as an entire, central region of the country I would never see, certainly not at this time and never as it was. I would add, in retrospect, that it was too early in China's conversion from its old economy and infrastructure to its new ones for anyone to judge how they would go.

However, as I felt that night debating Lee, I believe an insider's perspective can only take you so far. While I hadn't been in China for very long, I had been on my own without any guardrails keeping me penned in to the China my hosts wanted me to see. In a short time, I had seen many ugly and disturbing things many who had lived in China for years never had or would. If all you ever see of a country are the wealthiest regions and you never travel to the poorest regions, and in the poorest ways as I had, you couldn't possibly know that country, not really. And, of course, nor could you know it if you had only seen what I had, how I had, and less so now that so much of it has gone. All that's left of that world are the people.

I thought about both of those debates all through the night and well into the morning, when priorities interrupted. After breakfast, I began shuttle-bargaining between the UPS and DHL stores in the Lufthansa Center to see who would have the rights to mail home the scroll painting I bought in Xī'ān. Both offered about $40 shipping, almost double what I paid for the scroll, so it all came down to how to package it, because neither was equipped for anything that wasn't reasonably square, such as a tube. Sometime between my second and third visits, the women at DHL had devised a plan. I found some bubble wrap and we were set. I begged a few dollars off the price tag and then left my baby in their care. Alas, the package, a pretty solid, long triangular box that looked like a giant Toblerone bar, became not so mysteriously undone on its way through Chinese customs. They had naturally opened the package for inspection. It could just as easily have held a priceless antiquity as a cheap art school painting, so I can't blame them for that. I can blame them for not restoring the bubblewrap around the part they inspected or resealing the box correctly. The scroll was visibly damaged when it arrived at my parents' house. Thankfully, it ended up being the only package I mailed from China.

Blissfully ignorant of that future, I took advantage of the Lufthansa Center's one hour photo shop to process the rolls I had taken so far. I was not so blissfully ignorant of that past, but I knew enough to put it out of my mind until I saw them later.

Out on the town, I gave in and stopped at a Pizza Hut. I won't make any excuses about eating fast food pizza in China. This was therapy. In the past week, I had regained my health, mostly, my sanity, insofar as I was exercising patience with myself and others, and some weight, which I'd lost due to losing the first two and my failure to feed myself properly on my way to Běijīng. The greasy mess I ordered was too expensive and too small, but I needed it. I needed it and all of the American, fast food culture that went with it. And yet, it didn't look or feel like an American Pizza Hut. This wasn't some dump like it was for us at home (sorry, Pizza Hut, it was true). This was upscale. High class. I mean, the pizza and fries looked and tasted the same, but Chinese businesspeople came in suit and tie, eating their pizza and fries with a knife and fork. They even had armed security guards at the door. Why they had them, I don't know, but they were there.

As I exited, a woman was setting up shop selling bootleg CDs about ten feet from the Pizza Hut entrance. I doubt it was intentional, but it did make an interesting comment on the U.S.-China Trade Pact signed earlier in 1995, which promoted American chain stores and banned, among other things, bootleg CDs. I almost bought a couple of bootleg Beatles CDs for $2 a piece, but then I realized I'd be buying bootleg Beatles CDs and didn't.

I rode Jack's bike over to Yōnghé Gōng Lamasery. The place was small but beautiful. I completely underestimated how big the temple's 26 meter tall Buddha would be. It just didn't register. It was carved from a *single* sandalwood tree. The thing must have been as big as High Sierra redwood. And it was indoors. They had carved it first and built the temple *around* it.

I wish that had been the end of my day. When I picked up my photos, I was heartbroken. My worst fears had been confirmed. The defective shutter had resulted in uneven lighting and blurry photos.

Some pictures just came out black. Most of the ones from Guìlín and Kūnmíng were lost, as were all the ones from the roll that slipped the winder on Éméishān. Most of the shots from the black & white rolls from Xīníng, Xī'ān, rainy Tiān'ānmén Square, and the Míng Tombs came out, so maybe it had something to do with the color film? No? I don't know. I never will.

Even now, I can still remember what many of the lost shots looked like through the viewfinder. I couldn't go back, obviously. I had been keeping a journal as I traveled, mostly notes about people I'd met and things we'd talked about. Going forward, I would make sure to keep more detailed descriptions of everything I saw, if only to backup the pictures I took the rest of the way. I still had a long way to go.

MANDARIN LANGUAGE PRONUNCIATION
Lesson 4:

While the "Běijīng R" is often mentioned in classes about the language, the common example given being how "yī diǎn" (ee-dee-ann, meaning "a little") is pronounced "yī diǎr" (ee-dee-arr), the equally important "Northern U" is neglected.

In the north, they add an "EH", the suffix normally added in Mandarin to verbs to make them past tense, to nouns ending in "U". I heard this consistently throughout Xī'ān, Luòyáng, and Běijīng.

Examples:

- "Lù" (road) becomes "Lù-eh"

- "Gōngyù" (apartment) becomes "Gōngyù-eh"

DAY 33

Friday, October 6

Běijīng

•

I recovered quite a lot in Běijīng: my health, my wits, my sense of responsibility, and my patience with myself and others. I would have to remember not to surrender any of them so easily the rest of the way.

I enjoyed one last morning of Jacki and Jack's hospitality, for which I remain deeply grateful, and was out the door, pack on my back, at 10:30. With a three and a half hour cushion, I told myself I couldn't miss my train. Of course, I'd told myself that before. One half-hour, two wrong turns, and a taste of real, post-Conference Běijīng traffic later, my confidence had melted into doubt. I bravely worked through early difficulties with my tones and my driver's accent and managed to get to the PSB office to pick up my passport. The price tag on my shiny, new, one month visa? $3.

One short taxi ride later, I arrived back in traffic. We sat still for the better part of an hour, something all too familiar for the rest of us but still relatively new for 1995 China. My relief arriving at the station with an hour and a half to spare was tempered by having to spend the next half-hour tracking down where I should wait. No one working there seemed to know. Finally, the young woman at Left Luggage pointed out the train's number posted above the entrance to the correct waiting room, something new in my railway experience to that point in China. It seemed it was just as new to them, too.

Having found it, I had a leisurely hour to sit among my fellow travelers and watch while they tried to form a line they knew they'd never keep. I stayed seated past the boarding call, watching them try to squeeze themselves through the gates like toothpaste. I was in no rush, I had a Hard Sleeper ticket, a berth of my own. No mad dash to the train, no stepping on old women and crippled children, no Hard Seat to speak of.

On board, I was greeted by a pleasant surprise. While lying in my berth, I was hit by a Qīng Liè (Green Line) souvenir bottle opener, which had ricocheted off the ceiling and wall after the steward tossed it up at me like a bag of ballpark peanuts.

This wasn't the only perk about the Green Line. On these new trains, Hard Sleeper was in many ways superior to the hand-me-down Soft Sleeper cabins in the western provinces. From the color-coordinated wool covers, to the clean, green-gray uniforms of the crew, to the fact that this brand new carriage was unmistakably clean floor to ceiling, this was superior travel. One attendant even straightened out our shoes while we slept. The speakers, not loud at all, had been moved to a more central location in the car, so the only thing you really had to worry about was the headroom in the top bunk, which was still somewhat coffin-sized. I had asked for a spacious middle berth back in Běijīng, but they had assured me quite firmly that none were available. Both middle berths below me, as well as a few in other sections, remained empty for the entire trip. No matter, because the crew on the Green Line were kind and attentive, and isn't it service that counts?

The farther I headed through the eastern, coastal provinces with all of their "Overseas Chinese" investment, the newer and cleaner the trains seemed to be. That would turn out not to be so true, but soon enough these new trains would be the hand-me-downs and relics like the ones out west would be gone. Not every loss is to be mourned.

I fell asleep thinking about Shěnyáng, over 400 miles northeast of Běijīng by rail, and the long winter I almost spent there teaching English. That would have been a very different journey, and a very different book. This train was as close to it as I would ever get.

DAY 34

Saturday, October 7

Shāndōng Province, Qīngdǎo

•

They woke us around 5:30 AM, and this time the stewards made sure we stayed awake: they turned the lights on. We pulled into Qīngdǎo (Ching-dow) about 6:15 and then sat on our butts for half-an-hour while a steward pulled all of the fancy, new linens in our section. They had to get the train ready for all of the passengers heading back west. He clearly took pride in his work and in the results, something I would see more and more in the rapidly modernizing east. Only when he was done were we allowed to enter the city.

You may know the name Qīngdǎo by its Wade-Giles spelling, Tsingtao, and that from the beer introduced to the United States in 1972, the same year pre-Watergate Richard Nixon went to China to normalize relations. Now sold around the world, it originated here at a brewery built by the colonial English and Germans. By 1995, there were breweries all over China making beer from the same recipe, each brewery named for the city it was in. The beer we drank in Xī'ān and Běijīng was called "Beijing" beer. In Nánjīng, I would drink "Nánjīng" beer. It was all the same beer, but Tsingtao got the international name because that city had been a German colony.

It was easy to see why Qīngdǎo was such a popular resort for the Chinese. It was beautiful, a seaside destination that, exotically, had more in common with the resorts of its former colonial occupiers than the swiftly modernizing Chinese cities it drew its tourism from. There were clamshells and crabs on the sidewalk without a market nearby, the sounds of seabirds, waves lapping, and boats, and the smell of salt in the air. Yes, there were a few luxury high-rises starting to dominate the skyline, but I could really see the draw of this place.

DAY 34: Shāndōng Province, Qīngdǎo 167

Unfortunately for me, this combination of charm and growing wealth led to a problem. The first hotel I went to was booked up. "The delegation. Sorry," the receptionist said. The second hotel offered me a room where even the TV smelled like mildew, as if the room, on the fourth floor, had somehow been flooded. It reminded me a lot of my room in Xīníng, actually, which also had that peculiar smell. The third hotel had disappeared. I think it had been torn down to build a newer, more profitable one. The fifth hotel no longer accepted non-Chinese guests, while the fourth and sixth hotels had raised their prices to about $40 a night. So, four cab rides and lot of walking with my heavy pack later, I was back at the second hotel, the Haiqing, to see if I could do better on the second try. They did give me a better room, with no smell and a partially interrupted view of the Bóhǎi Sea, for only ¥210, about $25, the cheapest two beds in town.

Well, I'd had my inadvertent tour of the town, so I took a quiet stroll down to the waterfront. To my left, people were scavenging on the low-tide beaches. To my right, workers laying down the new sewage system under the street had just poked a big hole in a city water pipe; their ditch was quickly becoming a lake.

Back at the train station, I was greeted by what sounded like "Lo, sir! Lo, sir!", with vendors crowding around me on all sides. They weren't actually talking to me, though, it was the guides behind them hawking tours to Láoshān, the mountain attraction on the eastern half of the peninsula. I overcame the language barrier in time to figure out that getting from Qīngdǎo to Qǔfù, the ancestral home of Confucius, would take over a day. Instead, I would next go to Kāifēng, a city from the famed Silk Road which supposedly had the ruins of a 14th century synagogue. I could make Qǔfù an easy day trip from there. I bought a ticket to Kāifēng and then came back an hour later to exchange it when I realized that they had given me the wrong day. I really should have known better at this point.

From there, I was off to take pictures of the old, pastel houses in the hills, built way back in the 19th century when Qīngdǎo and most of Shāndōng province were a German colony. The cloudless sky had disappeared in the two hours I was inside. With the East European-style Communist blocks mixed in, the old, colonial section of town really did look like it belonged somewhere in East Germany. Up at the top of Xìnhàoshān, another local mountain attraction, were the Mushroom Buildings, built in 1989 to give panoramic views of the city and the bay. I stayed a while to take in the breathtaking views of old, colonial Qīngdǎo down below and the Yellow Sea beyond. This serenity, sadly, only lasted until I decided to take pictures of it. The bitter frustration with my camera shutter's refusal to close had only been made worse now that I knew what the shutter problems meant. Nothing from the park or my walk through the hills of colonial Qīngdǎo would come out, and I still couldn't afford a new camera, certainly not in a tourist town like this. Stupid camera shutter. Still, I had that time, and much as decades of neglect had made Běijīng's Míng tombs more attractive, Qīngdǎo's beautiful, well-maintained colonial architecture, which holds so much of China's too often neglected history, made it a place I was grateful to have seen.

I made my way back down through the winding streets to a market. Qīngdǎo's markets were stocked and loaded with dried shark fins, that and the city's contribution to food-on-a-stick, dried squid. I opted for some wonton soup, egg rolls, and stuffed eggplant, all for $1. I stumbled off with a sudden, huge headache, and with it the dread of a repeat of the train ride from Xīníng. I made my way back down to the waterfront, resting at an outlet where the inner bay joined the Yellow Sea, and recovered in time to watch the sun setting behind the high-rises sprouting on the western end of the peninsula. Funny how the sun always seems to speed up just as it's winding down.

DAY 35

Sunday, October 8

Qīngdǎo

•

I slept a lot last night. I woke only to brush my teeth and watch "An American Romance", a Horatio Alger-type propaganda flick made in Hollywood during World War II and now dubbed into Mandarin. It put me back to sleep. After a policeman knocked on my locked door to remind me to lock it, I went back to sleep again, safe and cozy, and woke up with the sun. And then I slept to about 8 AM.

I was out the door by 9 and by 9:30 my heavy pack was in the care of the surliest woman this side of the Old West. She was cartoonishly ornery, and she may even have had her own spittoon. She ran the Left Luggage room in the train station and when I left my luggage with her she all but snarled at me. Free of the weight, though, I was out roaming the streets and the Sunday markets. Sadly, while Qīngdǎo may have been filled with fresh air, interesting architecture, and friendly people outside of Lost Luggage, it was a resort *for* the Chinese and had just one, government owned, poorly stocked Antique Shoppe. Everything else, while cheaper than in Běijīng, was just cheaper, both in looks and quality. With time winding down to buy those special gifts, I could only hope better seas were ahead.

Directly ahead of me as I left the Shoppe was Qīngdǎo's waterfront, where the sun was shining on Sunday strollers. Crowds were back in the shallows, picking through low tide like it was the wreck of a Spanish galleon. Still, the air and scenery were great. Well, mostly. I thought I could see jellyfish floating in the shallows, but they were plastic bags. Jellyfish likely would have already been on somebody's plate by then, or sold in the markets along with the clams, crabs, shark fins, and squid. They were well stocked.

I stocked up on nuts, fruit, and cookies for the train to Kāifēng.

They would have to last. You see, I had indeed been wrong about the quality of trains in the east. They still had the same old ones back here, heading to and from poor cities and towns with the same, old, disgusting Hard Seat, which was all that would be available to me until I reached Nánjīng in four days, and there would be nowhere on those trains to buy food.

During one of my frequent trips to the station, I stopped back into Left Luggage to get my plane tickets. This time the Left Luggage lady really did snarl at me, though she didn't even have to stand. I called the United Airlines office in Běijīng from the Railway Hotel, the one that was full with "the delegation", and arranged to confirm my plane reservation from San Francisco back to Philadelphia after I returned from China. I was still planning on flying out of Hong Kong at this point, but that would soon change.

Back on the waterfront, I bought a bottle of Coke from a smarmy woman, who, not ten minutes later, angrily smashed somebody's lunch bowl down in the middle of the street. I took some quality time eating my own lunch, out of her reach, in the small park nearby that looked out over the water. That was the perfect thing to do in Qīngdǎo. For two hours, I simply sat looking out at the water and listened to the waves and the birds and took in the salt-air.

And then it was back over to the station to wait on the train and fight back the Hard Seat mob. Except, there was no mob. They were all mellowed out in Qīngdǎo (well, except for the smarmy plate smasher). Maybe it was the sea breeze and the relaxing oceanfront views, or maybe the train leaving Qīngdǎo for points far less glamorous had just been undersold.

I ended up swapping my whole three-seat bench to two old people for their two-seater, which was really more of a one-adult-and-one-small-child-seater. I'd have plenty of room to sleep, even if it was in a ball. The old couple had a nice army bag, smaller than the one I wanted, but just as good for my purposes. I decided to ask them where to get one once we got going. I hoped they wouldn't say, "Qīngdǎo".

DAY 36

Monday, October 9
Shāndōng Province, Hénán Province, Kāifēng

•

LARGE, SINGLE SLOB SEEKS TRAVELING COMPANIONS. LOVES ARE APPLES, CIGARETTES, CHICKEN IN A BAG, AND KARAOKE. CAN PROVIDE OWN ACCOMPANIMENT. This was midnight, and this not quite gentle giant, dropping the remains of all his loves on the floor while the stewards yelled at him to stop, wasn't even remotely the worst person I'd have to deal with tonight. In fact, by the end of it, I'd even come to like him.

He was sitting across from me in a train car that looked like it was being sent out west to die. It was nice at the start, when it was just us and the old couple with the Chinese army bag, the four of us spread out across three of the four Hard Seat benches in our section. With each stop, though, more ticket holders joined us, followed by the inevitable crush of Standing ticket holders. By 1 AM, all of that space we'd enjoyed leaving Qīngdǎo was gone. The old couple on the three-seater had been joined by an army officer and, literally, a snot-nosed recruit. His nose just ran and ran and ran. He had my sympathy. The slob got an old woman who had no idea how to open the train window but kept trying. I, on my small one-and-a-half-seater bench, had to that point been left alone.

But then, after we had all somehow managed to get to sleep, she sat down beside me. No, *on* me. I don't mind somebody using me as a pillow. Go ahead, lean, put your head on my shoulder as long as you don't drool. It's the legs I care about. In the cramped confines of Hard Seat, as I've told, it can get painful, especially if somebody, say, crushes your leg against a post, elbows your ribs, and then leans across you to make sure another person – in this case, the slob – sees her speak when she is talking. That sort of thing.

And could she talk! HI, HI, I'M GOING TO TALK AND TALK AND TALK AND TALK, NOPE, NOPE, CAN'T STOP ME, I'LL TALK AND TALK AND TALK ALL NIGHT LONG NO SLEEPING FOR ME OR YOU OR ME, ME, ME, ME, TALK, TALK, TALK, TALK, TALK. TALK.

On and on and on and on.

Here was something that highlights the differences between Chinese and Americans. In China, they wouldn't want to take the uncomfortable action of even politely asking her to be quiet. It went back to face and doubling the social error. The person's embarrassing themself already, so why compound the problem? This has its merits, but, like an unwillingness to stop others from cutting line, it can lead, has led, and will lead to the ongoing misery of others. For centuries. In the United States, by going to the opposite extreme, we have also put off solving problems. We want justice at any cost, even if it be justice itself. We want satisfaction. We want revenge. If we can't be happy, no one can. At this late hour in the United States, someone would have ordered her to shut the fuck up and woken everyone on the train doing it.

I, having picked up a clue or two in my five weeks in China, tried to work the patient, face saving route. I'd already had some practice earlier in the night, before the stewards started yelling at the slob for being one, when the dolt then sitting next to him loudly asked me some insulting questions about who I was and then complained that I should know the language. I had, in fact, understood everything he said, but had exercised the privilege of playing dumb and pretending not to listen in the hope that he would give up. We were all still awake at that point and the longer he went on, the less everyone else seemed to like him. Thankfully, he got off the train after staring at me for hours. Hours. He just kept staring. I hadn't given him the satisfaction.

This time, after the loud woman gave up trying to squash me and switched with the now awake old woman, I closed my eyes. I listened as she went on and on about how uncomfortable the seats were, about her socks, and about the snow that was falling as we passed near Jǐnán, the capital of Shāndōng Province. All of this went

DAY 36: *Shāndōng Province, Hénán Province, Kāifēng* 173

on for more than half an hour.

However. I couldn't fake sleep forever. When this loud-speaking woman, who was keeping me and the rest of the car awake while the rest of the train was sleeping, caught on that I was still awake, she tried to engage me in small talk and noticed I wasn't answering. Like the dolt before her, she turned to how I couldn't understand anything she was saying and how funny it was and how she couldn't believe I was traveling in China when I didn't even speak the language. Hours earlier and wide awake, this was an annoyance; now, dead tired and crushed into a corner, my best efforts to be patient and understanding of her profound ignorance and selfishness had reached their breaking point. To keep me awake by talking very loud at me was bad enough. To keep me awake by calling me stupid because I couldn't understand her? Oh, man. Oh, no.

I unloaded. I did not raise my voice. I did not repeat the mistakes I made in Luòyáng. I had had the time to think about what I would say and how I would say it. In no uncertain Mandarin, I pointed out the time and I pointed out that everyone else was trying to sleep, uncomfortably but trying to. And I pointed out that yes, oh, yes, I had understood every single word she had said. I did not, then, know how to say "Zhù kǒu!" (joo-koh, "Shut up!")[17]. I am proud to say I hadn't ever planned to use it. But here. But now. Now it didn't matter what language I used. It may even have been better that I used my own language, because the meaning in any language was clear. I took no pleasure in it, not in that moment and not now. As the Chinese would note, I was also embarrassed, especially after what I had been through and how I had reacted in Luòyáng. I didn't want to fight. I only wanted to be left alone. In the end, though, I had been insulted, out of petty ignorance, perhaps, but she was just going to go on and on insulting me, and with neck pain, back pain, and leg pain already making it hard to sleep, these insults adding to injury badly needed to stop. I spoke plainly and calmly, and then shut my eyes to sleep.

She didn't go quietly, as you might expect, but when she finally did we all quickly and happily readjusted ourselves for sleep. The

---

[17] "Bì Zuǐ!" also works.

old lady who couldn't figure out the window used my right shoulder for a pillow. The slob stretched his legs all the way under my seat. I was keyed up from the confrontation, so I watched the snow and a young couple trying to aim their infant's pee into a water bottle. I watched it all until I, too, finally fell asleep.

Not that I slept much. I nodded on and off until we reached Kāifēng. Only after the chaos of getting off the train did I realize I'd forgotten to ask the old couple about their army bag. There was nothing I could do about it then.

My next stop would be Qǔfù, so I bounced back and forth between the rail and bus ticket offices to get travel times. How much did they fear not knowing an answer? One woman at the train station actually ran when she saw me approaching her window a second time, and I'd been all smiles. Very cheery. Really.

Despite last night's snow, it was warm and sunny in Kāifēng. Out in the daylight, a determined pedi-cabbie had followed me from station to station to station, so I hired him for a ride out to one dump, the worst I'd seen, and then to a veritable palace, cheaper than the cheapest room in Qīngdǎo. He was a good guy, that pedi-cabbie. They were all good people in Kāifēng, the nicest people, even that poor, terrified woman in the ticket office. A pity it seemed there was so little to see.

I did see a lot of the town, though, more than I ever thought I'd get to. Why? Kāifēng looked like the last best chance I'd have to find The Bag. My big, gray L.L. Bean backpack had taken on quite a bit of extra weight at this point. Every souvenir I had purchased with the exception of the scroll painting from Xī'ān was now tucked inside. It was so full that the stitching on the seams was coming loose. I had completely resewn one of the seams already, top to bottom, so getting a second bag, any second bag, had become a necessity and I didn't want it to be one of those colorful, woven, nylon sacks I'd seen if I could help it.

So many people wore army surplus here that it looked like the town was under occupation. More likely, there was an army base nearby. I asked directions off a good lead on an army bag, which sent me from the western edge of town all the way back to the center. I

DAY 36: *Shāndōng Province, Hénán Province, Kāifēng* 175

had no luck, but I got in a lot of good practice striking up conversations with strangers, and these conversations taught me something it never occurred to me I had to learn.

When we non-Chinese think of the word "store", we tend to think of it as a structure, something with four walls, maybe a sign out front telling us what kind of store it is. In Mandarin, though, the word "diàn" means any place you can buy something, any place at all. It could be a building, sure, or a storefront, but it could also be a mat or blanket on the sidewalk. You had to specify exactly what kind of store you wanted, not by describing what you wanted but by using the correct name in Mandarin. Even with my dictionary, I couldn't find the right combination to ask for "army surplus store". So, I asked just about every person on the street where they thought the place to buy army surplus bags was, or just where bags were, and they all pointed to a place they'd seen people selling bags or, you know, point and tell me, "Zŏu ah".

And, of course, they all were right. A store was a store and if I kept walking, I would eventually find one. By the end of it, I'd seen every single kind of store Kāifēng had to offer. I was no closer to finding what I wanted and I could barely walk.

DAY 37

Tuesday, October 10

Kāifēng, Hénán Province

•

Yesterday's quest for "The Bag" had been both exhausting and disappointing. At one point last night, in a moment of desperation, I considered going four hours west by train back to Luòyáng, my absolute least favorite place in China, where I had last seen a full-size version of The Bag two whole weeks ago.

Well, that didn't last. Not liking where that desperation would have led me, I decided I wasn't going to worry about the Bag hunt today. It wouldn't be easy, since my tight-as-a-sausage big bag hadn't lost any weight or girth overnight, but I needed to slow down and see whatever Kāifēng had to offer without the distraction. I repacked yet again and made my way from the wonderfully hospitable Kaifeng Guesthouse over to the train station's Left Luggage room where I dropped off the big pack and took the unzipped, small pack once again for my tour of the town.

And there it was. Blocks from the station, folded and tied down on the back of a slow moving bicycle, there it was. I didn't know what to do. I froze, staring at it as it passed by in the street. That didn't last, either, but for a second I couldn't even think. And then I could. I saw it getting further and further away, so I ran.

I ran. No sense of shame, no sense of etiquette, no sense at all, I was chasing a man on his bike and he was not going to get away. Of course, he wasn't really going very fast. And then he stopped. I ran into the street and waved him down. He must have thought I was lost, or needed help, or was just crazy. In all fairness, I was a little of all three, but I knew exactly where I was: I was near The Bag. "The Bag"! Losing all remaining subtlety, I pointed and asked if I could buy it. He was shocked. Stunned. Confused. Why wouldn't he be?

DAY 37: *Kāifēng, Hénán Province* 177

"This bag?" he asked. "You want this?"

"Duì! Duì!" I told him, probably nodding like a maniac. I took out cash and started peeling off ¥10 notes like I was rich or something. He stopped me at six. His wife, who had been on her own bike, took their laundry out – this had been their laundry bag – and it, The Bag, was mine. In the middle of traffic, albeit incredibly light, Kāifēng traffic, with a patched hole, a buckle missing, and a rail sticker, The Bag was finally mine.

I was so happy. It was cheap, and I would have paid so much more. After all, hadn't Jacki said, "If you want it, and you don't think you'll see it again, just buy it"? There may have been something in there about, "as long as you try to stay within your budget",

but for what I got, paying only ¥60 – about $7.50 – was an unbelievable bargain. I had taken acquiring it to an extreme, but I cannot possibly explain how it felt being so close to completing that quest.

Everything was perfect the rest of the day. I took a picture of the man and his son to remember them – the wife kept her distance – and headed off with my two bags to Lóngtíng Park, where I basked in my petty success and took some shots of an old, brick bridge that went out into the middle of the lake and stopped halfway. It was a beautiful, tranquil park, filled with old men fishing for their dinner. I sat and enjoyed the sun for maybe an hour then made my way to the Dragon Pavilion, which was filled with ridiculous waxworks having a feast. From there, though, I could look out to the Iron Pagoda, which was a lovely sight. Built from brown bricks, not iron, it was almost a thousand years old and rose nearly two hundred feet in one of Kāifēng's parks. I had said that there was nothing to see, and, for the average tourist, sadly, the Pagoda, some small parks, and some odd waxworks aren't a must-see. At best, they were a non-Bag-hunting day trip. Still, the Pagoda is an impressive achievement.

There was, however, one more attraction that might be worth the time and effort, if only I could find it, the ruins of Kāifēng's Medieval synagogue, which I learned not one of those guidebook writers could ever really have seen. Wandering the neighborhood where the guidebook said it should be, I bumped into Bob Mung, a naturalized Canadian who had come back to his hometown to do some business and to buy his family a house. He insisted on showing me the actual "ruins" himself, which were not near where we were and which, it turned out, required permission and a guide.

You see, the actual "ruins" consisted of a plugged up well on the floor of the old city hospital's boiler room. That's it, or at least that was it according to Bob, who remembered it as a local "make-out spot" way back when he was a kid. We needed permission to enter from someone working for the hospital. We ended up being led through the boiler room by a man who, based on his uniform, worked there as an orderly or maybe a janitor. Honestly, I was a little worried about going to a boiler room alone with two strangers. I had taken bigger risks already with far less concern, but looking back I might as well have wandered into the train station in Guǎngzhōu. I needn't have worried; the boiler room itself was more of a threat. It was small, dark, filthy, and badly needed ventilation. I can't imagine why the kids making out might've come down here, other than knowing that they, too had somehow escaped with their lives.

The cap on the synagogue well looked like a manhole cover – it was about the same size and color – but with Hebrew script. I couldn't read what it said, but I guess the text described what it was and what had been there, and maybe who had made it and when.

We didn't stay long. Outside, Bob said the main reason they hadn't rebuilt the synagogue, which they had discussed, or accepted money from outside investors to build a new, better hospital for the people of Kāifēng was because they didn't want to hurt the business of the old, crappy hospital. It's a bit like refusing to upgrade old, slow, expensive-to-repair trains and infrastructure because you don't want to disrupt the terrible service[18]. I can't imagine they didn't eventually give in and build an entirely new hospital somewhere else in the city, but at the time they were stuck with what they had for reasons no one using it could understand.

What can people do but put on a better face? Bob asked this later, away from the hospital, as he and his neighbors chased away a bully who was tormenting a smaller boy. I watched with some pride for Bob and his fellow defenders, thanked him for his time and for getting me into the boiler room, and went on my way.

Heading back to the station, I passed the old river. It looked and smelled strongly like flat root beer: brown and sickly sweet. It crawled along so slowly, it looked like someone could be pulling it with a rope, like a donkey pulling a barge up a canal. As I watched it, and almost outpaced it, I passed an old woman whose face was so wrinkled she literally had her eyebrows and eyelids taped up, otherwise she'd have been blind. Not quite what Bob meant, but an example of making do just the same.

Traveling as I was, using overnight trains in place of hotels, I naturally tried to stay close to the train stations as my departure times grew near. After those near misses and that missed stop earlier in my journey, I didn't dare risk getting left behind because someone decided to arrive and depart an hour or so early. So, there I was, with my new Bag and my big, heavy old one, killing time in the station with almost six hours to go until the very estimated time of depar-

---

[18] American train systems, take note.

ture. I repacked as discretely as I could, rearranging my clothes, especially the still unused sweater and jeans, to serve as padding for souvenirs in the big bag, and transferring enough weight to the army backpack to manage them both together.

Bored, I went to the station's small shop and bought a pack of playing cards, pūkè, with images of famous heroes and warriors on them. One was mis-cut, so I brought them back. I don't know what I expected, but the vendor simply opened another pack, fished out a fresh card, and smiled as he gave it to me. I was surprised. I guess I shouldn't have been. With the exception of Luòyáng – STAY AWAY – all I had to do to get something in small cities like this was to be kind. It didn't hurt that I, tall and skinny with curly hair, a scraggly beard, and a big "Dà Bízi" nose was something of a novelty. Throughout the day adults and kids alike had stared and giggled and said "hullo" in that drawn out, pleasant way that vendors in touristy places had long forgotten. Despite the gawking, they all made me feel welcome. Kāifēng was a genuinely good town with genuinely good people. Well, except for that bully, but look what they did to him.

Then again, even in the most welcoming of places there were a few parents and old people so afraid of the foreigner that they hid their kids. One such couple was sitting on the bench behind me at the train station. They were busy preparing their son to be a serial killer, smacking him on the head and not listening to him to the point where he threatened *to stab his father with his toys*. I say "threatened", but the kid was *this* close to doing it. He tried. Maybe they weren't from Kāifēng. I choose to believe they were just passing through.

Eventually, I napped. I had to, because Kāifēng, like Yǎnzhōu tomorrow night, sold nothing but Standing tickets in Hard Seat class. That would be seven or eight hours both nights spent standing, waiting for a seat to open up, and/or sitting on the cesspit floor. I was lucky, I guess. I had the Newsweek magazine I bought in Qīngdǎo to tear apart and spread around to protect my seat wherever I sat. Tonight would be a test, for me and it.

DAY 38

Wednesday, October 11

Shāndōng Province, Yǎnzhōu, Qǔfù, Yǎnzhōu

•

So, there I was, only a thin layer of pages torn from Newsweek magazine separating me from the filth of the Hard Seat floor. Next to me among the waste and bugs were an old woman and a mother with a toddler, a remarkably bright boy who was learning fast and very, very communicative. The four of us sat on the floor together for the first three hours.

It amazed me how selfish and heartless some people could be, obsessed with their own comfort and holding onto room they wouldn't even use. They would rather let old people and young mothers with toddlers sit on the floor than squeeze in and share a little of their benches. It disgusted me more than the floor itself.

More selfish and certainly more heartless were the goons passing up and down the aisle, who kicked and stepped on us rather than lift their feet and legs just a little bit higher. They kept kicking and wiping their shoes on us until I, to the approval of the entire seated aisle, grabbed them by the ankles as they approached me and started "helping" them lift and keep their feet up as they passed over. It made me very popular and caught on.

Unfortunately, this was very much China with all of its extremes. Take what happened later. The old woman had finally been given a seat, and the mother and bright toddler had left the train. A very kind soldier, who had found a seat earlier, fought back the mob to offer it to me when another traveler left, either out of regard for my foot lifting or because I was a guest in his country. It was probably the latter, but I choose to believe it was the former. Well, as the soldier stood to do this, a man who had been sitting on the bench opposite him swooped in, took the soldier's seat, and wouldn't give it back. Everything I thought I understood about Hard Seat etiquette, that the seat was yours until you chose to give it away, had gone out the window. The seat thief's actions garnered a collective shrug. Still, the soldier insisted that I take the seat the thief had given up, so I did. A third person, seeing all of this, gave the soldier his seat and arranged to squeeze onto another half-seat himself. And the train just kept on going.

All of this happened around 4:30 in the morning. I slept on and off after that. I was anxious not to miss my stop, still two hours away. These overnight trains had been the price I paid for seeing these small cities and towns in daylight, and would be the rest of the way. It meant I never slept well, but it had made this journey possible. Still, three cities in three days – Kāifēng to Yǎnzhōu to Nánjīng, with a detour through Qǔfù – was crazy. It must all be high-speed rail now, just a few hours between each one, if that. I'd say don't do it, but today I don't think you could.

No sooner had we made it to Yǎnzhōu than I was fighting my way past the vultures coveting my seat. One drooling heap asked me four times, up close, if he could have it. I muscled my gray bag down from the rack and squeezed through the crowd down the aisle and out the door to the platform. I don't know who took the seat. Having gotten out, I wasn't looking back.

The new bag situation worked out great. Having repacked before leaving Kāifēng, I was able to spread my clothes and souvenirs around the L.L. Bean bag's combined big and small packs, and keep my camera, thermos, and other necessities with me in the army bag. I parked the L.L. Bean in Left Luggage for the day then trotted over to get my ticket to Nánjīng. This time, I made sure to stay at the window after I bought it. Sure enough, the ticket seller had given me a ticket for the right train at the right time but the wrong day. She wasn't even close, off by almost a week. She was very friendly, as was every person I met in Yǎnzhōu, but I wasn't staying there any longer than the train gods required.

Tonight's ticket in hand, I was off by minibus to see Qǔfù, ancestral home of the Kǒng family and their literal patron saint, Kǒng fū zǐ, better known in the West as "Confucius". No Kǒngs lived there

DAY 38: Shāndōng Province, Yǎnzhōu, Qūfù, Yǎnzhōu

now. Allegedly, they were chased out to Taiwan by the Communists, although the throngs of tourists who followed in the present day seemed far more terrifying. Yes, irony of ironies, this one time blight on the ideology of communism had been co-opted by that very same government, and the Communists were now making money off the Kǒng name.

The sleepy town of even recent guidebooks had now grown into a full-scale tourist attraction, all of it centered around making even more money off of old Kǒng. He might have been proud, although I have no idea what he might have thought about the rows of karaoke palaces and gift shops now lining the streets surrounding the Kǒng family compound as far as the eye could see.

The compound itself, by comparison, was fairly demure, though I still had to bob and weave through crowds of Chinese tourists just to see the famous stele and the larger than life statue of the Great Bearded One himself. The best part of the day ended up being the pedicab rides to and from Kǒng's mound-like tomb. Between rides, I had another fight with the camera shutter and met the souvenir vendors with the least imagination in all of China. Each of the forty or so shills held out the same book on Kǒng fū zǐ and the same Kǒng fū zǐ chops, as if each was the first I'd seen, all of them lined up in a row right next to each other like the area had been zoned for hawking. By the end, I started having fun with it, not that I wanted to buy anything. Other than pens and other knick-knacks emblazoned with the American flag[19], there really wasn't anything in Qūfù anyone other than the most devoted fan of Kong would want to buy.

Another minibus ride with another nice bunch of people – I had really good luck with the minibus crowd in China – and I was back in Yǎnzhōu. I actually spent more time in Yǎnzhōu than Qūfù. It was a poor town that had grown around the cavernous, two-story high railroad station. At night, dozens of bats flew around inside the station's high ceiling. Two young women at one of the junk shops around the station area tried to sell me a "money detector", which was just an ultra-violet light to bring out marks on big number bills. It never did work. They were so earnest, I felt bad, but I still didn't

---

[19] See SIGNS COMMUNISM WAS OVER, Part 3, following this chapter.

buy one. One of the other junk shops sold empty, used Tang and Nescafé jars to use on trains. And I thought people had brought theirs from home.

With the remaining sunlight fading, I sat out in the square across from the station surrounded by small monuments to workers and some representatives laboring over a hole in the sidewalk. As with Kāifēng and Xīníng, there appeared to have been an army base nearby, the streets filled with surplus surplus. I didn't see any Bags, though. Mine was the only one.

In front of me, three children, later joined by a fourth, were playing a game. The small boy covered his eyes while the others ran and hid around the square. Keeping his hands over his eyes, he called out, they answered, and then he wandered out to find them. If he ever came near, the others would run and hide again. He had no choice but to keep calling and keep wandering blind until he caught someone to take his place.

Yes, it was "Marco Polo". I don't know what they called it here.

SIGNS COMMUNISM WAS OVER
Part 3:

#9: (Post-Colonial Irony Division): In Kāifēng, the police directed traffic from beneath large umbrellas bearing the logo for BP, British Petroleum.

#10: One of the hottest selling items at train stations was a travel alarm-clock made to resemble a Motorola beeper.

#11: Also at the train station in Kāifēng: "Beverly Hills, 90210" bandanas!!

#12: The souvenir shops in Qŭfù were selling pens and other small items with American flag STARS & STRIPES designs.

DAY 39

Wednesday, October 11 – Thursday, October 12

Yǎnzhōu, Shāndōng Province, Jiāngsū Province, Nánjīng

•

It seemed that every day I spent in China I had two fewer until I went home. Today was no exception. It began as most days had, the night before, and it would be as tightly packed as my big, gray bag.

I had retreated from Yǎnzhōu's nighttime swarms into the relative safety of the station, with its high ceilings and insect-eating wildlife. As I watched and listened to the bats hunt for their supper, an old crank berated me in front of the entire, cramped Hard-class waiting room for having a Chinese army backpack while he and everyone else had to make do with their cheap, striped, woven-nylon bags. Did you laugh at me for building up my quest for The Bag so much? I wasn't kidding about how great they are, or how hard they were to find.

The crank wandered off, disgusted and probably looking for someone else to berate, but at least he sparked some conversation between me and my neighbors. The man sitting to my right had a copy of something you'd think China's railroad employees would be hunting down themselves: a national schedule of departures and arrivals. Then again, since no train I had taken had come close to sticking to it, maybe it was better not to know? It came as no surprise then that this train both arrived and departed late. I did laugh, though not at him. He deserved better.

What had come as less and less of a surprise the more I traveled here was how kind and generous Chinese travelers were. Old cranks and seat thieves aside, the vast majority were just like the soldier on the previous train and the man with his train schedules. On this train, even though it was crowded, another man gave me his seat. He insisted on it, just as the soldier had, and moved himself to sit on a bag on the floor. Yes, it could have been pity, either for a poor foreigner carrying obviously heavy backpacks or for a foolish foreigner being just stupid enough to travel in Hard Seat, but isn't that a kind of kindness and generosity? It certainly made me want to be kind and generous in return, and this was certainly part of the culture. I kept an eye on the seats around us, hoping to find one for him. The waitlist for a seat was shorter tonight, and it wasn't long before a soldier sitting across from us saw another seat open up, took it, and gave his seat to the kind man who had given his seat to me. It was nice to see everything work out for everybody, because that didn't happen too often.

I was able to sleep on this train, a first in Hard Seat despite some clod playing a loud hand-held video game behind me, and before I knew it we were in Nánjīng. We arrived early, too, because of course we did.

It was at this lovely hour of the morning that the city of Nánjīng greeted me with the taxi "travel surcharge" scam. It was real and, yes, it was actually sanctioned by the local government. The way it worked was this: at any arrival or departure point for long-distance travel, including train stations and airports, taxis were allowed to charge 50% more than the price advertised on the windows. This was applicable for transport to or from the airport or train station, just as it was in cities all over China and cities all over the world. So far, so good, so normal.

Ah, but here in Nánjīng there was a government condoned loophole big enough to drive a taxi through: Who was to say what or when was "to" or "from"? Generally, if you had luggage or a big backpack, particularly a heavy looking one, you had to be going to or coming from somewhere far away, the kind of travel that requires something big and heavy like a plane or a train to get you there. Right? That's just logic. That you were perhaps in the middle of your journey or even near the end didn't matter. That you might be going from one point in the city to another didn't matter. That you might be kilometers from the nearest airport or train station, as I was, didn't matter. As far as I had gotten from the station, taxi after taxi after taxi still offered the same "travel surcharge" rate. Even without a bag, I'm sure just being a foreigner in Nánjīng would have been enough to qualify. And why wouldn't they? It was 50% more money for the driver, and it had the government stamp of approval.

The main railway station was on the north side of Xuánwǔ Lake, and the hotel I needed to get to was somewhere south of it, so I'm sorry to say I gave in. Sort of. I had walked maybe halfway around the lake when I came across a three-wheeled moto-taxi, for which there was no "travel surcharge". It cost just ¥10, maybe a quarter of what I would've paid for a taxi. He took me directly, too, no loops around the lake, no friend-ly persuasion, no hassle at all. I gave him a 50% tip, and it was still cheap.

The hotel wasn't. I would rather have stayed at the university dorms, which were supposed to be cheaper and offered single rooms, but they were all the way across town and there was no guarantee there'd be a single or anything else for me when I got there. A month ago, I probably would have tried it, taking the time and the effort to save literally just a few bucks. That I would be able to afford the next two weeks in this expensive region was due in large part to making choices like that in the poorer ones, however much that backfired on my mental and physical health. A week recovering in the warm, dry, and comfortable home of Jacki & Jack Eyman had taught me a necessary lesson on the value of both. Here, I took what was offered. I paid ¥220 for a double, one of the cheapest rates for a proper hotel room in this city. With the added luxury of all-day hot water, I certainly had no regrets. Before taking advantage, though, I made sure to call home from the hotel lobby to let my parents know where I was and that I was safe. I then checked in with Jacki back in Běijīng to let her know the same.

Scrubbed clean, I went out to cash another traveler's cheque. On the way, I stopped for some boiled veggie jiāozi. Boiled jiāozi become water-heavy and very slippery, even for regular chopstick users. The choice was always either to stab at them and eat them like skewers, a popular local choice from what I saw, or to shovel them into your mouth with your chopsticks like rice, with the plate or bowl held up to your mouth. It was a bowl here, which helped a lot. I experimented with both and was just grateful not to have dropped any

DAY 39: Yǎnzhōu, Shāndōng Province, Jiāngsū Province, Nánjīng 189

on the floor. Small victories.

When I arrived at the bank, the exchange windows had closed for their own jiāozi session, so I crossed Zhōngshān Lù, named for favored son Dr. Sun Yat Sen, to use the phone at the local five-star hotel. Having now seen the beauty of Nánjīng with my own eyes and having a chance to slow down and enjoy it as I had in Běijīng, I decided that completing my circuit of China with a return to Guǎngzhōu and then Hong Kong wasn't what I wanted anymore. I called the United Airlines office in Shànghǎi to see about flying to San Francisco from there instead.

Happily, the cost to change my flight wouldn't be much more than I expected to spend going all the way back down to Hong Kong. The flight would be a day earlier, on the 27th, but I'd have three extra days in this region, which somehow almost felt like too many. For all of this, I wouldn't have to worry about traveling long distance in Hard Seat again, the seaworthiness of a ferry back to Hong Kong, or what to do and where to stay in Hong Kong when I got there. I would also not be traveling through an area I knew to be higher in crime laden with souvenirs in heavy bags. I'd miss out on seeing prehandover Hong Kong in the daylight, which I now regret, but again, at that time with all I then knew or thought I did, it felt like it was worth it.

Back at the bank, I met a Brit, Allan Steele, waiting and waiting in the short exchange line. They were very thorough. Allan was in town for a conference, a very fashionable thing for major Chinese cities in 1995,[20] and then planned to travel the country with a friend. He had "borrowed" his copy of our mutual guidebook from his local library back in England. He wasn't supposed to take it out of town, let alone all the way to China. As unreliable as it was, I warned him about what to ignore and recommended he make sure to visit Guìlín and Yángshuò, to which I sadly now also wouldn't be returning.

Having the same plans for the day, we went to find a bus out to the Nánjīng Massacre museum. The guidebook had listed what bus number to take, but naturally had neglected to mention where in the

---

[20] A banner in Nánjīng: "Welcome Friends of Industry & Commerce Circles of the Five Continents *To Have A Talk*" (italics added for emphasis)

city that bus might be found. There weren't any bus route maps to be had, so we looked instead for a moto-taxi, now known to be the cheapest and most reliable option around. The driver of the first one we found told us, bravely and honorably, that he was illiterate, didn't know the city, and that we should look for somebody else to go longer distances. Maybe not much of a career in moto-taxis for him, but here's hoping he succeeded with that or something better eventually. The next driver was just as forthright but knew the city and got us there, no problem.

In the West, we refer to the Nánjīng Massacre as "The Rape of Nanking". Our memories of it consist of graphic photographs and newsreels from the 1930s. Our grandparents and great-grandparents may have tut-tutted and shaken their heads at the horrors they read about in newspapers or maybe glimpsed at movie theaters before the cartoons if they weren't in line for popcorn, but no one lifted a finger to stop it. For them and most of the world, if they even knew what was being done, it was something that disappeared when the newsreels ended, something safely far away from the world outside the theater.

For the Chinese and residents of Nánjīng in particular, it was anything but. For them in the present day, it was still close, still fresh in their minds, every bit their own Holocaust, every atrocity just as malignant as those that played out in Europe in the 1930s and 40s, in the Balkins and central Africa in the weeks I was traveling through China, and in places we may fear talking about right now. For them, "Never Again" applies to everyone.

Entering the grounds, the museum appeared small, with low, pale, sterile buildings and sculptures rising out of the sea of pale, sterile stones covering the museum grounds. It all made sense once we went inside. The museum proper was a level below, displaying the contents of a mass grave: piles of white, sterile bones, the same bleached white as the stones directly above, in room after room. An estimated 200,000 men, women, and children were slaughtered in less than four months amidst looting and sadistic brutality, including widespread rape.

The numbers may be debated, but proof of it is on full display at

DAY 39: *Yǎnzhōu, Shāndōng Province, Jiāngsū Province, Nánjīng* 191

the museum, including gut-wrenching films shot by the Japanese occupiers themselves, just as the Nazis did, just as those convinced of their right to genocide always do. It's what they do to tell themselves it's normal. It's what they do to justify what they know they should not be doing. And it was all just as painful to see as any concentration camp in Europe.

I thought about Katsuo, the Japanese student I met on the train to Kūnmíng, and the museum exhibit we saw there on the Japanese occupation of Yúnnán province. The Japanese government's inability to own up to what they had done even decades later, let alone their inability to offer a sincere apology for it, had led to a skewed portrayal of Japanese people in Chinese culture. In movies, television shows, and books, the Japanese still played the same role they played in 1945: an almost alien embodiment of evil. Recently made films and shows I saw in China showed Chinese heroes in the present day and even in a science fiction future still fighting Japanese soldiers forever dressed in 1931-1945 period uniforms. The soldiers in those stories still raped and pillaged, just as they had in Nánjīng. Katsuo's generation weren't being taught this history. How they were supposed to deal with it when they came across it, as he had, I don't know.

Allan and I next went down to Zhōnghuámén (China Gate). It was a remnant of Nánjīng's medieval walls and, like the park atop the walls surrounding Xī'ān, it offered a view of the city's rapidly growing, modern skyline. We talked about football, all kinds, and baseball. It was getting dark, so he took a bus back to where he was staying, we hoped.

I walked on, stumbling across Fūzǐmiào (Master Temple), a kind of cross between a temple and Coney Island meant to draw Chinese tourists with all of its gaudiness. There, I bought one of those tiny silver boxes with a lid made from a chunk of broken ceramic tile. The vendor initially asked $45 for it, seeing

192 AN INCREDIBLY FOOLISH AND DANGEROUS THING TO DO

my face for being a foreign sucker. I smiled and gently began to negotiate in Mandarin. I paid about $4.

A long walk took me all the way back to the boiled jiāozi shop. They were really nice people, and the locals loved it. After dinner, I called home about the change of plans. My final tally for the day's calls? $35. The length of those calls? About seven minutes. Between everything I'd seen this long day and how close I was to going home, it really didn't seem like too much.

Garbage Can, Nánjīng, 1995

DAY 40

Friday, October 13
Nánjīng
•

I overslept, again. After my long, busy day yesterday, I guess I needed it. I got out the door at 9:30, which felt late but left me plenty of time to see just about everything.

Down Zhōngshān Dōng Lù is a public park that used to be the Imperial Palace of Zhū Yuánzhāng, the "Hóngwǔ Emperor", founder of the Míng Dynasty. What time hadn't done to the center of the world, the 19th century colonial powers had, shelling the palace into rubble to put down the Tàipíng Rebellion, which had been headquartered inside.

Fought from 1850 to 1864, the rebellion had many causes: a starving population, loss of confidence in the Qīng dynasty's rule, the Christianity-based religious ideology of the Tàipíng rebels, and, as ever, charismatic demagogues promising quick and easy answers to long term, difficult problems. The catalysts driving and uniting those four reasons, though, were escalating abuses by those same colonial powers, principally among them the forced trade of opium. While it may not have been introduced into China by the British, they would exploit it to fund their seafaring empire and fought two Opium Wars to maintain the trade of it in China

193

and with it increased access to China's resources. The second of those wars, fought during the late 1850s, brought the French, Russians, and Americans in on the fun, with each of them gaining "concessions" in Shànghǎi and other port cities. When the Chinese surrendered in 1860, the French stayed with the British to "stabilize" the opium-free territory held by the Tàipíngs.

And so it was here, at this once opulent palace of emperors reduced to rubble by gunpowder-fueled cannons, that good, Christian soldiers from Britain and France killed other good, Christian soldiers from China, once again to maintain the trade of a drug meant to create dependency and thus weaken the colonized Chinese. The irony of it all was that the Tàipíngs' rejection of the colonizers' opium and greedy brutality, as well as the Qīng's corrupt government that enabled it, was inspired by the work of Christian missionaries from the same countries they were fighting. I couldn't tell you how many Chinese viewing the ruins beside me knew the history, who died here and why. I have to believe they're taught some version of it, certainly more than we are.

Inside the park, amid the ruins, there was dancing. It might seem inappropriate based on what I just wrote, but this was also a public park and was probably better known for it as historical sites often are. Last night, in the regular park between my hotel's gate and the canal, there had also been dancing. The music had been a traditional, Chinese melody set to a Samba beat. The dancing had been beautiful, with some very polished performances. Here today, they put more contemporary songs to the test, with some people taking instruction as if it was tài jí. I enjoyed watching them for a while, but then they played that song. The first line went, "Zou-zou, zou-zou, zou-ah-zou!" and, no matter what style or tempo you played, it retained the same "Yo-Aye-Kippie-Aye!" rhythm. It was played everywhere: parks, stations, trains, McDonald's. The Chinese just couldn't get enough of that song; I just wanted to chew my ears off.

Making my escape, I took a moto-taxi to see Zhōngshān Líng, the imperial-style Mausoleum of Dr. Sun Yat-Sen. It is, quite literally, China's answer to Mt. Vernon. The Chinese like that they were able to transcribe the names "Sun" and "Sen" into "Zhōng Shān", which means "Middle (or Central) Peak". Dr. Sun was at the time of his death the central, towering figure for the newly quasi-democratic people of Zhōngguó, the "Middle Kingdom". Even Máo and his followers agreed, Zhōngshān was a fitting name. Whatever their public stance on Dr. Sun's Kuomintang (National People's Party) and Sun's protegé, the corrupt, militaristic dictator, Generalissimo Chiang Kai-Shek, the Communists would not hold the power they hold today without the 1911 revolution led by Dr. Sun. That he was buried in the style of an emperor on a mountain dead center in a park almost as large as the rest of Nánjīng didn't hurt the symbolism.

Every day, thousands flocked to see the view of Nánjīng from the top of the steps and Dr. Sun's Lincoln-Memorial-esque statue on top of his sarcophagus. They came from countries all across the globe, and they all lived in dread fear of the mausoleum employees. The employees were already plenty rude to their own countrymen, so anyone "too stupid to speak the right language", beware. I was mocked, vulgarly, by a ticket-taker for not understanding her thick, regional accent[21]. I knew she was asking me about my ticket, and I could guess she was asking about the student price, but to her my hesitation was enough to make me a moron. I remembered Luòyáng, and while I was still pretty bitter about that I did my best to suck it up. I smiled like the idiot she thought I was, thanked her, and went inside.

The site itself is impressive. The mausoleum at the top of the Purple Mountain is big and white with a blue tile roof and a view of the world. Dr. Sun, another Christian rebel, never sought imperial-style power for himself, but his successors – Chiang, Máo, and every Chinese Communist Party leader to this day – have all enjoyed his reflected glory and the power that comes with it. After all, hasn't every leader of China, crowned or not, been revered this way? Don't they all carry the "Mandate of Heaven"? For them, the view from the top is very different.

I descended to see the Hóngwǔ Emperor's tomb, located on the map at the foot of the mountain. I figured it would be a quick walk and was again wrong. A half-hour passing areas closed off with

---

[21] See LANGUAGE PRONUNCIATION, LESSON #5, following this chapter.

barbed-wired led me to the third and entirely skippable section of the Hóngwǔ compound. There was nothing of the tomb to see, only a huge mound and a gift shop. After a break from the heat under the shade of a pagoda, I wove my way over to the other side of a hill. As with the intact Míng tombs in Běijīng, the "Path to Heaven" leading to this tomb was lined with male and female representations of animals carved in stone. It took a while to find them, but they were quite impressive, too.

It was getting late and I hadn't eaten lunch, so I took a local bus back into town. This one was almost empty, which made it a safe bet for ¥1. In town, I walked, walked some more, had some ice cream while I walked, and then walked even more. When I reached the park by the Drum Tower, I rested and had some peanuts while I worked out my possibly too optimistic plans for Shànghǎi. If I could pull it off, I would be staying in the perfect place, a hotel near the airport, the United Airlines ticket office, the antique stores, and the new subway that could take me all the way to the Bund, all for $30 a night in the old French Concession. I had everything worked out perfectly and a back-up plan for when that didn't work, because when had anything worked?

Allan had told me he would try to have dinner tonight at some place called the Black Cat, a Yángshuò-style backpacker hangout in the university area near the Drum Tower. It seemed like a good idea. The backpacker hangouts in Yángshuò and Xī'ān had been great places to meet and eat meals with people, and, as a bonus, if I found anyone heading to Hong Kong, I might have been able to swap the $95 HK I no longer needed with someone going there. So, using the information in our shared guidebook – I know, I know – I went off to find it and wasn't at all surprised to find that I couldn't.

I looked some more, wandering into the university area. It was here that I came across one of those things that makes traveling, even with all of its hassles, so much fun. I had just written-off Nánjīng as having next to nothing but cheap, touristy junk. I'd had that very thought in the park by the Drum Tower. And yet, out of nowhere, in what I guess was the middle of the university section, in a little cubicle of a corner store mostly selling school supplies, I found beautiful,

DAY 40: *Nánjīng*

hand-painted scrolls. Oddly, hand-painted scrolls were rare in Nánjīng. Three or four scrolls here were really good, and not one was smudged with dirty fingerprints, a common problem in coal-burning China. I was caught by a small, narrow one with purple and yellow flowers hanging just inside the door, and the asking price started out pretty low. I, however, still had trouble understanding the Nánjīng regional accent. The shopkeeper tried, but I stepped out to refresh my art store vocabulary before I returned, because I really wanted that scroll. I wanted it bad. I came back and, as an introduction so I wouldn't lose leverage on the first scroll, I asked about another I liked, green and black bamboo in the same style and size with the same calligrapher. It was the same price. Then it hit me: my brother and sister-in-law's wedding gift! Why not get both, a package deal?! They balanced each other perfectly! I knew what I'd be willing to spend, and although she claimed that she'd have to call the artist – I originally thought she was saying that she'd have to call her husband – I hoped she'd go lower if she knew she was selling two and not one. It turned out they were part of a Four Seasons set with two other scrolls I didn't want. In retrospect, I should have bought them all, but I didn't need them and honestly I didn't think I could afford all four. I played up the "poor, student traveler" bit, tugging at my frayed shorts, and I finally got my price on the two. Our accents got in the way, but communication was made. Unfortunately, she didn't have boxes, so she had to wrap them in brown paper like a couple of hoagies. I had plenty of space for them in the new rubber-lined army bag, where they would be protected from the elements.

I again tried to find the Black Cat, passing prep work for the 3rd Chinese Urban Games, to be played in Nánjīng the following week, a coup for the city. Signs for the games were up in front of one of the many, new five star hotels sprouting across the city, one that might well have buried the Black Cat months ago. I ducked into another jiāozi shop just in time as a rush of hungry locals enveloped the place. Here they fried up meat jiāozi by the hundreds, scooping out ten delicious dumplings per order. I had four orders and I was happy.

MANDARIN LANGUAGE PRONUNCIATION
Lesson 5:

The accents I heard in Nánjīng not only dropped the "H" from Mandarin words as they did further south but also the "O" off of the end of words. These differences may have something to do with Nánjīng being close to southern China and also within the region around Shanghai and its Wu language dialect, Shanghainese. Maybe? I really don't know, I can only describe what I heard and what worked when I said it.

Examples:

- "Duō shāo qián?" (Dwoh sha-ow chi-en?), an abbreviation for "How much do you want to spend?", became "Du sa jian?" (Doozuh jen).

- "Wō yào chá." (Woah ya-ow cha?), meaning "I want tea.", became something like "Weh ya za?" (Way'za?). I think? I still don't know.

DAY 41

Saturday, October 14

Nánjīng, Jiāngsū Province, Shànghǎi

•

I overslept. Again. One of the smart things I'd done before coming to China was to buy a wristwatch with an alarm, the $40 Armitron that Suan, my self-appointed guide in Guìlín, asked me about. It was a great watch, but the alarm had stopped working. The hourly chime still worked perfectly, somehow, but the alarm defied all testing. It was as if a little gremlin was following me around, refusing to let any one piece of technology I brought with me work correctly.

And it was raining.

Time was tight. If I wanted to catch the 8:30 express, I had to get going. I caught a moto-taxi and, after a tour through town and a perilous crossing of the causeway that snaked across Xuánwǔ Lake, which through the dense fog might as well have been an ocean, I arrived at the train station with enough time to buy a platform ticket at the information window.

Which is what I would have done if they hadn't just renovated the information window as well as the entire foreigners' ticket office right out of the station. I would still get to pay the tourist price, only now I would have to wait in what could only generously be called a "line" and choose between Soft-class or Hard Seat. The Soft-class ticket office still existed, way off on the right, but I found that they had neither tickets nor clues. When I asked where I could buy a ticket, they pointed vaguely in the direction of Tibet and I followed it over to the left side of the station where I saw a policeman. He listened politely, nodded, and then pointed right back where I came from.

All I wanted at this point was an information window or booth.

Either would do. Here, my Mandarin definitely failed us both. "Wǒ zhǎo chá hào tái tíng", is what I think I told him. It does not translate to "I am looking for the information booth", even though that is what the individual words mean. The correct wording is, "Wǒ zài zhǎo fúwù tái" (something like, "Woe sigh jow fu-woo tie"). A phrasebook beats a dictionary every time. I repeated the wrong phrase and, not understanding me, he again pointed behind me. I pressed him for details and he became flustered. "Over there, there, that way," he mumbled, his finger flailing around like a puppy dog's tail.

A good natured passenger saw the display and, I assume wishing to prevent injury to someone's eye, asked where I wanted to go. I told him. He pointed in the exact opposite direction as the policeman. I wasn't taking any more chances, so I took him by the hand and asked him to show me. This, of course, was a chance itself, in that grabbing somebody's hand like that is extremely rude in just about any culture. I'd been grabbed more than enough in China myself and I hated it. I, of course, wasn't trying to sell him anything, but I still shouldn't have done it. Luckily, he took mercy on me and, once he freed his hand, he walked me over.

It turned out that the information window – "xìnxī chuāngkǒu" ("shin-she chwang-koh") – not booth, was exactly where he had pointed: across the main hall, through a door, and all the way on the far side of the smaller next building over, inside some makeshift, slipshod room only a few seemed to know about. Twenty minutes after I reached the station, it only took me thirty seconds to buy a ticket for a train that left when I was still going around in circles with the policeman.

Now that I wouldn't be able to get into Shànghǎi until the middle of the afternoon at the earliest, I called my first choice of hotels to reserve a room. "Sorry," they told me. "We don't accept foreigners anymore, except Overseas Chinese." They would, however, gladly recommend some $50-a-night hotels for me. So much for Plan A. My second choice, only because it was far from the airport and the ticket office, was the Pujiang Hotel, just across Sūzhōu Creek from the northern edge of the Bund. Today, it is once again a fancy and expensive hotel bearing the irony-rich, colonial era name, The Astor

House Hotel, but back in 1995 it was still an inexpensive hostel with dorm beds and large lockers for every guest. They said that they'd try to keep a bed available, but who knew?

Some very kind people, including a Chinese-born Frenchman and a man who had lived in Canada, helped me get on board the next express train and find a seat. We had some interesting trilingual conversations while we were waiting. The train was one of the brand new, European-style double-deckers; no Hard Seats in sight, Soft Seat only. The car was tattooed with a million ads. Ones for Coca-Cola were on the head-rests, the seats, the doors, and the windows. There were also ads for a canned thing, either lychee nuts or some kind of mollusk, with an American flag as its background. I couldn't tell if the Chinese were importing them from the United States or just using the flag to sell them. I made the mistake of drinking some absolutely lousy train coffee, but made up for it by impressing myself with my acquired language skills. I was sitting next to a nice, young couple who were traveling with their toddler. I applied what I had learned in Nánjīng and picked up parts of the couple's conversation and everything from their toddler, although that was mostly "Bù yà!" (Don't want!), the most toddler thing a toddler could say.

It was a pleasant ride in. The countryside west of Shànghǎi, soon to be consumed by Shànghǎi's expansion, was beautiful. Chinese farmers were burning the waste of their harvests, dotting the fields with thousands of small fires, and leaving, for us on the train at least, the sight of black, circular stains in the fields and lingering smoke the rain failed to stop.

We arrived in Shànghǎi at a quarter to three. I had told the woman at the Pujiang reception desk "between 2 o'clock and 3 o'clock" over the phone. I was certain I'd be late, but there wasn't any sense worrying about it, not then. They'd hold it or they wouldn't. I found a moto-taxi outside the station, one of the ones with a back-facing seat and no canopy. Anything that had to stay dry was safe in the rubber-lined Bag, so I didn't mind. I really just wanted to get there fast. Of course, being a moto-taxi, so did he, and we were off through the rain. He started so fast I nearly fell off the back. Fifteen wind-blown, rain-soaked minutes later, my new best friend parked me outside the Pujiang Hotel. No problem. They had saved a bed for me way up on the top floor. I would get used to the climb. I dumped my stuff in the sizable dorm locker that went with it and bolted back out into the rain to catch a bus out to the Shanghai Centre, the massive home to both the luxurious Shangri-La Hotel and the shopping complex that included the United Airlines ticket office, celebrating its fifth anniversary that very day.

I made my way across the bridge over Sūzhōu Creek and down the Bund, a promenade built in the late 19th century for Europeans and Americans staying in the elegant hotels and working in the banks and trading houses that lined the colonial concessions. The buildings, mostly designed in that period's Beaux Arts style, are beautiful, which may explain why they survived the Cultural Revolution when so many others didn't. I didn't intend to stop, but I did anyway, to watch a rain-soaked percussion troupe perform in bright yellow costumes. Not once did they lose sync, even in that heavy rain.

Having nothing in my pockets to pick – it was all in pouches under my clothes – I took the #71 bus out to where the guidebook said the Shanghai…oh, yeah, that's right, it was completely unreliable. I think I was just using it out of habit at this point. I stepped into one of the local four-star hotels to ask for directions. A few people later, the concierge pointed off somewhere behind me, just like the Soft Sleeper clerk and policeman had in Nánjīng. I don't know where he was pointing. Mostly, it was just out the door. He then handed me a tourist map and packed me into a taxi.

And here's why moto-taxis were so much better than regular taxis. This guy drove me around in circles, trying, in vain, to milk the meter over a short distance, and then he tried to keep the sizable change when I paid the fare. The poor doorman at the Shanghai Centre stood waiting in the rain, holding the door open while I made the driver give back the rest of my money, though he'd only do it piecemeal, ¥10 at a time. I never did get all of what he owed me back, but I did get the receipt, which showed he was fudging the numbers to get a bigger portion of the tip, the rest of which I guess went to his bosses. I know they usually dealt with careless businesspeople's expense accounts and therefore got away with this all the time, business as usual, but I wasn't paying with other people's money. Well, United Airlines didn't treat anybody like that[22]. They confirmed my ticket changes, and the surcharge I paid ended up being less than the original estimate. That squared away, I went back out into the downpour and headed back up the road the taxi bringing me from the south had come down, only to realize I was, in fact, walking *north,* because taxis. I turned around and went back down past the Shanghai Centre, where I came across a row of storefront "currency exchanges". They looked official, like something you might see at an airport, but based on the convenient-to-the-Shanghai Centre rates they were offering, the only thing they seemed to want to swap was whose pocket your currency was in.

As tempted as I was to walk all the way back to the Bund through the rain – soaked straight through to the skin, I was actually starting to enjoy it – I was certain I'd get lost, so I found a Bund-bound bus.

And then, much to my disappointment, I got off the bus to get something to eat. We'd been passing hole-in-the-wall restaurants filled with locals and it seemed like a perfect opportunity to try Shanghainese cuisine. I'd heard stories everywhere I went in China about how good it was – "The best in China!", they swore – but what I had this first night was awful. Awful. This wasn't one of the overpriced tourist traps near the Bund, either, it was a jiāozi stall with fluorescent lights and a menu written on the wall, as reputable a sign of quality as I'd seen everywhere else I'd been. Eating jiāozi was a thread I had sewn throughout my journey and, with the obvious exception of the "yāzi" misadventure back in Xīníng, it had been one of the consistent joys I'd had regardless of other troubles. In this first taste of Shànghǎi, though, they were just about inedible. At this seemingly for-locals restaurant, they made them with par-boiled celery, which made them taste like bad tuna salad. Wretched.

Maybe I just didn't understand? Maybe I'd just had the bad luck to pick the one jiāozi stall in all of Shànghǎi where they did this? Or maybe this was just a very, very, very local delicacy? Mercifully, I never came across it again.

---

[22] Again, this was 1995, I can't speak to anything you might experience now.

I wandered back out into the rain and used my best regional accent to buy myself a flavorless ice cream cone, you know, more like iced milk. It lasted, with my left hand protecting it from the rain, the rest of the way back to the Bund.

The beauty of the Bund in the misty rain, especially at night with the lights playing off the colonial architecture, cannot be overestimated. It was breathtaking, even with oblivious legions of Chinese tourists snapping away in front of the huge FujiFilm ad. I took my time walking back up to the Pujiang. I couldn't get any more wet, that was certain, and I didn't know when I'd get another chance to see these buildings this way. The new buildings across the Huángpǔ River in the Pudong New Area development zone were lit up, too. The Oriental Pearl TV Tower, then as now, dominated everything

DAY 41: *Nánjīng, Jiāngsū Province, Shànghǎi*

else on the far side. A poster advertised some guy named "Big Jim", who was hosting another one of his "world famous Booze Croozes". It seemed I'd missed it. I wasn't sorry.

When I finished my ice cream and the roll of film, I finally made my way back across Sūzhōu Creek to the hostel. It was then that I discovered the one drawback to staying in that room on the top floor: the hotel's neon sign was right outside our windows. We had access to the roof, though, which offered views of the Bund, and the Pudong New Area.

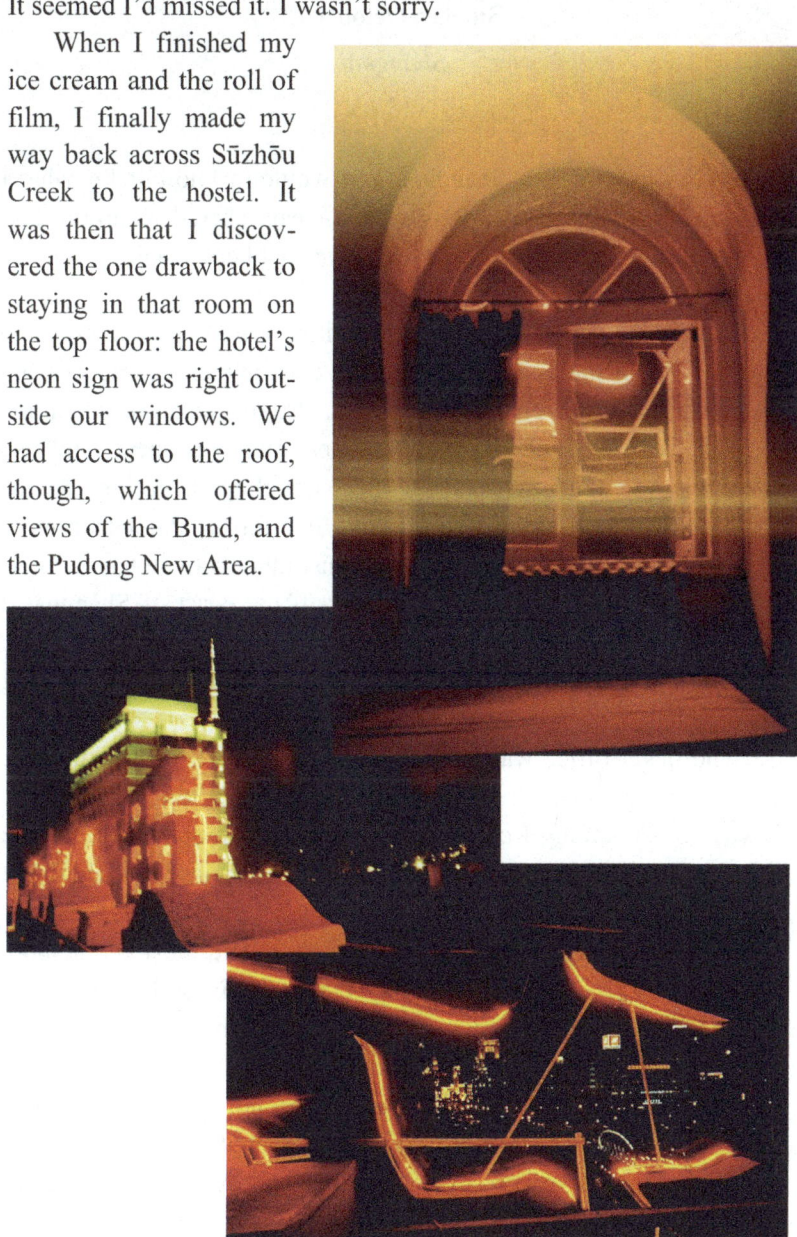

DAY 42

Sunday, October 15

Shànghǎi

•

Six weeks in, I was in Shànghǎi. You wouldn't know it for what I was spending. My dorm room, with a clean, shared bathroom and private locker, was one of those lucky breaks I kept tripping over.

The other breaks, however…

It was Sunday and the rain had disappeared. I took my time strolling down the Bund's promenade, enjoying the warm sun and watching everyone else do the same. There were some foreign tourists, like me but maybe with a lot more money to spend, and also some Chinese tourists, many of them traveling in groups. At the south end of the Bund was the ticket office for the Pǔtuóshān ferry. Pǔtuó-shān, one of the four holy Buddhist mountains in China, is on an island in the Zhōushān archipelago off the coast of Shànghǎi. I had learned enough from previous ticketing failures not to wait, so while I took enough time to enjoy the sun, I didn't waste any getting down to business.

The ticket office was open and the staff was friendly, but there was one problem which would not go away until I left Shànghǎi and it was not something I could justifiably complain about: the man in ticket window only spoke Shanghainese. This being Shànghǎi, that shouldn't have come as a shock or a surprise, even in 1995. Shanghainese is a dialect of the Wu language group and most people born and raised in Shànghǎi naturally learned it as their mother tongue, or at least they did before widespread tourism and migration from poor, Mandarin-speaking, alternate-accented regions to the eastern cities became a thing. He tried, I tried, but nothing, not Mandarin – Běijīng or Nánjīng accented – or English or even the writing and pantomime that had done me so well before, got through. After ten minutes of starts and stops and shrugs and apologies on both our parts, another English speaking man came over to help. Unfortunately, all he managed to do was clog my ballpoint pen writing on his palm. When I asked him for the ferry, he replied, "Ohhh, the ferry!", and said what I imagine was the word in Shanghainese to the ticket seller. Then, like some rehearsed comedy routine, they both pointed straight up. "Upstairs," the man said.

Upstairs, I was helped by a native of Pǔtuóshān. He said the ferry, a hydrofoil like the one I took upriver to Wúzhōu my third day, actually left every night at 9 PM, not every two days at 3 PM as the wildly inaccurate guidebook claimed, and that tickets could be bought one or two days in advance, but not, for whatever bizarre reason, day of. So, once again, I found myself reworking my itinerary. Hángzhōu, once first among these destinations, would now be last. Rearranged, I would now spend three more days in Shànghǎi, then four on Pǔtuó-shān, followed by four in Hángzhōu before returning to Shànghǎi to fly home. I'd have to skip Sūzhōu and its famous canals – looking back, a clear mistake – but as I figured this out I wasn't sure I could afford to go there and still do everything else. Whatever the plan was, I'd have to come back tomorrow to buy the ticket to Pǔtuóshān if I wanted to do it at all.

I spent the hours through lunchtime wandering towards the west side of town, stopping for a delicious bowl of celery-free wonton soup with a group of old men who flagged me in. This had to be the Shanghainese cuisine everyone had been so high on. The broth was rich, the wontons small and savory, with green and white vegetables, it was one of the best meals I'd had since my first day.

Moments like this are what traveling should be, for guests and hosts and food. My hosts and I didn't talk much because they, too, spoke little but Shanghainese, but they were kind and generous and I'd like to think I'd always do the same for anyone visiting my hometown. I don't generally sit in front of my building with a big pot of soup, but that's probably on me.

With Shànghǎi's food reputation restored, I headed back towards the center of town and somehow stumbled across the Shanghai Antique and Curio Store. It's still there, and if you go to Shànghǎi, make sure you make time for it. In its three showrooms, it has a collection of Chinese art better than most museums. They had genuinely antique scrolls of paintings and calligraphy, painted fans, sculptures, carved wooden furniture, silk clothing, and more, and all of it was priced for museum-sized budgets. I took my time taking it in. I wanted to give myself as much time as possible just in case I couldn't find it again.

Further out and farther north, I then stopped in the Shaanxi St. Antique Store, where I met Mike, a student from Boston, who was buying an expensive, old clock. I saw a pair of large baskets, the kind that need a pole to carry, one basket over each shoulder. They were missing their brass fittings and needed some restoring, so I appraised them as best I could and went to work. I might have succeeded, but I never stood a chance. From Mike's expensive purchase, to the shopkeeper's "friend" who appeared to occupy her while I stewed, to her obviously long experience in dealing with accommodating well-funded foreigners, all hope was lost. She wouldn't settle for less than $85, and at one point tried to sneak a higher price back into the bidding. I couldn't complain, not really. Even as I haggled, I understood there was no way I could actually consider buying them. They were nice baskets, but where could I even put them back home? They were huge. And even paying just $50 or $60, I'd still have to ship them, which would have tripled the cost at the very least. She said I wasn't poor, which was true, but I would have been if I had thrown my money around like that.

Circling back by way of Nánjīng Lù, which was and remains Shànghǎi's main retail shopping street, I made it back to the Bund by nightfall. I bought myself a chocolate ice cream cone from a teenage girl working in a stall about halfway up the promenade. The fragile cone crumbled in my hand before I even had a chance to taste it, leaving a chocolate blob on the pristine sidewalk. I stepped back to the window, but the girl was more interested in her own lipgloss than helping, and even told me as much in her own, sweet and charming way. She handed me replacement ice cream in a paper wrapper without a cone, told me to get lost, and turned her back on me.

Do I believe that someone in the past had scarred this girl the same way that horrible, young ticket seller in Luòyáng must have been? No. This was just another petulant teenager with a crappy food service job she doesn't even want, the same as they are the world over.

I took my handful of ice cream and liked it, and I didn't look back.

DAY 43

Monday, October 16

Shànghǎi

•

I marched down the Bund this morning to get my ticket for Pǔtuóshān. The Bund was clean. From the arcades to the Greco-Roman bodies with Chinese faces in the reliefs that lined the strip, the Bund was clean. If anything could serve as a final sign that communism was over, it was the Bund, not that it was clean but how the statues and monuments once built to celebrate the birth of the Communist state now served as its gravestones, mere tourist attractions like everything else around them, historical backgrounds for tourist snapshots. The colonial era banks and hotels that once represented the evils of capitalism and enslavement by colonizers once again seemed to represent the ultimate Western virtues of individual wealth and conspicuous luxury. At night, the well-lighted, old buildings represented status in the new Shànghǎi as much as and maybe more than any of the shiny new towers rising across the river. Away from them, so as not to ruin the view, there were so many different advertisements on the Bund from foreign, capitalist economies, especially ones from Japan and the United States, that a person couldn't spit without hitting one. Of course, doing so would likely be against the law now in hyper-capitalist Shànghǎi, just as it is in Singapore, then one of its main investors and role models.

Back at the Shànghǎi to Pǔtuóshān ticket window, another English speaking attendant helpfully translated between me and the same Shanghainese ticket seller who had been down at the main window yesterday. I wasn't yet sure how much time I wanted to spend in Shànghǎi, but yesterday I had decided on three more days, so I bought a second class ferry ticket for the 18th. There was so much to see and do here, right? Well, maybe if I had known the city better or had a better guide book, but I did not.

From the ferry building, I made my way down to the Yùyuán (Yù Garden) Bazaar, a shopping district dressed up to look more "Chinese" than China, like a pre-fab Chinatown in an American or European city. There, I hoped I might be able to find those elusive antiques and quality souvenirs at reasonable prices, but no, it was just the same junk tourists, most of whom appeared to be Chinese. It was a fact that in the larger cities the genuine buys were all centralized, thus ensuring a captive, higher-priced market for anything of actual value. Liúlíchǎng market in Běijīng was an excellent example. You might think cramming everyone into the same zone would force competition and lower prices, the way it used to be in New York with its lighting district, its cooking supply district, and its famous fashion and flower districts, but no. In these captive marketplaces, everyone just raised their prices, the way it now is with airlines, supermarkets, and coffee chains: one raises prices, the others watch to see if they get away with it, and then the rest all raise their prices, too. In Shànghǎi, I would have to go to the "official tourism zones" to find what I wanted, and then either not be able to afford it or give in and pay through the nose.

To escape the punishing crowds – I lost count of the number of people who turnstiled me and my backpack out their way – I retreated to the Rénmín Gōngyuán (People's Park) in the then-center of town. Despite half of it being a concrete slab, likely meant for rallies in the old, actually communist days, this was a very relaxing spot, seemingly far away from the madness that filled the streets outside. It offered a chance to sit back and breathe, or at least think and reflect. I reflected, watched some people playing cards and chess, looked at the map, and decided that I'd better get back to that ticket office as quickly as I could to trade my ferry ticket for one leaving tomorrow. For someone like me, with neither business in Shànghǎi nor a permanent home nor a lot of money to spend, the city actually had little to offer. At this time, at least, there were no museums or historical sites of note, and little nightlife beyond the Chinese opera and acrobats, either of which would push my travelling budget and wardrobe for a single performance, and hunting for better, celery-free jiāozi. Five days here was simply going to be too many.

Rushing back to the ticket office, I still managed a detour to where the other, guidebook-listed antique store in Shànghǎi no longer was and then to the No.1 Department Store, located among the newly built, glass façades on Nánjīng Lù. I found nothing I wanted, so I zig-zagged back to the ferry office in time to exchange my second class ticket for a cheaper, more-crowded, third class ticket on tomorrow night's ferry, for only a two dollar surcharge on top of the third class price.

Having managed one fewer day here, I strolled back to the hotel to pick up my laundry. I expected a big bill, given that the 5th floor attendant appeared to be scamming the hotel on the receipt, which she tried to hide from me, but the price was nice and cheap, just ¥34.10, half of which, about $2, went into her pocket. Relieved and wearing clean clothes, I went back out for dinner and, in some little corner shop I almost missed, I found perfect, carved wooden boxes for my brother and sister-in-law's jadeite chopsticks, which I had been carrying wrapped in paper since I bought them all the way back in Yángshuò. I didn't try too hard to bargain, because they were exactly what I wanted and they were cheap enough already.

Out on the Bund, the night could turn ugly if you weren't careful. Vendors, beggars, and wandering "money changers" were everywhere, all of them trawling for rich tourists and blocking the entrances to buildings and the sidewalk in front of you. To say that they swarmed like gnats may seem too much, but there they were, swarming. It ended up looking and feeling a bit like the "guesthouse" hawkers when I first landed in Hong Kong. I don't know how many times I politely said, "No", as I wove my way through them back to the hostel, but I guess they'd heard the word enough in dozens of languages to see it coming. Most didn't even wait for me to finish, they just stepped back out of my way and moved on to their next target.

DAY 44

Tuesday, October 17

Shànghǎi

•

I got out early and had some breakfast. It's how a normal day should start, and, for better and worse, this would be a normal day for me in China. I left the full gray pack at the hostel, checked in their luggage room and waiting for me to retrieve for tonight's boat to Pǔtuóshān. Leaving Shànghǎi early had changed my plans for my parents as well as me, so I called to let them know I'd be out of touch while I was on the island. Pǔtuóshān was popular and must have had international phones, but I had no idea if there'd be one I could use.

Another $12 in phone charges later and I was on my way across town to the Jade Buddha Temple. Apparently, the buddha wasn't really jade. That should have hinted at what else I'd find there, but like so many lessons here, it was one I'd only learn through experience. The souvenir shop inside actually did have the best selection of scrolls and collectibles I'd seen outside of the Curio Store, which in a consolidated market such as Shànghǎi explained the high prices for things such as a two-foot-wide, hand-painted, watercolor goldfish scroll: ¥3,800 here, compared to ¥2,000 elsewhere and everywhere. I browsed anyway, treating it more like a museum even though it had few actual antiques, none of which seemed close in quality or age to what the Curio Store had.

Not expecting to find anything, of course, I did. I found a great scroll for my parents, one with every variation of hànzì for "Longevity", as in longevity in life, happiness, love, fortune, etc. It was a beautiful piece, about the width and length of the scroll I mailed home, with a brown silk border. It was priced much higher than the goldfish, but low enough that I hoped I could get it down just a bit more, maybe even in the range I'd paid for the others.

Ah, but this was a temple, and they tell you no bargaining in temples. That would be disrespectful. Well, these people weren't monks, not even fake ones dressed in robes like on Éméishān. This was a business with official government credentials, which meant that line was nonsense. In a side room seemingly designed to keep bargaining safely away from the ears of other potential customers, the vendor fed me that exact "no bargaining" line, right before he dropped the price by 1/6th. At this point, I wavered, entirely a tactical move, part of the haggling pantomime we both surely knew. What he offered was actually close to my price, just a few dollars off, so I figured a little time considering his offer might wear him down. The price, as it was, was at the top of my range, good enough really, so I wasn't worried. I excused myself to "think about it", stepped out into the main showroom, browsed for a minute, and then wandered back in for what I expected to be the traditional final round of bargaining.

Nope.

At this point, it was the vendor who stepped out, stepping back in with an English speaker and another very tall, very large man. And here it was: a simple, reasonably pleasant transaction had now become an awkward "Good Cop-Bad Cop" routine.

Even as I tried to speak to the English-speaking Good Cop, Bad Cop THUNDERED, "BÙ!!" (NO!), and pointed at the price the vendor had written on the sheet. I stopped. Three of them, one of me. I was either going to stop and defend my dignity, or cow under and let them bully me. Well, "Bù" to that.

I didn't miss a beat. I turned to Good Cop and told him, very calmly and very politely in both English and what Mandarin I knew, that I was now not going to buy anything, and that by bullying me they had not only lost money but had also lost face. As Chinese in a Buddhist temple, they should know enough to conduct business in a respectful manner. Instead, they had cost themselves a sale.

And then I turned to leave.

Good Cop, seeing his cut slipping out the door, quickly made after me and gave me a tour of the main showroom, kissing my ass the whole way like the pro he was. By the time we'd circled back to the side room, Bad Cop was predictably gone, leaving just the three of us to see if I would ever, ever change my mind. I don't think any of them took what I said as anything more than another tactic, and I guess using face like I had can be. It can be a tactic for getting people to show respect, but also one for gaining leverage. In the moment, I had meant the former, but I have no doubt they only saw the latter. To them, making the sale was all that mattered, and I had spoken their language.

Seeing this for what it was, I knew I would only be left with this ugly experience if I didn't buy the painting. I couldn't teach someone who wouldn't learn, and I wouldn't lower myself the way I had before, so I bought it at their last offer and got out. All I have to say is, don't ever go to the Jade Buddha Temple. Don't reward ignorance and disrespect. I know that it's been thirty years as I write this, and I may have bought something myself, but if you haven't gone and I can save you from having to learn one thing from a brutal experience, let it be through writing this far too belated review.

Angry, I retreated to a local restaurant for a bowl of soup and some tea. The local spots in Shànghǎi were, as they were everywhere in China, warm and welcoming places to pass time. Even the place with the awful celery dumplings had been pleasant. I sat and stewed there until I was calm again, said my farewells to the kind people inside, and was off to Lǔ Xùn Park.

My moto-taxi driver, like all the others I'd have today, took a straight route on a map and turned it into a tour of Shànghǎi. He clearly wasn't trying to get more money out of me – it was a flat price – he was just lost. I saw everything I can think of, from bike shops to more bike shops to houses being prepared to be torn down to houses that should have been long ago and somehow still hadn't.

When I finally arrived at the park, I was happy to find myself in the middle of the Minorities Culture Festival, with dance and music performances by ethnic minority troupes from across the country. Little children on their fathers' shoulders mimicked the dancers' movements, many of them pretending to be one girl who was pretending to be a peacock. Thousands of miles between their homes had been reduced to this dialogue between a performer and her audience. It was an unqualified success, and not just because they pulled it off.

Around the enormous park people were playing chess, dancing on their own, or taking rides around the lake in boats shaped like UFOs. At one of the shacks dotting the park, all dedicated to one tribe or another, I was beckoned inside, behind a long line of Chinese and Europeans, with the call of "Lǎowài! Qǐng, lǎowài!" The phrase literally means, "old outsider", "old" being a formalization like using the plural "you" with a stranger in European languages. In theory, it's just a way of saying, "Hey, person I don't know, can I have your attention?"; in practice, it comes across as something closer to "Hey, foreign idiot!", even with the word "Qǐng" (please) thrown in. I think the ones who wanted to take a picture with me meant the former. I think.

Another couple of hours in the park and I was ready to head back to the hostel. I was walking and had just picked up a snack of egg rolls when, after smacking a few people by accident with the Longevity scroll box sticking out of my pack, I again bumped into Mike from Boston, walking his bike. Mike from Boston was actually born in Westchester, north of New York City. He was in China studying Mandarin. He told me that these shiny, new buildings all around us and those scamming little taxis buzzing all around the streets had all only just appeared in the past two years. Cheated by a taxi? You couldn't find one to cheat you back in 1993. Now, of course, you couldn't avoid them[23]. He led me down to the Friendship Store on Nánjīng Lù, which was apparently had been little bigger than a shack just two years before, then rode off.

It was just about 7 o'clock and getting dark now. I retrieved my heavy bag and began my trek down the Bund to the ferry terminal. I got to the gate about 7:20 only to hear that the ferry to Pǔtuóshān had already left.

Of course, it had.

It was only now that I looked at my ticket. Yes, I know, I admit

---

[23] The characters "Ta" and "Xi" on Chinese TaXis can be translated to mean "Smoking Tower", literally "Tower" & "Smokes".

DAY 44: *Shànghǎi*

it, I hadn't bothered until this point. But why should I have? Had I not been told twice on successive days by two different shipping company translators, in English, that the boats left at 9 PM? 9 PM. Had I not been told, in English, to be there no later than 8 PM? 8 PM. Yes, I damn well had. So, why the hell should I have looked at the goddamn ticket?! Well, this was China in 1995 and despite experience after experience, lesson still not yet learned, it seemed, by them or me.

There was one possibility I could think of, just one. Had I been given a stamped ticket? You see, planned time changes for train tickets would often be stamped on existing tickets to save money. *Planned* changes. This was a ferry, but the same, thrifty stamp usage might also have applied. Fine. I looked at my ticket. No stamp. It was just a ticket for the ferry, stamped "晚上 9 点" (9 PM). So, what was it? What did I do wrong? What did they do wrong? Why the hell hadn't I been at the dock waiting for that boat at 9 o'clock in the goddamn morning?! Had I gotten comfortable and careless again? Had I slipped and not heard them right? No. No, there hadn't been anything to mishear, I had it in writing and I hadn't written it down wrong. It had only been the time of departure, "9 PM". Then why was it wrong? How was it wrong?!

The simple, easy answer I settled on in that moment, desperately needing one as I stared at that ticket and scrap of paper, was that the ticket sellers and translators were idiots and I, in my own idiocy, had just wanted to believe that they weren't. I had made the mistake of wanting to trust someone, of wanting to believe that someone in this country's screwed up transportation system just wouldn't screw up, and in doing that I had only screwed myself. That had to be it. I had gotten too comfortable. Worse, I had gotten careless. I had forgotten "xiǎo xīn". Again.

But, no, I was wrong about that, too. Very wrong.

It turned out that the ticket sellers and translators had seemed so confident in what they were doing, had looked like they had done everything correctly, and had seemed so clear in their answers was because they were, they had, and they had been. It turned out that neither they nor I had made any mistake at all. Someone else had, long before I ever even spoke to them.

The mistake someone else had made was failing to give the people selling the ferry tickets in the ferry ticket office an updated ferry schedule. The one they had in the ticket office, the one with the time they had given me for today, was wrong, and no one had thought to give them a new one, stamped or otherwise. No one. The only ones who knew the current schedule were the the ones piloting the boat and the ones taking the tickets down at the dock, which was where I realized just how broken their transportation system was and why. And it was there, in the actual words of one of the ticket takers, that I make my case:

"The people in the ticket office have nothing to do with us."

Think about that. He thought it was funny. He meant it as a defense, of course, of himself and, frighteningly, of systemic failure. "[They] have nothing to do with us." Those words in any culture translate to one thing: *It happens all the time, and we don't care.*

I felt stupid. I had wanted to believe so hard that it could be different here in this "modern", "Westernized" city. Maybe I had been lulled by it feeling so modern and Western, so familiar? If so, I had taking the wrong lessons from my experiences, colored no doubt by my own prejudices born of traveling back home. My experience at the United Airlines office had been so smooth[24]. They were so organized, so efficient[25]. It had been so easy[26]. But no, not here, not in this transportation system, not yet. Some people communicated quite well. Some people believed things could work. They were the ones up in the ferry ticket offices, and all of their hard work had been undone by a couple of stooges down at the docks and whatever idiot decided that their own ticket offices didn't need to know their own schedule.

What then, did I do? Now knowing the actual departure time, or so I believed, would I spend another day in Shànghǎi and take the next boat? Hell, no. I went back upstairs, got my money back, and

---

[24] OK, seriously, this was 1995.
[25] It was such a different time.
[26] I urge you to accept that all airlines seemed so much better at customer service back then.

DAY 44: Shànghǎi 219

took a long, long moto-taxi ride almost to the train station. This, I have to say, was the one truly bad moto-taxi experience I had in China. Along the way, the driver took us down the wrong side of a median to a dead end, and then tried to pull the entire moto-taxi over the median. I pointed out the turn-off fifty feet behind us and in no time we were two blocks from the station, where he stopped. He claimed, even as other moto-taxis whizzed past us going to and from the station, that he wasn't allowed to go any further. I suspect he really meant he didn't have a permit for his rig or even a license to drive it. It was a growing city with growing tourism, and people like him were flooding into Shànghǎi and other eastern cities everyday.

Between his excuses and that side-show over at the ferry terminal, I was plenty mad now and prepared to argue my case as long as it took. After ten minutes of firm, lawyerly persuasion – I had no Bad Cop to back me up – he conceded the fare and I heaved my two, heavy bags over my shoulders to walk the two, very long blocks to the train station. I walked the two blocks, and then I walked one more when the Soft-class waiting room attendant told me I'd have to buy my ticket over at the Longmen Hotel across the street. By the time I'd dragged myself and all that weight over to the hotel's ticket office, it was literally closing time. A few minutes after 9 o'clock, when I should have been leaving on the ferry to Pǔtuóshān, I squeezed back out the office door with a ticket to Hángzhōu on the 2:55 AM train, Soft Seat.

My plans had changed, again. I would now have to go back to the original, time-wasting schedule I thought I'd gotten rid of a few days ago. Just another normal day in China, October, 1995.

DAY 45

Wednesday, October 18

Shànghǎi, Zhèjiāng Province, Hángzhōu

•

They woke me several times, each time a different station steward making his rounds. They all wanted to know if I really had a ticket and what time it was for. I have to say, it was something new. At least, it felt that way. They certainly wouldn't have done that out in China's old west. When the last guy woke me at 2:30 AM, my train was in. The "Soft Seat" car looked like it belonged out west, filth and all. I could see why this one ran while most people were asleep. We left ten minutes early and pulled into Hángzhōu ten minutes late.

Outside the station in Hángzhōu, I hopped a pedi-cab in the direction of the Huanhu Hotel. Like my driver out to the station in Shànghǎi, he also stopped shy of our destination, pulling up in front of a newly opened Kentucky Fried Chicken franchise, but he at least offered a decent excuse: he didn't know where the hotel was. He didn't want to admit this, of course. It took five long minutes asking and re-asking, trying to rephrase the question every way I could think in case I was asking it wrong, before the growing crowd of curious locals and I all learned that not only did he not know where the hotel was, he didn't even know which street he was on. He did admit it, though.

Out I went onto the street with my bags and I started to walk. Suddenly, the pedi-cab driver built up the courage to ask a policeman across the intersection and, having the answer, dragged his pedi-cab up to where I stood, waiting to cross the same street. He begged me to get back on. I appreciated his effort, as well as that he overcame his obvious fear of the policeman, so I did, and he peddled us about fifty feet across the intersection to the Huanhu.

The rates at the Huanhu had changed drastically from the ones quoted in the guidebook. In just two years, the rate for a single room had risen from ¥86 a night to ¥420 (about $11 to $52). It was an okay hotel, but not nearly that okay.

Out the door and back across the street, to the left of the KFC, was the Xihu Hotel. It was definitely a step down from the Huanhu. None of the rooms had their own baths. As for the rates, a Chinese tourist could have a single room for only ¥60. Although I was traveling alone, as a foreigner I was only allowed to rent a double for ¥144, still a clear bargain compared to the Huanhu. The rate included a 50% surcharge for no one sleeping in the extra bed. Oddly, had two foreigners stayed in the same room together, the rate would only have been ¥96. It made sense to somebody.

I dropped my bags on my extra bed then waited back in the hall for about forty-five minutes for the attendant to clean the room. Only then could I reenter and sit. A few minutes rested, I made my way down to the front desk to see if I could make a phone call. They told me it would ¥28 per minute, the same as in Shànghǎi, but they couldn't get the phone to work. I went over to the Huanhu, but they didn't even have the courage to try. So, no call.

I walked down to the south side of Xī Hú (the West Lake, namesake for my hotel) to find a bike to rent, but I couldn't find one, so I came back up the east side of the lake into town and stopped in a bank to change money for what I hoped would be the last time. While I was at it, I traded my now useless Hong Kong currency to a Chinese man who I think was saving up for a vacation.

Kuai in hand, I spent what was left of the afternoon hunting for gifts to take home. Way up the street from the hotel was a small day market. It looked more like a flea market or yard sale than anything else, tables covered with old, used things people hoped somebody else might want, all of it priced to move. And like most flea markets and yard sales, little of it would. After browsing for a while, I found a very old, very used, lidded porcelain bowl. Its blue, hand-painted, Míng-style decorations included the Xǐ (Double Happiness) design, the symbol of matrimony, making it a perfect wedding gift for my oldest brother and sister-in-law. However, it was also filthy and had a chipped crown.

My first thought was to look for some new, clean version of it, maybe at the Friendship Store in Shànghǎi. If I was lucky, I might find one in a store here. So I left, but as I walked I began to think about Jacki Eyman's advice about paying for value and not letting rare things go. I was pretty anxious to get that design, and no matter what the condition was it would be a great gift because of how I found it and brought it from so far away. The farther I walked towards the north end of town,  the more attractive its age and that chip made it feel. It had been given and used before. It had been part of people's lives. Chipped, it also seemed closer to the China I had experienced. And, perhaps most important considering Jacki's advice on paying for value, it was actually pretty cheap. I trekked all the way back, coughed up a couple of extra bucks because the vendor knew I really wanted it, and it was mine.

Of all the gifts I bought in China, it would be the one I was most proud of, even beyond the scrolls, which were more special than I knew. It would also, naturally, be the one I feared breaking most. It had survived decades and at least one marriage before it got to me with only a few, small chips, but I spent the rest of the day terrified of bumping or dropping my Chinese army backpack. I needn't have worried. It was strong. I think the only regret I'll have about it was washing off the dirt. If only there had been a way to preserve it. It lost a bit of its history and character without that dirt. It still looked great, but somehow less like itself.

DAY 46

Thursday, October 19

Hángzhōu

•

The open, public shower at the Xihu hotel was yet another experience I hadn't anticipated. There were four of us, each minding his own business, not so much avoiding each other as ignoring each other. It was functional. And cold.

Clean, I went for another try at calling home. This time was the same as the last: they couldn't get hold of an operator. They did, however, recommend a place to rent a bike.

Up the street, at the Hángzhōu Overseas Chinese Hotel, I went through the whole routine of trial and seat adjusting before I hearing the price. They wanted ¥4.5 per hour, which doesn't seem like much now, but it was more than I had paid for entire days everywhere else for better bikes. Still, I had to get over to Hángzhōu's Shangri-La Hotel, the promised land of International Direct-Dial on the other side of the lake. I approached the three pedi-cabs by the corner and asked them, one by one, what it would cost for a ride to the other side. "30 Yuan," the first one told me. "30 Yuan," the second one told me. "35 Yuan," the third one told me. Some joke.

So, once again, I walked, and I'm glad I did. I quickly found the causeway over the lake that led to the Shangri-La. The path across the water looked and felt like a boardwalk at the seashore, and the views were breathtaking. The causeway also led me to the Provincial Museum, said to be housed in the former buildings of the Míng emperors' vacation home. I could see why an emperor, or anyone, would want a vacation home here, but I couldn't see anything about the buildings that looked even remotely that old.

The museum contained some good, informative exhibits, including one about the mostly forgotten Recovery Party, which was a small group of militant intellectuals who tried to incite rebellion in 1907, four years before Dr. Sun Yat-Sen succeeded. Most of them were killed in an attempt to assassinate a general of the imperial army. As usual, though, the exhibits I had come to see, including a whale skeleton, were all closed. From Kūnmíng to Běijīng to Nánjīng to here, every museum display of a skeleton, be it dinosaur or whale or whatever, had been under renovation. One trip to the American Museum of Natural History should tell you why if my suggestion hasn't already: the opening of China to the rest of the world had revealed just how out of date and possibly incorrect their museum exhibits had all been. Still, the rest of the museum was worth it.

At the Shangri-La Hotel, on the northwest shore of the lake, I was able to call home with my phonecard for the first time since staying at Jacki & Jack's. With my scheduling contortions straightened out, I walked all the way out to the Temple of Inspired Seclusion, which was possibly the most inaccurately named place on this planet. If anything, going to it inspired seclusion. It was easily more crowded than the Forbidden City had been on a national holiday, and almost all of it was tour groups. This was one of the big sights for Chinese tourists and had been given the full treatment, including a new theme park with plaster replicas of every other tourist site in China, rows and rows of booths with tacky souvenirs, and even more tacky souvenir hawkers roaming and tugging on everyone's sleeves.

That, though, was not the main attraction. The reason so many tour groups and hawkers broke the inspired seclusion was the Golden Buddha, a twenty foot tall statue of Siddartha with royal blue hair sitting in the lotus position and backed by a wall of saints, buddhas, bodhisattvas, warriors, and everyone else, almost all of them surfing on the backs of various animals. The golden statues lining the walls weren't bad, either. Take away everything that had been added for the sake of tourism, and this would be worth a visit all by itself.

I'd been walking for five straight hours at this point, so I sat down to take a break. No sooner had I settled than I became a tourist attraction, too. Fans of "Dà Bízi" seemed to be everywhere. Some hung out across from me, staring. Others snuck up next to me and posed for pictures as if I was one of the statues dotting the grounds outside the temple. A few of them even asked my permission. A smattering of giggles later, I took the bus back to the area around the Shangri-La. I had thought of stopping in one of the parks, but the lingering clouds now burst into a downpour. I ducked into a snack shop and watched as already soaked bikers paid for cheap, yellow parkas even as the rain was stopping.

When it had, I headed back around the lake and promptly made a fortunate wrong turn. I stumbled across an antique store where they were completely honest about the age and price of everything. I couldn't afford anything there, but I learned a lot about what was genuine and what was not. It mirrored much of what Keith Culvert told me in Běijīng, covering patina and foxing and markings, hand painted and stamped. I decided to put that education to good use and headed back where I thought the day market was. And then I got lost, again. I passed through some other shops, all asking unreasonable prices, before finding myself in a tea shop where I received my second valuable free lesson of the day.

The shop specialized in Lóngjǐng tea, the local varietal considered by many to be the "Premier Cru" of Chinese green teas. After some false starts, I learned that leaves picked before the Qīngmíng Festival, taking place some time between late February and early April, are at the peak of flavor, and those picked later are considered overripe, having an inferior, "burnt" aroma. I also learned that only leaves picked directly west of the lake, in a region of hills similar to a wine region, could be named "Xī Hú". The rest were named after the province, Zhèjiāng. The best Xī Hú went for between 10 and 20 cents per gram, though around tourist centers and Friendship Stores the prices were obviously much higher. The prices in this shop would end up being on the high end for Hángzhōu, but the shopkeepers had taught me a lot about their product, so I'm glad I bought mine there.

I was very lost by now and continued all the way down to the south end of town before stopping and doubling back. I cut over to what amounted to Hángzhōu's "Main Street". Just past 5 o'clock, after nine hours of walking, I finally stumbled across where the day market had been; only the grid painted on the street for the tables remained. The market was only only a couple of blocks from my hotel, so I could come back in the morning if I wanted.

At the jiāozi bar facing the market, I was happy to see that I could read the hànzì menu, mostly variations on chicken. By this point, I'd better have been able to. As I ate, I noticed vendors setting up a night market out on the grid in the street. In an hour, it was packed again, with vendors and people looking for bargains. Unlike the household bric-a-brac sold during the day, at night there were tiger paws, monkey skulls, and other sorts of art-carved animal parts, along with a broad assortment of terracotta teapots, most of them brand new.

In San Francisco, they sold these teapots in high-end stores. Some designs were true works of art, elegant, perfectly balanced, and seemingly weightless. Others were gaudy, touristy junk, with painted tree-trunks, fruit, blue clamshells, and "bamboo" weaves. All were priced between $125 and $225. In Shànghǎi, the same designs sold for only $50 each, and they were still a rip-off at that price. The ratio of elegant and balanced to touristy junk was decidedly in favor of the junk. They wouldn't fetch 50 cents, let alone dollars, at an actual yard sale. The locals didn't even use them, they used plain ones, nothing fancy, nothing extravagant.

I browsed among those and then found a modern yīn-yáng design on one of the impressive and balanced tables. The yīn-yáng motif had been worked into the relationship between the pot and the handle, as well as the flat handle for the lid. The saleswoman asked less than $5. I countered with $2 and change. Deal. Done. And it came with a protective cardboard box.

DAY 47

Friday, October 20
Hángzhōu

•

I didn't want to leave Hángzhōu. I'd like to have spent time by the lake, a day or two, just sitting, just sitting and relaxing. I'd earned it. However, I had things to do and, once again, other places to be. I'd finally found a use for all of my unused cold weather clothes: wrapping fragile souvenirs, all of them now in the core of my big, gray bag. I checked out and stored the big bag in the Xihu Hotel's storeroom. They didn't like doing that sort of thing, so they gave me until 5 PM to retrieve it. I'd still have to work something out since I'd be taking a 2 AM train, but it gave me about nine hours to shop.

I ate the breakfast course at the jiāozi bar from last night – you go where you know the food is good – and then hit the day market to test my new antiques knowledge. Sadly, I think I'd already bought the only "antique" thing worth buying, the lidded wedding bowl, so I wandered around checking for tea using that new education. I found that, like good antiques, good tea was hard to find. By the end of it all, I found myself way up at the north end of town, at the local boat and bus terminal. Accepting my failure, I decided to return to the lake, where I could at least get some sitting done.

About an hour into my walk, I realized that I'd made yet another wrong turn, all the way over to the west side of the lake. I'd started out on the east side, so that was some wrong turn. I turned left and quickly, or not so quickly, found myself back at the northwest corner of the lake, down the street from the Shangri-La Hotel and approaching those parks I'd wanted to visit before yesterday's rain.

The first one was full of school-kids on field-trips to see the "senic spot" [sic]. Little kids, big kids, teenagers, it was a place for children of all ages, which, surprising for what I had seen in China, had no cheesy rides, just greenery, quiet pavilions, and the lake. I was happy that they kept – or was it left? – the spot so "senic".

As I sat by the lake, some teenagers snuck over and did the Dà Bízi-tourist attraction thing. They weren't intrusive like the tour groups had been at the temple, so I didn't mind. I really would have stayed there longer, but the clock – or was it meter? – was running out on my pack. On my way back east, I bought some porcelain chopsticks with blue, Míng-style applied decals for my brother, John. I didn't even bargain for them, especially after all the trouble the shopkeepers went through, practically turning the shop over just so I could leave with the best, matching pair. They even gave me a box for them, albeit from a balsa wood fan.

I double-timed it back over to the Xihu and begged for more time to keep my big pack in their storeroom. The uncommonly-kind streak continued, and I now had until 8 PM. I dined once again at the jiāozi bar and waited for the night market to set up shop. Tonight, I was coming back for the plain, classically designed, terracotta teapots.

I started out buying a ceramic, soup-size bowl for John that I thought would be nice for his new place, wherever that would be. I had bargained for another bowl first, mostly just to warm up. Both bowls started high, but I held to my price and the hams selling the bowl I bought settled low, thinking they'd suckered me on a bowl with a chipped rim. The rim really was chipped, but I was buying it for the hànzì somebody had carved inside of it, something they also apparently considered a defect. We probably would, too, if the words had been scratched in English. They told me not to worry about it, or the chipped rim – "Méi guānxi, méi guānxi,", the older one said (It doesn't matter, it doesn't matter) – to which I replied, "Nǐ zhème shuō, dàn wǒ shì mǎi tā de rén." (You say that, but I'm the person buying it.) This was all stock dialogue for the bargaining process. Like the wedding bowl, I liked this bowl because it had a history. The damage told a story. Sometimes, it was better that the sellers didn't appreciate that.

I spent the rest of my time lapping the tables up and down the block, looking for unusual or refined teapots. I'd found a small pot

DAY 47: *Hángzhōu*

earlier, swept back, with a brass-horn-like mouth, but it was a little lopsided. I might have bought it if the guy hadn't been such a macho jerk about bargaining. I saw it all the time. It was men, for the most part, bargaining as though their manhood was at stake. They'd rather lose the sale than look weak. Not too bright; these weren't things anyone needed. At least this guy didn't employ an angry giant, like at the Jade Buddha Temple. The women, for the most part, seemed to ask, "Is this the best price I'm going to get?", and didn't mess with pride or face unless you really pushed their buttons or their man-child husbands were around. More than once, including with the bowl I bought tonight, I saw the wife "zetz" her stubborn husband, something my Mom loved to do to my Dad, a poke that translated to, "Quit being an idiot!". In this case, it meant, "Quit being an idiot! Take the money!"

The terracotta pot I ended up buying hours later was a very normal, very plain, beautifully refined design. It would nicely offset the yīn-yáng pot I bought last night. I paid ¥30 for this one, after spending almost half an hour trying to bargain down below ¥20 with the same vendor for another pot. Why pay ¥10 more? It was her own pot, the one she was still drinking tea from. It was her idea. She saw me admiring it and made an offer, which I accepted without bargaining. It had the clean, simple lines I was looking for and, crucially, was the only one of its design I'd seen. Oh, and it had a history, something I think she did appreciate.

It was already past 8 o'clock, so I ran back to the hotel's storeroom, grabbed the big, gray pack, and pedi-cabbed it over to the train station. The lines were long and few, so I thought I'd try my chances with a platform-ticket. The woman in the information booth sent me outside and around the corner, where the young woman in the ticket window, despite holding a stack of platform tickets, sent me back inside again. The woman in the info booth wanted to go on break, so I had to hold the plexiglass window open and repeat the situation over and over until she gave up trying to send me back, came around to my side, and took me over to the ticket window herself. She took my ¥1, gave me a platform ticket, and then chewed the young woman out while I made my way back to the waiting area.

The Soft-class waiting rooms, all but empty, took up almost the entire main building of the very small train station. I couldn't get inside Soft-class with only a platform ticket, so I staked out a claim in the Hard-class waiting area outside and napped until about 1:30 AM, careful as always to use my bags as pillows, protecting them with the weight of my body. At 1:30, I wandered around the corner and found the small, indoor Hard-class waiting room, oddly not as clean as the one outside but with an electronic departure board. There, some Chinese teenagers doted on me and made sure I got on the train.

In the long line of jockeying passengers, which for all its activity didn't move, I met Greg, a Swede, who had been working most of the past year in Shànghǎi and was only now starting his travels around the country. He said that after almost a year in Shànghǎi he hadn't learned much Mandarin or Shanghainese because he hadn't had to. I was legitimately stunned, but I guess I shouldn't have been, not with China's growing, international, capitalist financial services sector. He'd only been able to buy a standing ticket, so I figured I'd avoid the inevitable sea of people and try for something in Soft Seat, which was almost empty. No, no upgrade. It must have been where the conductors and stewards slept. One of the kids found me a seat in one of the rear cars, but Greg, unfortunately, had to sit on his bag near the toilet.

DAY 48

Saturday, October 21
Hángzhōu, Zhèjiāng Province, Shànghǎi

•

We left a little after 2. It would only be three hours or so and then I'd have a bed. Some others couldn't wait that long and bedded-out on the floor. To keep them company were cockroaches; one of them, big and red, was the size of a mouse. No joke, it was three or four inches long.

When we pulled into Shànghǎi just after 5 in the morning, it was still dark. The conductor who had waved me onto the train didn't seem to care too much about making me buy a ticket, so I went through the tug-and-puzzle routine again and passed through the platform exit home free. There was a kind of justice in it; this would be my last train ride in China.

I bid Greg goodbye and good luck then lugged myself and my heavy bags over to the highway, where I learned the buses wouldn't start running until 6. It wasn't too long before a moto-taxi found me and offered to take me back to the Pujiang Hotel for a reasonable fare.

Along the roadside, old people were stretching on guardrails before beginning their early morning exercises. When we arrived at a quarter to 6, the entrance to the Pujiang was still locked. Vendors sat out front sorting through the day's newspapers, while more old people were practicing their tài jí and fencing in the street. I sat and watched for a while, until a cabbie pointed out that the side door of the hostel was open. I thanked him, went inside, and got myself a bed way up on the sixth floor. The elevator wasn't on yet, so I climbed the stairs all the way up. In my stupor, I'd gotten the room number wrong, but I finally found it, placed my bags in my locker as softly as I could, found my bed, and gratefully fell asleep.

I woke around 10 and made my way down to the ferry terminal to buy a third class ticket to Pǔtuóshān for tomorrow night. The ticket again said "9 PM", but I knew the actual schedule now, I hoped, so I would be getting to the wharf closer to 5. Maybe 3. If I actually did anything tomorrow other than go to the ferry terminal, I'd be pressing my luck.

From there, I went back to the Friendship Store. They had terracotta teapots there that might have held three of four times as much tea as the ones I'd bought. They were being sold for $2000. Yes, this was a larger teapot, but $2000?! This was a teapot no Chinese person would ever want to use. Out on the street, down past the "President Hotpot Seafood Restaurant" and onto Nánjīng Lù, I saw a version of the yīn-yáng teapot I had bought for $2, same size, same design, being sold for $45. $45, and it wasn't even well made! The symbols were off-center and the handle was lop-sided, but it was conveniently located and next to pots that cost $2000, so $45 had to seem like a bargain to the right tourist.

At the "Guo Hua Chinaware Store", I bought some black, lacquer chopsticks. They were extra cheap and looked it. I only bought one pair, but I could always go back to the Friendship Store and get some nicer but much more expensive ones if I wanted.

Between lunch and dinner I napped and then read Russell Watson's interview with Chinese Premier Jiāng Zémín in Newsweek's October 22nd issue: "Storm Warnings: Jiang Makes It Clear That His Summit with Clinton Won't Go Smoothly". This was the interview in which Jiang described the Communist Party's power – and by extension, his own – using the words "Mandate of Heaven", the term first used by emperor Qín Shǐ huáng to describe his divinely blessed hold on power and the lives he controlled. I think Newsweek dropped the ball in not pursuing his choice of words and analyzing them. It was good work in getting the interview, but without the analysis it just read like a puff piece: "Please, Premier Jiang, tell us your perfect Sunday."

I followed dinner at Mickey D's – I promise, it was because it fit my budget – by strolling back along Nánjīng Lù and people watching with a cone of mint ice cream. That was all I ate here, all anyone seemed to be eating here in Shànghǎi: junk food. The unisex fashion statement among teens in Shànghǎi at the time? Dyed-red hair, a bit like the Jello-dyes kids were playing with back in the States. There were also a lot of men growing out the few facial hairs they had, especially mole-hairs, as long as they could. I guess that went along with extra long finger nails as a pre-Communist tradition of some sort. All in all, it felt like a walk through any city's downtown.

When I made it back to the Pujiang, I cleaned myself up, sorted my clothes by what I expected to wear and what would best protect all of the pottery I now had, repacked again, and slept.

That is, I slept until some loud men, Turks, I think, came in around midnight. It should have been hard to sleep after that, but it's amazing what you can get used to.

DAY 49

Sunday, October 22

Shànghǎi

•

I'd spent my last Saturday in China. My last Sunday would mark my seventh week completed on this journey. What better place to spend a bright, warm Sunday than at the zoo? Now, the Shanghai Zoo as located on the map wasn't so easy to get to. I started out taking the #71 bus, which didn't go to the zoo but got you going in the right direction. On the bus was an old, blind man playing the harmonica. He wasn't all that bad and he wasn't playing that "Zou-zou zou-zou, yippie-kai-yay" song, but he did manage "Seasons in the Sun", somehow, so I gave him all of my loose Fen, both paper and coins. At this point, better to be rid of them.

I took the bus as far as it would go and then, under a shady span of the new superhighway, I found a moto-taxi to take me the rest of the way. The farmland that once circled the city limits was giving way to luxury hotels and apartment blocks for businesspeople who preferred to stay closer to Hongqiao International Airport. Soon enough, Hongqiao would be replaced and downgraded to a domestic airport and no one would remember these farms ever existed. We avoided the late-morning traffic jam that filled out Hóngqiáo Dàjiē by driving along the sidewalk, and arrived at the zoo gate around 10:30.

Never could I have imagined what I had come to see. Sadly, it was something that I had to have seen to understand this rapidly vanishing version of China. The Forbidden City, Moon Hill, and the Great Wall are timeless representations of China, but the trains out west, the blocked off museums under reconsideration, the new construction consuming farmland and replacing hútòngs, and then places like this zoo, these were the China of 1995: China caught in transition between past and future, between a culture of shared poverty and, starting in the east, one of aspirational comfort and conspicuous consumption.

The Shanghai Zoo was not a zoo, but one part zoo, one part amusement park, and one part garbage dump. Inside, people lined up to roller skate, ride the ferris wheel, and have their pictures taken with cardboard cutouts of Marilyn Monroe, then-American President Bill Clinton playing the saxophone, romance novel cover model Fabio, and others. At the front entrance, they also had their pictures taken next to some decaying, stuffed monkeys dangling from a makeshift tree branch – very popular – and a statue of a brave soldier protecting his horse[27]. A few feet from the statue, in letters three feet tall, was a sign that announced, or pleaded, "ANIMALS ARE OUR FRIENDS".

Given what I saw inside, no one understood. Visitors would crowd around cages and pens to pelt poor, helpless animals with fruit, bread, and garbage. One guy beaned a hippo on the head with an empty Sprite can. The animals tried to hide, they tried to sleep, they tried to do anything in cages not much cleaner than Hard Seat rather than deal with these wretched people. The tiger, fierce and savage beast in the wild, appeared traumatized; it awkwardly paced back and forth in a concrete cage not much bigger than it was, never stopping. Those animals that dared approach the savage creatures watching them were teased with offers of food that were either drawn away or launched at them. The panda, alone in its cage like most of the species here and one of the few species protected by glass, simply lay on its back, asleep or pretending to. I could sympathize, I'd been there myself.

And there was litter. Everywhere. The orangutan made less mess. In fact, it didn't make any mess at all. It tore open the plastic

---

[27] A common, derogatory joke among Chinese was that the Cantonese will eat just about anything. There was some truth to this in that Cantonese cuisine includes a number of options northerners might scoff at, but it also revealed a prejudice among northerners about southerners, something common in just about every country on the globe. They would joke that the soldier wasn't protecting the horse in battle but from hungry Cantonese.

bags of food thrown at it, ate the contents, filled the bags with water from the moat separating it from the visitors, washed the food down with a swig, and then neatly laid each empty bag down on its bag pile, all of this while a crowd of people ooked and awked and threw him more food to put on his show. The path they threw the bags from was strewn with more them, empty, like the bags the orangutan was so careful to stack, and discarded. Of course, this was his home, so it only made sense he would want to keep it clean. The littering herds of gawkers were only passing through.

 The center of the park was notable for its amphitheater and lake. The billboards above the amphitheater gate showed bears on motorcycles and other carnival sideshow attractions no one here would ever see. As for the lake, they had recently drained off the top layer of water to reveal hills of swampy muck and silt from shore to shore. It didn't look like they had any plan for it, but it's hard to imagine anything I saw here remains now. Like China's modern trains, stations, and museums, the Shanghai Zoo of today is probably state of the art, for the animals as well as the people passing through.

 Only an hour after I arrived, I was on another bus headed back to the city. This bus ran as far as Nánjīng Lù, just past Changde Lù. I stopped for some lousy Chinese fast food, bought my night's supplies for Pǔtuóshān, and found myself again back on the Bund around 3 in the afternoon, already thinking about getting my bags down to the ferry terminal.

 As I sat on a bench looking out at the Oriental Pearl TV Tower, an old man and his wife engaged me – really, commandeered me – to speak some English. He had arrived in Shànghǎi thirty-eight years before as a university graduate, his assignment given to him by the Party. He'd learned Shanghainese, his wife's native language, and now, with joint-ventures everywhere, he wanted to work on his English, which was already very good. He did lack some common idioms, so I taught him a few. As our conversation turned to the Chinese's "lack of manners" – his words – the man sitting next to me on the other side, oblivious to our conversation, ashed his cigarette on my right foot. I couldn't say if that was timeless or not.

SIGNS COMMUNISM WAS OVER
Part 4:

#13: PLAYBOY designer sportswear outlets

#14: JEANS WEST clothing stores

#15: Hat stores now sold baseball caps bearing the logos for DISNEY and WARNER BROTHERS, as well as Major League Baseball, National Football League, National Basketball Association, and National Hockey League teams.

#16: Children pictured on toothbrush packaging not only had white teeth but blue eyes and blond hair.

#17: "AMERICAN PISTACIOS!" [sic], were sold in packages with the image of an American flag.

#18: Big American Cadillacs roamed the streets of Běijīng and Shànghǎi.

#19: Car Alarms. Who said there was no such thing as private property in "communist" China? Can there be theft in a world without it?

DAY 50

Sunday, October 22 – Monday, October 23
Shànghăi, Pŭtuóshān

•

At 5 PM, I again made the long trek with my bags from the Pujiang Hotel down the Bund to the docks. The boat? Still there. So, I sat as the crowds grew until 8:45, when we all finally piled onto the boat. 9 PM, it turned out, was the actual departure time. This time. My ticket was good for a three-person cabin. The other two persons, a not all that considerate, hormonal teenage couple, crashed in just after 9. And then, as you might have guessed, we left late, but only by half an hour or so. The kids eventually let me sleep and woke me up for good at 7 in the morning. We docked at Pŭtuóshān about fifteen minutes later. It was about ten hours for the trip, two hours fewer than advertised. I didn't trust the ferry company to pull that off again, so I'd still be leaving on Wednesday.

After I paid my ¥20 fee to enter the holy village, I was harassed by someone from the Sanshengtang Hotel, one of the two "official" hotels for lăowài. Following me with an "I've got you" grin, he apparently thought he had some kind of claim on me and would not leave me alone, repeatedly stopping me, shoving brochures in my face, grabbing me by the arm. Twice, I pushed the brochures away from my face, but he kept pushing them back. The last time he did, I was asking an Englishman advice on where to stay when he brought the brochures right up in between us and again grabbed my arm. Normally, I would just keep telling the man, "Bù!" and "Bù yào!", as I had been, and walk away, but he was preventing me from walking away and literally wouldn't let me go. I shook him loose, knocking his brochures to the ground, and pushed him away.

It bothers me that I feel that I should have to defend myself for having defended myself, but I understand why. If I was watching myself in that situation, not having seen what led up to it, I would be uncomfortable. I know what led to it, and I still feel uncomfortable. At the same time, I know that I genuinely felt threatened in that moment. I was alone and far from home, and someone repeatedly grabbing you has to have a limit.

Taking the Brit's advice, I hit the village off to the right of the main road. Carrying my heavy bags, I was in pain by the time I reached the first hotel. I had thought of leaving the heavy stuff locked up at the Pujiang or the ferry terminal while on Pǔtuóshān, but I just didn't trust the security, not after all I'd been through and not with my now large collection of souvenirs. "Méi yǒu," said the man at the first hotel, and "Méi yǒu," said the man at the second. They had rooms, just not for me. So, why then were the signs advertising room rates in English? It was for the "Overseas Chinese" who couldn't read hànzì.

Fed up, I continued over to what looked like condos, old and cheap, but condos. It was a beautiful day, not a cloud in the sky, which lent them a Mediterranean look, sort of. Out in front of one of them, I saw some people having breakfast in a café area, so I parked myself at one of the tables. After an unnecessarily drawn-out ordering of tea, I had some cold doughnuts and stewed while I waited.

Just then, a portly Chinese tourist sitting at the table next to me stood and decided to pick up my ceramic-laden L.L. Bean pack to see how heavy it was. He didn't ask, he just did it. And then, having lifted it, he dropped the bag back down about a foot onto the cement patio. I don't believe he meant any harm, but I don't think he considered it, either. Seriously, who does that? I snapped at him for being a disrespectful idiot and he, rightly embarrassed, turned his attention elsewhere. Mercifully, the ceramics, all wrapped in my thickest, softest clothing in the center of the bag, survived.

The woman who ran the tables recognized that I needed a place to stay and pointed to the house next to us. On cue, out popped a woman and I had a room. They asked under $10 for the room, clean with a television, so I took it. Knowing what I'd have to pay elsewhere, it seemed like a huge bargain. I had asked them not to clear my tea while I checked in, but I guess I took so long they thought I wasn't coming back. The table lady showed up with only the worthless guidebook I'd left on the table, the only thing I left I didn't care about keeping. With a rosy smile, she asked $5 for the less than continental breakfast. It was a helluva lot for a helluva little, but I figured what she really wanted was a well-deserved commission on the room, so I gladly paid it.

After some personal time to check on the ceramics and clean myself, I was back out in the sea of Chinese tourists. I got stares everywhere I went. It wasn't so much that I wasn't Chinese, it was that I was the only one wearing shorts. Even in the sun and heat, not a cloud in the sky, they still wore slacks, with some sporting dress jackets, too. It was not the first time semi-formally dressed locals had looked at me like I was a barbarian – the beard and curly hair didn't help – but there were so many of them this time I genuinely felt a little embarrassed myself.

I found the tourist center over a hill and, combined with the stares outside, came to terms with the reality of this island: it was intended almost entirely as a resort for Chinese and Overseas Chinese businessmen and their wives, and it would be packed with tour group after tour group in their semi-formal best everywhere I went.

Leaving the tourist center, I bumped into the Brit again. He introduced himself as Jeremy. He and I briefly exchanged opinions about the island and the mainland before we were joined by Katharine, a Frenchwoman who was traveling with him. A Filipino trading in textiles had bought them lunch yesterday and had invited them out again. Jeremy and Katharine invited me to join them. They were wary of accepting another free meal. They weren't sure what the expectations were on the part of their host. I understood, or thought I did. I was treated to two free meals back in Guǎngdōng, by Taiwanese businessman and guardian angel Frank Lu and then local Zhàoqìng businessman Jack Ho, so I knew the outcome might just be a free meal. On the other hand, my Swiss roommates in Chéngdū had been tricked into paying for an entire, large dinner.

It ended up being the former. The Filipino was waiting at the outdoor restaurant with two Chinese businessmen and invited us to join them. I suspect that sharing meals with foreign travelers in front of prospective business partners was a good way to impress Chinese businessmen of one's wealth and confidence. The Filipino, and probably Frank, too, had used us as props in a bit of business theater. If that had been one of Frank's reasons for inviting me along, I can't complain. I feel like I got the better half of that deal. As in Guǎngdōng, it was a good meal, all seafood and all fresh. The razor clams we had, which Jeremy being English called "razor fish", might have been the exception. They were very small. Jeremy suggested that they weren't mature, perhaps the result of overfishing in the area. After some shots of cheap liquor, the Filipino paid and left with the Chinese men.

The three of us remaining exchanged stories and ideas on China. Katherine had been to China only the year before and said prices everywhere had at least doubled. And the guidebooks? We all agreed, even the newest ones had to be hopelessly out of date. It was unavoidable, normally, but in a country changing as quickly as China was, a book released while we were sitting there would have already been obsolete.

Jeremy and Katharine went to find a beach to wait out the day until Katherine shipped out. Before they left, they warned me about the crowds at the foot of the holy mountain. It was easy to follow one group or another that appeared to be going somewhere and get lost. After several false leads, I found the entrance to the path up the mountain by a temple, where I surprised a monk – a "monk"? – and some tourists by telling them that I actually wanted to walk up. They had all assumed, the "monk" included, that everybody took the minibuses parked at the base most of the way to the top. The exceptions were the actual Buddhist pilgrims who would walk all the way from the dock to the temple at the summit, stopping and kneeling in humility every step along the way and up the mountain. I passed a few of them as I climbed the stone steps. It looked painful as their knees came down, but they prayed, pushed themselves back up, took the next step, and knelt again. I arrived late enough in the day to avoid most of the tourists, but I still had to struggle against a few waves of people heading down. Two of them recognized me from the Shànghǎi ferry terminal and stopped to say, "Hi". I had been there so often, I wondered from which day.

My camera again gave me problems, building my frustrations beyond the customary levels brought on by the rudeness of arm grabbers, price gougers, and bag droppers. This was all eased by a humorous pantomime exchange, as some novices watched me reload my camera. I reached the temple at the summit as planned, just in time for the sunset. The east coast of Zhōushān Island across the water was bathed in hues of yellow, orange, and brown. I took half a roll from the western face of the peak to make sure I got even one frame right.

Descending into night on the eastern side of the island, the colors just a few feet below the peak transformed into shades of purple, green, and black.

At the bottom, a closed snack bar designed to look like a temple, its orange string of bulbs the only source of light.

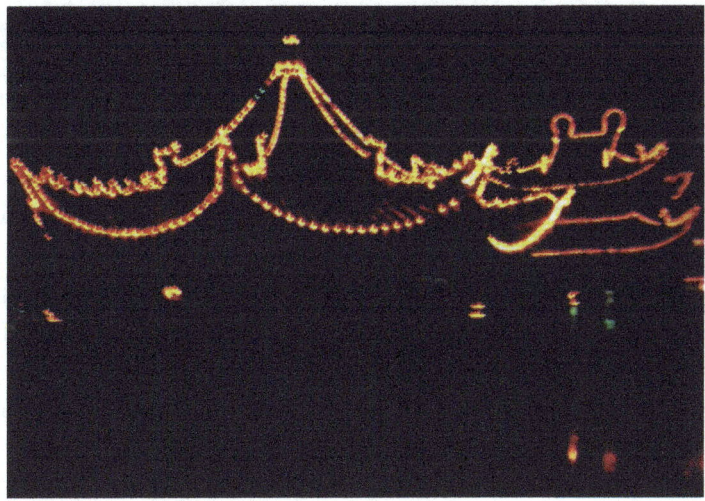

And then, finally, alone in the darkness, I found my way back to my room.

DAY 51

Tuesday, October 24
Pǔtuóshān

•

It was cloudy. This was true, but it wasn't why I decided to leave Pǔtuóshān after just one day. Nor was it the souvenirs, which were all just cheap trinkets, poorly made and overpriced. It was the people. Now, that's not a nice thing to say, but it was as true as the weather and the souvenirs.

To be very clear, I'm not talking about the Chinese and Overseas Chinese tourists, although they never did stop staring. I'm talking about the locals, the people who lived and made their money on Pǔtuóshān, this holy, Buddhist destination. What I had tried to dismiss as just another arrivals gauntlet like in Hong Kong or Xī'ān, I had since learned was something more like I found in Liúlíchǎng market in Běijīng or the Friendship Store in Shànghǎi. On crack. We were in a closed system with limited options and no means of escape until the next ferry, and the people here had taken that as license to squeeze every last Fen out of every person who came off the boat.

Remember yesterday? I thought I'd lucked out on a $10 room, but then it was another $10 for a bowl of rice, and then another $10 for a cup of tea, and then they demanded $10 more for bottled water but gave me a discount to $5 because they "liked me". This had nothing to do with me not being Chinese. The Chinese tourists got it just as bad, if not worse, because most of them were on package tours where the markups could easily be bundled and hidden. Whenever you dread the next interaction with anyone, it's time to go. I passed on breakfast and considered myself lucky to get a ticket for the 5 PM boat.

Repacked for the flight home, or so I thought, I went out to find some more of that tea I almost had yesterday when I arrived. The lesson from this island's price gouging was to insist on being told an exact price before agreeing to buy anything. For just some tea and a pastry, I did this more times than I could count. Each time, the person would pretend not to hear me no matter how many times I repeated the simple question, "Duō shāo qián?" ("How much does it cost?"). They kept trying to get me to sit down, as though that made it a binding contract. If you sat, they seemed to want to believe, it was your choice, you had committed to something, you had submitted to them. They relied on this, on making guests feel powerless.

Yet again, people had managed to turn a holy Buddhist mountain into a place to exploit and abuse people. This, though, was worse than the "monks" at the temple hotels on Éméishān. These people had made every moment adversarial. In the long term, I would like to think that meant a loss of business and a loss of tourism, but in a captive, closed market with religious appeal, that's never the case. Here, we were all meat to them, and with a steady supply coming in and no expectation of seeing any of us ever again, they had no incentive to change. They likely won't ever have to. I held my ground and each time, finally and reluctantly, they told me prices they knew I'd never pay.

Jeremy passed by and told me how he'd just paid through the nose for a breakfast smaller and worse than the one I almost had yesterday when I arrived. Of course, he hadn't asked first. It came as even more of a shock to him because last night he'd gone back to the restaurant where we had lunch with the Filipino and, with the Filipino's good word, he hadn't paid that much. It seemed that was the only way you paid a reasonable price here, if you knew someone who hooked you up. Even more fed up than I was, Jeremy was going down to the dock to wait the whole six hours for the boat rather than spend any more time or money with these people.

I grabbed my bags and paid the landlady, who had lost all of her charm now that I was leaving, and joined Jeremy about noon. It had taken me an hour because I had to find this woman to pay her directly or risk having her send a couple of thugs down to the docks to break my kneecaps.

Jeremy and I spent the next few hours comparing stories, cracking peanuts he'd brought from Shànghǎi, and cracking jokes about each new wave of unsuspecting tourists. Jeremy noted that, between tourism, fishing, and business from the nearby naval base, this "quaint, charming place" must draw in a comparative fortune, and it wasn't even the high season for tourism. I wondered if the people waiting for the ferry yesterday had seen us coming in and laughed at us the same way. They must have.

After 3 o'clock, we ventured over to the waiting room, already packed with people. I napped for an hour, then sat and watched as somebody playing with the light switch convinced almost everyone that the boat was boarding. No doubt eager to leave, they climbed all over each other to get ahead in line. Having seen this show play out in train stations across China, I stayed put with Jeremy on one of the rear benches. They squeezed and squirmed against each other for almost fifteen minutes before an actual ferry employee came in and opened the gates, and then they all squeezed their way down to the dock and the gangplank, nearly squeezing some people right into the water as they did. I was as eager to escape this place as any of them, but I was patient and held back.

At long last, I got to my bunk in a room with eight other people, including two unfit parents and their unbelievably loud and spoiled little girl. Even after her parents exhausted themselves and fell asleep trying to please her, she went on for two more hours keeping the rest of us awake before she, too, finally fell asleep. In all honesty, as eager as I was to leave Pǔtuóshān behind, I would have been grateful to have been kept awake all night, by her or anyone, if that was the price I had to pay.

DAY 52

Wednesday, October 25
Shànghǎi

•

I barely slept on the ferry, though not because of the girl. I had a lot of nervous energy, I think because I knew I would soon be going home.

Beyond that sunset on the mountain peak, my time on Pǔtuóshān – and anyone else's – was a complete waste. I can't speak for pilgrims, but that whole island felt like an insult to everything they believed in. It made me wonder if all of those wrong tickets and delays and institutional stupidity down at the ferry docks had been the universe telling me not to go. Determined fool that I was, I was never going to listen.

We arrived back in Shànghǎi three hours late if you counted the time it was supposed to take, but only one hour late if you counted the advertised time of arrival. Still, it allowed me to watch the sunrise over the construction sites in the Pudong New Area from the ferry lounge. I had my bags and made sure that I was one of the first off the boat. Good thing. A steady stream of Chinese poured by for no less than fifteen minutes before Jeremy finally managed to squeeze out. He and I then made the trek up the Bund past the morning exercisers to the Pujiang.

My packs' combined weight was starting to get to me. With the scrolls, pottery, and other souvenirs added to everything I brought from home, it felt like I was carrying a whole other person. By the time we reached the bridge over Sūzhōu Creek, I was starting to feel like a long distance runner struggling to make it to the finish line. I think I had only overpacked for the trip by maybe a few pounds, and that was the clothes for cold weather I was now using to protect my souvenirs, so I didn't know what I could or should do. I'd be home in a few days, I reasoned, so I resolved to tough it out.

We arrived at 7 o'clock, just as the hostel entrance was being unlocked, and were both dormed in the same room I had my first time through. I had to find a phone to call home, so I cleaned up and headed back out. The Peace Hotel, famous for handling international business travelers, didn't have a phone I could use, so I had to head out once again to the Shangri-La Hotel and its business center.

I took the #71 bus out as far it would go, although this time "as far" wasn't very far at all. The driver decided to take his break starting at midtown and told everyone to get off. The Chinese passengers were just as confused as I was. Fortunately, at the time, the Shangri-La Hotel towered over all of the other buildings in the area, so I quickly made my way over and up to the fourth floor, only to spend ¥20 for a call that didn't even get through. That's business, I guess. They told me I'd have to come back and try again later.

I ducked into a wonton soup bar around the corner for some breakfast and returned to the business center just before 11 to read newspapers and wait it out. That morning's issue of China Daily had little to say, and the latest International Herald Tribune was still forever a week or so behind the times.

Finally, just in time for lunch, my call went through. I very quickly caught up with my parents and John, I settled my travel plans all the way back to my parents' house and then celebrated the call, my upcoming flight, and my impending freedom by gorging myself at the nearest Mickey D's. Yes, this time it was entirely because it was American fast food, which with so few opportunities remaining to eat authentic Chinese food was clearly a silly choice, but in that moment, I didn't care, I was giddy, this was a victory lap, and I think mentally I already had one foot out the door and American fast food was the first step. Maybe the second. It felt good.

I then wandered back through shops I'd seen on previous walks, hoping I'd find something I'd missed the first time through, or maybe something I'd seen and let go. Shaanxi Lu Antique Store still hadn't sold those baskets I no longer wanted. At another, smaller place, I met some very nice storekeepers over a cold 7-Up, and then, across the street south of Rénmín (People's) Square, I came across what I thought might be another good break. Here, though, I was once again very wrong.

It was, literally, a hole-in-the-wall shop, a window where you stood out on the sidewalk and looked in. The old woman had chops (carved stamps) and other small things, a little over-priced but good enough that I thought I could live with it. I'd put off buying the chop long enough. Time was running out, and so was the selection. She had one I liked, a carved oval that fit the fingers nicely and was equally nice to look at and also through. I wanted to bargain, but...

"No! No bargain!!" she shouted, a bit aggressive, but basically the same pantomime from the other shops. I fidgeted, my side of the performance, I thought, but then this "nice, old lady" started to hound me, pressuring me with "Yào bù yào?!"s left and right: "Do you want it or not?!" Left at that, I might have said, "Shì de" (Yes). She pushed it though, and then her husband joined her, and then it got ugly.

I had already decided to buy the chop, so I asked quite innocently if it came with a box, which it should have if it was worth what she was asking.

"Yes," she said.

"With or without a box?" I asked.

"With," she replied. What she actually meant was, "Yes, it comes with a box, but you have to pay extra for the box." And how much extra would I have to pay for that box? Well, quite a lot actually, because the box came with the chop and they wouldn't let me buy the chop without the box, especially now that I had asked about it. It just about doubled the already unreasonable price. The price gougers in

Pǔtuóshān would have been proud.

Right here was where they really started to bully me. When I took too long thinking about it – honestly, it was more sticker shock than performance – the husband reached through the open window and started poking me in the chest. Hard. To him, I was just another walking bag of money, and how dare I not spend what I was told. Every time he poked me in the chest, the less I wanted that damn chop. I loathed it. This wasn't like the scroll I bought for my parents at the Jade Buddha Temple. They'd only tried to intimidate me with a comically bad good cop/bad cop routine. This jackass was physically assaulting me and demanding my money. He wasn't going to get it.

I hated them. In that moment, I truly hated them. And then I remembered Luòyáng and how I had felt that same way, and how I had acted in that moment, and how ashamed I still was. I couldn't do that again. I wouldn't. I walked away.

I needed something I knew, some place I felt safe. In my anger, my thoughts turned to the Shanghai Antique and Curio Store. I could never afford anything there, but that was the appeal: they wouldn't expect me to. When I reached it, there was only one other customer, a Chinese man browsing in the first showroom. It was quiet, the first two showrooms every bit as peaceful as a museum. I needed that.

I crossed the street, my mood lightening as I climbed the stairs to their showroom for scrolls, prints, and fans. There, I was greeted by the wonderful old man who managed the showroom. Just how wonderful? He told me he remembered me from when I visited two weeks earlier. I could imagine being hard to miss in China, but hard to forget was different. We hadn't even spoken. I saw some folios the Store had published of scrolls from the past two hundred years, so I bought one for my brother and sister-in-law and another for myself. He went through every volume they had just make sure I could get the best two.

When I'd paid, he walked with me towards the stairs. There, we passed a glass cabinet displaying some hand-painted fans, each costing hundreds or thousands of dollars. I told him how much I admired them. With this, he launched into an explanation of the symbolism behind them, some things I'd learned back in grade-school and long forgotten, but much of it new. The central fan portrayed green bamboo. Bamboo on a scroll or fan, he told me, stood for good fortune and longevity. Officers would have scrolls and fans painted with this design in hopes of improving their rank and of having a long career.

The bamboo reminded me of the two scrolls I bought in Nánjīng, so I told him about them. I described them as best as I could, one with green and black bamboo like on the fan, and the other with purple and yellow flowers, and how I felt they balanced each other visually. I didn't mention the other two scrolls from the set, they didn't seem important. The flowers, he told me, symbolized prosperity. Not bad, I thought, I'd gotten my brother and sister-in-law scrolls that meant good fortune, longevity, and prosperity; not a bad wedding gift. Then, over in the corner of the cabinet, I spied the exact flowers, almost as if the artist in Nánjīng had used the ones on the fan as a model. "Orchids," he said. "They stand for a bride just as bamboo stands for a groom."

I think I almost fell down.

Only then did I tell him about my brother and sister-in-law. I hadn't known any of this when I first saw the scrolls in Nánjīng, they'd just looked right. They felt right. "There it is," he said. "Of course," he said. I think his smile was almost as big as my own. I was only sorry that I had to go. He invited me to come back any time so he could tell me more. He wished me a safe and happy journey. I couldn't thank him enough. He was such a sweet, warm person. He made my day. I think he may have made my whole trip.

Euphoric, I floated over to the Friendship Store, stopping for a soda on the way and toasting passers-by. At the store, I browsed the instruments some more, the clerk giving me yet another free lesson, telling me about the names of the instruments, about how to play each one, and about the reasoning behind the pricing, much of it, as you'd expect, being materials and craftsmanship. They were still too overpriced to consider buying, but I was glad I had stopped in. On my way out, I bought two sets of lacquered chopsticks, matching pairs, one for my parents and another for my brother and sister-in-law's maids of honor/best women. They, too, were overpriced, but I felt so happy I didn't care.

Exhausted, I passed out back in the dorm, then woke to pack and repack and then repack again as I learned both what the airline weight limitations on luggage were and that I had no idea how heavy all of this stuff really was. The others in the dorm, including an Austrian who thought China was amazingly clean, tried to help me by lifting my bags and guessing. They were all sure I'd be okay and, just as important, no one dropped them when they were done.

DAY 53

Thursday, October 26

Shànghǎi

•

This would be my last full day in China. I wish I could have been more reflective on that as I spent it. I understood its relevance, the sense of something ending, the anticipation of going home after what felt like a year, but I was still too close to it all to understand how I had changed, or if I had. For better and worse, I had gotten comfortable. I understood enough of the language to get around, I'd learned what I thought were the limits of everyday Chinese kindness and cruelty, and my own limits in accepting both. This day, this last full day, would be a lot like my first full day in many ways: I was in it, I was still finding my way, and there were unforeseen dangers, not all of which I would manage to avoid. Whatever happened now, I would have to adjust so I could finally make it home safe, if a little less sound.

Last night, in anticipation of flying home, I removed my three-weeks' beard. Today, I had no game plan. I was going to wander, to take Shànghǎi in one last time and let it lead me where it would. I figured that my best chance at finding the last things I needed would be down at the Yùyuán Bazaar. It opened late, so for the first time in a while I slept in. Well, I slept longer. I was still out by 8 AM. Since I'd repacked my bags for the flight home – I was certain for the last time – I took just the camera. I wound my way through the twisting streets of Olde Shànghǎi that led into fruit and seafood markets, braving the crowds one last time. When I arrived through the Great South Gate (Dà Nán mén), the entrance to Yùyuán, the food shops were the only things open. I took some shots to fill out the film roll, but the camera was still screwing me on the first shot after every layoff of a minute or more. The batteries were fine, or so the camera said. I knew the odds of successful shots were low, but the light was good so I tried.

A few stores opened at 9. I passed time browsing through stores selling cheap clothing, luggage, and souvenirs for tourists while I waited for the music and antique stores to open. At last, one of the music stores opened. They had a snake or lizard skin sānxián, which looks, plays, and sounds a bit like a jangly banjo. It was $10 cheaper than at the Friendship Store but they were sold out. I asked about the display model, but the saleswoman said they didn't sell them. I then asked to see a small pípa, which resembles a slender-backed lute. The reluctant saleswoman sighed and moped her way into the back, returning with something that looked nothing like the display model.

The reality of display models was they looked like pictures on a box showing you what your kit model might look like if built in a perfect world. What you got from the back room was what you might build yourself, if you had no skills or experience whatsoever. This pípa had a bunch of broken frets. The saleswoman suggested they could be fixed with glue and went to get some, which only suggested that this happened all the time. I wasn't buying anything you had to glue together right there in the store. I flagged down the store manager and he stopped her gluing so she could bring out a larger pípa.

Here, once again, is why they did not sell the display models. The one hanging next to the sānxián looked great; the one they brought out looked anything but. He made an effort to convince me that they were the same, just that the wood was a different color. They clearly weren't even the same kind of wood. The display model looked like some kind of maple; the one he was pushing looked and felt like balsa. I wasn't buying it, his pitch or the pípa.

On my way out of Yùyuán, I stepped into the self-proclaimed "largest antique store in China", which naturally didn't have any. I did, however, find some tiny terracotta teacups to go with my tiny terra-

cotta teapots.

The only hitch was the young woman behind the counter, who while very nice had a problem with math. When I added two more cups, bringing the total to six, she got confused and raised the price for each cup over the original price. To her credit, she got another saleswoman to help and I got my cups. Even so, I was very disappointed that these were all I had to show for the walk down.

I decided to take a route back through side-streets I hadn't taken before, hoping I might get lucky one more time, and wouldn't you know it, I did, I caught a break. Not a cheap one, not by far, but for the quality, very much yes. I stumbled across the National Musical Instrument outlet store, just a small shop with guys playing cards in the back room. The instruments were much better than any at Yùyuán or the Friendship Store. The sānxián went for $20 less, but I didn't go for that, especially after the proprietor tore away loose and upturned lizard scales trying to make it look better. My eyes were drawn to a pípa, with better wood and better everything. Even after they added to the price with a padded bag and extra strings, it was more than worth it. One of the men from the back room even tuned it for me and played a song for the audience of shoppers. The tuning certainly wouldn't last the three flights back to Philadelphia, but the song was a nice touch. Yesterday, I had promised John an instrument for a gift, not knowing what that instrument might be, and today I had it.

I returned to the safety of the Pujiang, adding the terracotta teacups and pípa to the locker in my room before heading back down to cash a traveler's cheque, #27, my last one. I had to wait behind a long line of Japanese students to do it, but I didn't mind. With my morning's haul safely tucked away with the rest of my things upstairs, I only had a chop-set to buy and I would be home free. It wasn't even noon yet. I had time to wait in line, time to wander, and time to eat one last, leisurely lunch.

Now, the Chinese didn't have a word for "jaywalking", at least not in 1995. There were no laws for it, either. Streets in Shànghǎi were as crowded as any other city in the world, and as in those other cities it was customary to wait for a bus or car to stop at an intersec-

DAY 53: *Shànghǎi*

tion and cross in the gap behind it. I was headed back up a side street towards Nánjīng Lù when a bus did just that. As it settled to a stop, a middle-aged woman already waiting started to cross behind it. She was followed by a middle-aged man and then me. It seemed safe, because if the bus wasn't moving, certainly the car directly behind it wouldn't, either. I mean, no more than the bus, right?

Wrong. Yet again, and nearly for the last time, I could not have been more wrong.

As the woman passed between the bus and the taxi behind it, the taxi inched closer. I didn't think much of it, cars at lights inch forward all the time and there were about six feet between the bus and the taxi, so the middle-aged man and I kept going.

As best as I can guess even now, the taxi driver hadn't just been inching closer, he'd been marking his territory. That was his space. His. He'd been threatening us and we just hadn't caught on. No sooner had the middle-aged man and I gotten between the two vehicles, the taxi driver took his foot off the break and hit us.

He hit us!

He hit both of us, the middle-aged man and me. My legs were knocked out from under me and I ended up on the car's hood. I looked in the taxi. The man in the passenger seat was just staring at me, his jaw hanging like I'd dropped from the sky. The driver was screaming something at me, I don't know what. He was shaking his fist. The middle-aged man was hopping on his right foot to the far side of the street, holding his left knee as he did.

I looked down and saw that there was now maybe half the space between the taxi and the bus than there had been before. When I pushed myself off the hood into the gap, he did it again.

He hit me again. Again!!

I was back on the hood and the gap between the taxi and the bus was down to about a foot. The middle-aged man, his left hand still on his knee, was already going through the motions of indignation: his right fist was clenched and shaking at the driver, he was shouting and gesturing at where he had been hit, but he was doing so from the safety of the far sidewalk. I have no doubt he was angry, but he still kept his proper, public reserve.

The taxi driver wasn't paying attention to him, though. He was still focused on me. He'd gone from shaking his fist to pointing at me and sticking his chin out as he cocked his head. He was still shouting insults at me, too. I think they were. I can't imagine he had anything else to say. His three slack-jawed passengers weren't saying anything.

I looked over at the middle-aged man, now losing some of his reserve and shaking both his fists at the driver. A small crowd was gathering around him, which probably helped. I slid myself off the side of the car hood this time, onto the street. I didn't want him to hit me a third time. If I had slid down between the taxi and the bus again, I have no doubt he would have. He would have taken it as a challenge. He would have crushed my legs between them and he would have felt good about it. How many has he hit since?

By now, the driver was leaning out his open window, still pointing at me and screaming insults. I didn't say anything. My knees were in a lot of pain, but I could walk. Or at least hobble. I took two painful steps over and hit him. I aimed for his head but only caught most of his arm and maybe the back of his head as he deflected my punch. I didn't try another. As I found out later, I shouldn't even have tried the first. The only way you got a taxi license in 1995 Shànghǎi was if you were a member of a gang. Supposedly, they all had guns in their cars. Certainly, knives.

The crowd had grown, a few helping the middle-aged man, now seated on the sidewalk, and the rest shouting and shaking their fists at the taxi driver. My whole left leg was sore by now, but I made myself walk. I could walk, which was lucky. Of all the luck I'd had in China, good and bad, the luck of being able to walk away from that taxi was possibly the best luck I'd had. I didn't want to be there another second. Some people in the crowd asked if I was okay as I passed. I nodded and muttered thanks, but I didn't want to talk to anyone. I calmed some as I limped away, doing my best to let it go.

And yet, even as I write this, I still have difficulty wrapping my head around it: a man hit me with his car on purpose.

What kind of psycho intentionally hits people with his car?!! Nothing I had experienced in my life, let alone the past two months, could have prepared me for this. Nothing. I had seen gangs at home and outside the train station in Guǎngzhōu, and smartly kept my distance. I had faced off against two sets of muggers in Barcelona and found ways to escape. I had been in a car that spun out across a sidewalk into a parking lot after another car ran a red light and hit me, and walked away. Before this, the biggest threats I had faced here had been a tree root outside of Yángshuò, suspect dumplings in Xīníng, and yesterday's windowfront chest poker. Well, those and my own naive stupidity. No, nothing could have prepared me for this.

Passing the Friendship Store, I spied the Day & Night Friendship Store, a small, bowling lane of a shack offering an assortment of seemingly lower quality trinkets at Friendship Store prices. But there it was. Hobbled and pissed, I had found it, the chop: only 35mm tall, yellow-green jadeite shaped like a karst hill rising out of the rice paddies near Yángshuò, it had a richly dressed woman in red ink and calligraphy in dark green carved into it. I would only later learn how timely and relevant to my entire

journey finding this had been. The calligraphy was a famous poem from the Sòng dynasty by Sū Shì, "Prelude to Water Melody"; about a lone traveler missing his loved ones, it was written and set during the Mid-Autumn Festival [28]:

> How long will the full moon last?
> I raise my wine cup and ask the azure sky,

---

[28] Translation by Qian Jia, based on Tang, Guizhang 唐圭璋 (ed.). Quan Song Ci 全宋詞. Vol 1. Beijing: Zhonghua shu ju, 1965, 279; The Global Medieval Sourcebook

258   AN INCREDIBLY FOOLISH AND DANGEROUS THING TO DO

Which year is it tonight?
I want to ride the wind and return,
yet I fear that in the jade and crystal mansion up there,
so lofty and high, one cannot stand the cold.
I rise and dance with my own pure shadow;
am I still in the world of men?
The moon turns at the vermillion pavilion,
hanging down at the carved window
and shining on sleepless me.
It cannot have pity on men,
yet why does it only become a full moon
when people are apart?
Men grieve, rejoice, separate, and reunite;
the moon dims or brightens, waxes or wanes.
Since antiquity, such things have never been perfect.
We can only hope that all our friends and families
can live long lives,
Looking at the moon together, across a thousand miles.

- Sū Shì, 1076 CE

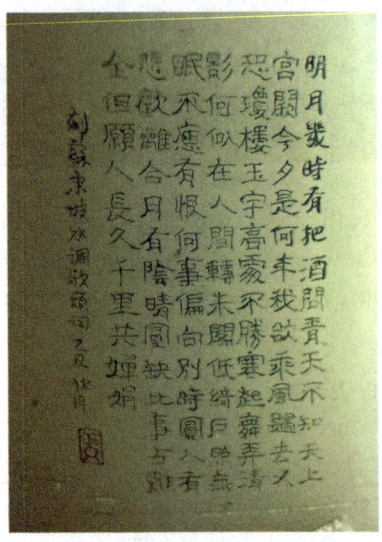

Again, as with the scroll paintings I would give my brother and sister-in-law, this seemed fated somehow. I couldn't read the poem. I had only chosen the chop because of how it looked, because of its shape and color. The carvings were detailed, and on something so small that took considerable skill. After what had just been done to me, the smart thing to do would have been to pay a little more just to have it and get it and myself back to the safety of the Pujiang. Had I known about the poem, I certainly would have, but then the shopkeeper started to lower the price a little too quickly for his own good, from ¥500 down to ¥100 ($12), not a bad price for any day. I was tempted to take it right there, but I offered ¥90, just to see if I could get it lower. With all I'd spent at this point, a dollar or two wasn't much, but, again, I'd just been hit by a car, twice, and I needed a win.

He tried to play out the passive-aggressive machismo routine, putting the chop back in the case and avoiding eye contact as he walked to the other end of the shop. I stood my ground, literally and figuratively, making eye contact whenever possible, a pleasant, hopeful expression on my face masking the pain running up and down my barely mobile left leg. He stood down by the door for a while, paced, stepped outside to spit, paced some more, and checked his merchandise, glancing back only a few times. I was sweating him out, and I had him. He finally came back and took another look at the chop. He took me over to his calculator and typed in a last ditch "100". I cleared it and typed in "90". He gave in. One more, "C'mon, 100," eked out of his mouth when I gave him the ¥100 bill, but I had him, and it was over. I paid twice as much today as I would have paid yesterday at the window shop, but he threw in the silk-covered box for free, as it should be, along with a full inkwell in its own silk box. And, performative passive-aggression aside, he was pleasant. He didn't hit me once, with his finger or a car. That's a low bar, I know, but for today I'd call that a win.

It was 2 PM on my last full day in China. The universe had spoken, and this time I was listening. I was most definitely done.

DAY 54

Thursday, October 26 – Friday, October 27

Shànghǎi, Hongqiao International Airport, Tokyo-Narita Airport, Over the Pacific Ocean, Sacramento Airport

•

My long, last day in China began very much the same as my first: the day before and with me in a lot of pain. It was 3 o'clock in the afternoon. I had limped my way back to the Pujiang to rest my leg and repack one last time. The others in the room with the exception of the bearded Frenchman in bed #1 had planned their evenings and now, while they waited to head to dinner, it was time for war stories. I had already told them about the psychotic taxi driver, so I warned them about Pǔtuóshān and the chest poker across from Rénmín Square. I also told them about the Antique & Curio Store and where to find everything from teapots to telephones in Hangzhou, because we should always make sure to share those things, too.

A young man from San Antonio told us how he'd had his pocket delicately sliced open by the person sitting next to him while he and the other passengers were distracted by a very probably staged fight in the back of their bus. Stealth, subtlety, and planning were the keys, and all, including the local authorities, could be involved. To illustrate this point, Jeremy told us about his friends in Guǎngzhōu, instructed by their bus' ticket taker to sit by the window. They obeyed, the window opened, and out flew one of their bags like so much garbage from a train. It had been a sting from the start.

We all wondered how long it would be before the thieves' ambitions proved deadly. My taxi story hadn't helped. If anything, it was a warning we all needed. We all had neck pouches, but how long before our shirts and even ourselves might be sliced open to get at whatever riches we were hiding, the riches all tourists must be hid-

DAY 54: Shànghǎi, Hongqiao International Airport, Tokyo-Narita Airport, Over the Pacific Ocean, Sacramento Airport

ing? If it was true in other countries, why not here? With all of the money flooding into the rapidly expanding eastern cities and the poor from the south and west flooding in looking for jobs, crime was bound to rise, not because they were poor but because even with all of the new construction there weren't nearly enough jobs to go around and high unemployment always leads to higher crime. It wasn't the kind of thing you wanted to think about while you were here, or anywhere.

By 6 o'clock, they'd all gone out except the Frenchman. I remained and would remain; I still had to repack two or three more times, and I needed to keep weight off my sore left leg. The Frenchman had been in this room for three weeks, including my first stint, but we hadn't really spoken. He was a very interesting man, big, burly, hairy, imposing, and friendly. He gave me his newspaper and lent me his alarm clock for the night to make sure I woke at 5 AM for my flight.

The Austrian and the Dutchman came back at 10 o'clock, having seen something I should have seen but somehow in all my time in Shànghǎi hadn't: the Chinese acrobats. As we had done the other day, the Dutchman and Frenchman took turns picking up my big pack, the best way any of us had to guess the weight; both of them agreed that it was under the limit. Over, under, I had no idea, but then its weight was the only thing I had to judge it by. I knew it had gotten heavier, but that was all I knew.

By midnight, I'd finished my final repack and apologized in advance for waking them all in the morning. I slept light, anxious after everything on this trip not to miss this flight. Up at 3 o'clock, up at 4:47, the Frenchman's alarm made it final at 5 in the morning. I worked fast and was out the door in time to find that no one else in the hotel was awake at 5:20. I found the night manager, who called somebody who called somebody who could return my ¥50 key deposit, also known as cab fare.

Out the side door at 5:40, the first taxi of the day spotted me and pulled over. I held up the fifty. "All I have," I said. It wasn't true, but I was offering the whole thing. He accepted it and helped me put my bags in the trunk. I was on my way.

Back then, Hongqiao Airport was all the way out past the western edge of the city, but it was early, so early that we were just about the only car on Hóngqiáo Dàjiē, the highway out to it. Rush hour to rush hour, the road consisted of a traffic jam, but at this hour the ride out took all of twenty minutes. I arrived just after 6 o'clock, the cabbie landing himself a giant tip out of the ¥50 I'd given him. Nice guy, too, since neither of us had to worry about the money. Maybe that was what Máo had been aiming for all along?

My early arrival placed me five hours ahead of my flight, three before I could enter the check-in area, and one full hour before the airport officially opened. I waited, first in line, paid the then ¥90 foreigners "airport tax", and then waited beside the airline check-in desk watching the lines grow behind me. I used the baggage scales to see how I'd have to adjust my packing before checking-in. The combined weights of my bags came to about 80 lbs. My big, gray L.L.Bean backpack, which I would check onto the plane, came in at 55 lbs, more than anyone at the Pujiang had guessed but under the then-airline limit for American carriers[28]. I'd have placed more inside, but the items I'd stashed in The Bag, which I would be carrying on along with the pípa, were either fragile or necessary for the flight. Anyway, anything more might have burst the seams.

And then, at long last, check-in for my flight opened. It went quickly. I filled out my customs card and passed through security before I knew it.

It only hit me later what a moment that had been. I was really leaving. Of course, it also occurred to me in that same moment that I already had. Airports all look more or less the same. They're meant to. You enter, you go through the same motions, repeating the same steps at the same desks, kiosks, lines, shops, and gates that you find at every other airport. You don't leave a place from an airport, you leave going in. I had already left China hours earlier back on Hóngqiáo Dàjiē, watching the rapidly disappearing fields west of Shànghǎi blurring past in the dawn sun.

---

[28] Yet again, please remember that this was 1995.

DAY 54: *Shànghǎi, Hongqiao International Airport, Tokyo-Narita Airport, Over the Pacific Ocean, Sacramento Airport*

For the short flight to my short layover in Tokyo[29], I had a seat by the emergency exit, leg room and all. Never had I needed it more. I couldn't raise my left leg, much, but it helped. The wait to board the flight to San Francisco was only about an hour, enough to change the time on my watch for the first time since I arrived in China but not much else.

At the gate, I met a Canadian YMCA liaison who'd spent two months in Wuhan before taking a very quick, very far tour of the sights in northern and eastern China. He'd picked up some kind of cane at the Běijīng airport. It had figures either carved or molded down from the wooden, knob head. It was nice, but neither of us could figure out what it was made of. I liked the layover, not necessarily the hassle of it, but how it broke up a long flight. After so many long train rides, the thought of breaking them down into smaller pieces seemed very appealing.

Of course, how could I have known what the layover would really mean? The overhead bins on the second, wide-body plane were much larger than on the short-haul jet we took from Shànghǎi, more than large enough to accommodate my pípa and a few bags. Fine. But here, far from all that was China and every frustration I'd had traveling there, I could only watch as some stupid, American businesswoman heaved up her wheeled carry-on right into the pípa. She just flung it up into the bin like she was practicing the Olympic hammer throw, without a thought to what might be in there already. I had placed the pípa way up on top of another bag in the back of the bin, so anyone sliding their bag in from the front wouldn't have touched it. It released a sickening chord as the suitcase hit it. She didn't look. She didn't think. She didn't care. I can't imagine anyone ever asked her to, before or since.

And here was when the final, hard-learned lesson of my journey really hit me. I had gone to China to see this foreign culture, this post-colonial, post-communist society, this world so different from

---

[29] In Mandarin, called "Dongjing", meaning 'Eastern Capital", with Běijīng being the Northern Capital, Nanking the Southern Capital, and Xī'ān, formerly Xijing, the Western Capital.

my own, and what I'd come back with was the realization that they're exactly the same as us. Take away the advantages and disadvantages, the riches and the poverty, the new technology and the hand-me-downs, and you had the same kind, thoughtful strangers you find all over the world and the same goddamn idiots throwing heavy cases on top of musical instruments because they weren't looking, weren't thinking, and didn't care.

Really, I should have expected it. I should have exercised xiǎo xīn one last time and anticipated someone else's carelessness. I should have held onto the pípa until everyone else was on the plane and found a place for it then. As I'd later see, it had suffered a dent in its lacquer. It didn't look like much, it didn't even feel like much, but for all I'd gone through to get it and how far I'd be taking it to give it to John, it felt like a lot. It was one last reminder to do better myself.

I don't remember much of the flight going back. I know that we crossed the International Date Line, briefly returning us the 26th before turning once again to the 27th, but I'm pretty sure I slept through that. The pilot announced we'd be early, coming in at 9 AM instead of 10. Of course, we would. We were flying west to east, so I knew it would be faster, but after every departure and arrival in China, something about that just felt right.

Of course, that was before the fog in San Francisco and Oakland sent us all the way to Sacramento, where we had to wait in the plane on the tarmac until the fog cleared. You see, while Sacramento has long been the capital of California, for some reason the airport wouldn't have facilities for processing international travelers until 2006. This was especially unfortunate for everyone on the plane who were from Sacramento. For them, after traveling so many hours and having come so far just trying to get home, it must have felt like nothing ever worked at all.

Yes, it really did feel right.

EPILOGUE

The days after my return to San Francisco were something of a blur. I spent a few days with my oldest brother and sister-in-law at their house on Grove St, cleaning myself and my clothes and learning to recognize myself again. I had lost a lot of weight that first month, about 20 lbs from being sick and not eating enough. Despite getting healthy and staying healthy the rest of the way, I hadn't put much back on. Carrying two heavy packs had played a part. The sight of me had come as much of a shock to everyone back home as it had been to the Eymans in Běijīng.

I did manage to lighten my bags a decent amount by giving the newlyweds their many gifts: the jadeite chopsticks from Yángshuò; the long, handmade, steel wok spatula from Xīníng; the lidded, porcelain "double happiness" bowl from Hángzhōu; the bamboo and orchid scroll paintings from Nánjīng; and the art folio from Shànghǎi. They had survived a lot to get there. Sadly, the bamboo painting didn't survive too much longer. It was destroyed a few years later by my brother through a kind of carelessness I had now become all too familiar with.

The scroll for my parents fared much better; it still hangs in their home. The silver hairpins and wooden compass have aged well, too. John happily received his porcelain chopsticks, pípa, and bowl, graciously downplaying any dents or chips he might have seen in the latter two. I stayed with my parents for another month before using the rest of my savings to move to New York, where I still live today.

• • •

It has been thirty years now as I write this. The time has helped me better understand why I went and how the journey changed me. It has also clarified and in some cases softened my opinions on what I did and what was done to me. In that sense, I am still on that same journey, still in China in 1995, still experiencing it, still visiting and revisiting memories and lessons learned just as I continually packed and repacked my bags, never quite coming to a final understanding.

The lessons didn't come all at once. Like the migraines that come from wine and the rage that came from the strain of traveling sick and alone, they took time to come together and only revealed themselves later. Some lessons took years to take root, and only then when I was ready to listen. There would be relapses, where I seemed to forget what I had learned only to have to be reminded, and there would be times watching others that brought lessons I had learned back to me and even improved upon them. Never has it been a straight path.

And I never did become a journalist. The closest I ever came was editing sound on documentaries and writing a blog on decision-making and other behavior in politics: politicaltheatre.net. I applied for entry-level positions in New York for over a year, but, my experience in China and acquired language skills gave me no advantage in finding a job. They all still insisted on a journalism degree. I considered it, going back to school for the only credential they seemed to want, but I had started to wonder if journalism was what I wanted. If I had avoided getting that degree for so long, maybe I needed to listen to what I had been trying to tell myself.

As I understand the industry now, I'm pretty sure I would have hated it. The flaws in the industry were already on public display back then, with the business side increasingly throttling the reporting and analysis that the public badly needed in exchange for continued access, something politicians and business leaders have increasingly exploited at the public's expense. Too often, America's papers and networks of record have come to resemble the credulous propaganda of China Daily and the inoffensive, delayed reprints of the Herald-Tribune, and we can see where that's led us.

Yes, I would have hated it. I would have seen the flaws in that system and insisted on trying to fix them even though I had no power to do so. That seems to be my nature. Among the many things I should have learned about myself by now, that much is inescapable. I would have seen institutional failures and co-workers who seemed to stop trying and I would have repeated the same mistakes I made dealing with the trains out in China's west, complaining about avoiding avoidable mistakes to the point where I rendered myself miserable and just about unemployable, which is itself an avoidable mistake. In fact, this is what I did in the jobs I eventually had, though I managed to maintain a career in one of them, somehow.

So, in the end, I ran away and didn't escape anything. I only postponed it. My year preparing for China and two months there proved incredibly valuable for my life and especially my personal growth, but I still faced the same uncertainty when I returned. All of the questions I had before I left remained, but none of the stories I'd convinced myself were answers seemed plausible anymore. If anything, having set those fantasies aside, my uncertainty had only grown. That was something I'd have to learn to live with it.

For me, maturing has been about trying to find solutions to broken systems in a productive way. Even if I fail, and I have mostly failed, I do so with the understanding that those industries, workplaces, and relationships haven't really been so different from the railways back in China. As trite as it feels to write this, we all fail for the same reasons in the same ways.

I have not returned to China and I don't know if I ever will. I know how much it has changed, especially out west, and I've seen pictures of places completely transformed from my memories. I couldn't say how much the people have changed, but I imagine they've followed the course I saw them starting down in the east, one of aspirational, consumerist comfort and convenience, never asking how or the human cost. So, yes, capitalism, but also communism for the cadres and the life of a mandarin in the imperial court.

Can they ask questions, though? Can they look at what they've done and created, and, seeing the flaws, admit their mistakes? Recognizing those mistakes, can they fix them? I had to ask myself those questions, in China and once I came home, and then again as I wrote this. I asked them about China and I asked them about myself.

Many of the answers I thought I had proved to be just as unreliable as the stories I told myself before I left home and the sometimes laughably inaccurate entries in that thoroughly discredited guidebook. The answers that held and proved true were the ones that described things we all do, the mistakes we all make for the same reasons, but also the kindness most of us show others in need. The truths I found inevitably were the constants we all share. If we have failed the same ways, then it stands to reason that we may succeed in the same ways, too.

One of the truths I have carried forward with me is that to succeed in anything I have had to overcome my own kind of authoritarianism, the one I in my immaturity held over myself. I had allowed it to drive my decision-making to go to China, which ultimately proved good, but I had then allowed it to compel me into situations I hadn't thought through while I was there. It led me towards adaptations in behavior and expectations that maintained my problems rather solving them. It made me afraid to admit my own mistakes until I was so deep into them that I had no choice but to seek help to find a way out. Learning to ask those questions and learning to listen to what I was trying to tell myself in asking them was the key to breaking free of that child I was.

I have come to see that pattern, of shifting my thinking from short term needs and solutions to long term ones, a pattern that I had seen in colonialism and now saw in myself, as being as much the journey as anything as I saw or tasted or felt while I was there, and that last, incredibly valuable step of asking questions and listening to the answers was this particular journey's ultimate destination. I have from time to time wandered off the path towards it, or been misled by those I wrongly trusted, and I have discovered both wonders and pain as a result, but I have always found my way back. Whatever else I brought back with me, that was what made all of this worth it.

ACKNOWLEDGEMENTS

I must, of course, thank my parents, Stephen Ward & Judith Allen, for their love and support before, during, and since my two months wandering on the other side of the world, when it felt so much farther away than it does now.

And I must thank Jacki and Jack Eyman, not only for their generosity in giving me their home, their food, and everything I needed to recover physically while in Běijīng, but also their patience and compassion in giving me the space to recover mentally and emotionally, as well.

And then there is the debt I shall never be able to repay to everyone in China who helped me along the way, among them locals, tourists, and perhaps especially the transportation workers who struggled in a flawed and sometimes broken system long before I arrived and who tried their hardest in spite of it long after I left. Of the Chinese (and Taiwanese), I should single out a few for special thanks: Frank Lu and Chen Chongjing, who saved me when I arrived and delivered me safely out of Guǎngzhōu; "Mum", who seemed to save everyone passing through Xī'ān; the wonderful man from the Shanghai Antique & Curio Store, who was so thrilled to share his knowledge and his love for the art all around him; and every man and woman who waved me over to feed me from their own tables with no expectation that we could communicate or would ever meet again. To everyone named here and everyone else: Thank you

And finally, I wish to thank all who have helped and encouraged me in the writing of this book. It is one I kept putting off, with false starts and other half-efforts. For the longest time, I never felt sure I had a story to tell. I hope, at long last, I have written one worth reading. If I have, it is due in no small part to all of you who urged me to continue and especially those who read the book in an earlier stage and asked the hard questions I needed to listen to:

Emily Simoes, Katrina Monzón
Arthur Herskovitz, Diana Athena

Thank you

– Daniel Reiver

GLOSSARY

More of a phrasebook than a glossary, this should hopefully give you a better understanding of words you'll need to know traveling in China.

中国	Zhōngguó; China
普通话	Pǔtōng Huà; The Common Language (aka, "Xiàndài Biāozhǔn Bànyǔ", aka, Mandarin)
汉字	Hànzì; Character Script
你好	Nǐ hǎo; hello
再见	Zàijiàn; goodbye
请	Qǐng; please
对不起	Duì bu qǐ; I am sorry
没关系	Méi Guānxì; it doesn't matter
对	Duì; correct
是的	Shì de; yes
不	Bù; no
要	Yào; want
不要	Bù yào; don't want
要不要	Yào Bù yào?; do you want it or not?
没有	Méi yǒu; do not have
酒店	Jiǔdiàn; hotel
房间	Fángjiān; (hotel) room
多少钱	Duō shao qián; how much (does it cost)?
一点	Yī Diǎn; a little

芬	Fēn; 1/100 Yuán
块	Kuài; money; any currency
多谢	Duō Xiè; many thanks
谢谢	Xiè Xiè; thank you
泻泻	Xiè Xiè; diarrhea
	(yes, they are pronounced the same)
臭	Chòu; ugly, unpleasant
美	Méi; beautiful
好	Hǎo; good
不好	Bù Hǎo; bad
好不好	Hǎo Bù Hǎo; OK?
很好	Hěn hǎo; very good
非常好	Fēicháng Hǎo; excellent
好得别得料	Hǎodé Biédéliào!; better than expected!
	(always spoken with discerning taste)
马马虎虎	Mǎmǎhǔhǔ; "half horse, half tiger",
	meaning, "neither good nor bad"
不错	Bù Cuò; not wrong
大	Dà; big
大鼻子	Dà Bízi; "Big Nose"
小	Xiǎo; small
小心	Xiǎo Xīn; to be careful; focused
火车	Huǒchē; train
票	Piào; ticket
站台票	Zhàntái Piào; platform ticket
站飘	Zhàn Piào; standing ticket
硬座	Yìng Zuò; Hard Seat
软座	Ruǎn Zuò; Soft Seat
硬卧	Yìng Wò; Hard Sleeper
软卧	Ruǎn Wò; Soft Sleeper
飞机票	Fēijī Piào; airline ticket
信息亭	Xìnxī Tíng; information booth
哪里是	Nǎlǐ shì; where? or, where is it?
走	Zǒu ah; walk; coloquially, "Go straight"
	or "Keep going"; really, "I don't know"

Glossary

信息亭	Xìnxī Tíng; information booth
哪里是	Nǎlǐ shì; where? or, where is it?
走	Zǒu ah; walk; coloquially, "Go straight" or "Keep going"; really, "I don't know"
直的	Zhí de; straight
向右	Xiàng yòu; to the right
向左转	Xiàng zuǒ zhuǎn; to the left
在前面	Zài qiánmiàn; in front
在后面	Zài hòumiàn; in back
上	Shàng; upper
中	Zhōng; middle/central
下	Xià; lower
北	Běi; north
东	Dōng; east
南	Nán; south
西	Xī; west
京	Jīng; capital city
胡同	Hútòng; alley, side street; neighborhood
路	Lù; road
街	Jiē; street
大街	Dàjiē; avenue/boulevard
门	Mén; gate
江	Jiāng; river
湖	Hú; lake
山	Shān; mountain
牌坊	Pái Fāng; archway
寺庙	Sìmiào; temple
清真寺	Qīngzhēn sì; mosque
寺院	Sìyuàn; monastery
小偷	Xiǎotōu!; Thief!
小头	Xiǎotóu!; Small head!
公安局	Gōng'ān jú; Public Security Bureau

老外	Lǎowài; literally, "Old Stranger"; colloquially, "Foreigner"; really, "Foreign Fool"
扑克	Pūkè; playing cards
茶	Chá; tea
水	Shuǐ; water
热水	Rè shuǐ; hot water
冷水	Lěngshuǐ; cold water
啤酒	Píjiǔ; beer
葡萄酒	Pútáojiǔ; wine
酒	Jiǔ; liquor
臭酒	Chòu Jiǔ; unpleasant liquor
饺子	Jiǎozi; wrapped dumpling
包子	Bāozi; stuffed dumpling
米粉	Mǐ Fěn; rice flour
面條	Miàn Tiáo; noodle
担担面	Dān-Dān Miàn; dan-dan noodles
油条	Yóutiáo; fried dough sticks, like churros
肉	Ròu; meat
猪肉	Zhūròu; pork
牛肉	Niúròu; beef
羊肉	Yángròu; lamb
鱼	Yú; fish
鸡	Jī; chicken
鸭子	Yāzi; duck (make sure it's duck)
患	Huàn; danger, misfortune
囍	Xǐ; "Double Happiness", the symbol for marriage, given at weddings

About the Author

Daniel Reiver lives in New York City. He writes fiction, non-fiction, some poetry, and the occasional essay.

He is also the author of the novel Black Star.

Made in United States
Orlando, FL
21 November 2025